Britain

modern architectures in history

This international series examines the forms and consequences of modern architecture. Modernist visions and revisions are explored in their national context against a backdrop of aesthetic currents, economic developments, political trends and social movements. Written by experts in the architectures of the respective countries, the series provides a fresh, critical reassessment of Modernism's positive and negative effects, as well as the place of architectural design in twentieth-century history and culture.

Series editor: Vivian Constantinopoulos

Already published:

Finland
Roger Connah

Forthcoming:

Brazil
Richard Williams

France
Jean-Louis Cohen

Germany
Iain Boyd Whyte

Greece
Alexander Tzonis and Alkistis Rodi

Italy
Diane Ghirardo

Japan
Botond Bognar

Netherlands
Nancy Stieber

Spain
David Cohn

Switzerland
Stanislaus von Moos

Turkey
Sibel Bozdogan

USA
Gwendolyn Wright

Britain

modern architectures in history

Alan Powers

REAKTION BOOKS

Published by Reaktion Books Ltd
33 Great Sutton Street
London EC1V 0DX, UK

www.reaktionbooks.co.uk

First published 2007

The publishers gratefully acknowledge support for the publication of this book by the
following:
  Graham Foundation for Advanced Studies in the Fine Arts
  The Paul Mellon Centre for Studies in British Art

Printed and bound in Great Britain by Cromwell Press, Trowbridge, Wiltshire

British Library Cataloguing in Publication Data
Powers, Alan, 1955–
  Britain. – (Modern architectures in history)
  1. Architecture – Great Britain – 20th century
  2. Architecture, Modern – 20th century 3. Modern movement (Architecture) –
  Great Britain
  I. Title
  720.9'41'0904

ISBN-13: 978-1-86189-281-2
ISBN-10: 1-86189-281-0

Contents

SPIRIT OF MODERNITY: *"HOW'M I DOING?"*
SIR HENRY WOTTON: *"HEY, NONNY NONNY"*

Pressed to explain further a drawing apparently richly symbolic, the artist said the gramophone represented the voice of MARS, the cactus its insistent repetitions, and the figures at the back some architects over-entangled with display. The sheep may be taken to be either a bored and indifferent public opinion or the rest of the architectural profession. Sir Henry Wotton's famous tag it will be remembered was the nucleus round which the Exhibition was formed.

Introduction

What's your proposal? To build the Just City? I will.
I agree . . .
     . . . O show us
     History the operator, the
Organiser, Time the refreshing river.

Lines from *Spain 1937* by W. H. Auden, quoted in the brochure for the opening
ceremony at Linton Village College, Cambridgeshire, 14 October 1937

The way that the history of architecture is conceived changes constantly. A subject that may appear narrow in its focus can extend almost indefinitely into the social and intellectual history of all times and all places.

Fundamentally, it is a history of buildings, but these do not tell the whole story. Behind them are people, ideas and social pressures that increasingly have become an essential part of the way in which architecture is written about. A catalogue of works is a fundamental basis for history, but this book is conceived in addition as a history of ideas, reflecting on architects' own motivation and on the way that modern architecture was received and understood outside the profession.

The title of this series of books defines 'modern' as its field, but gives 'architecture' a plural form, as if to encourage multiple readings of both words. Unlike some of those who have written on modern architecture, I have doubts about the value of defining the term too closely and my pluralist scepticism (something I believe to be necessary for a historian) is probably evident in the way this book tells the story. The received view is that the 'white hats' of Modernism are lined up against the 'black hats' of otherness, under whatever name. Over time, I have looked quite closely at representatives of both sides, and tried to fill out the middle of the field, an area often shunned by the advocates of black and white alike. It is in the nature of the brief for this book to concentrate on the white hats, but I have deliberately looked along the boundary line where they can sometimes fade to grey. This is important in my view, because the lack of widespread popular acceptance of Modernism in Britain since its inception cannot simply be ignored or dismissed as the stupidity of the unenlightened.

Gordon Cullen, cartoon of the MARS Group exhibition of modern architecture, 1938. The theme of the introductory section, suggested by Godfrey Samuel, was a reinterpretation of Sir Henry Wotton's paraphrase of the Vitruvian triad 'Commoditie, Firmeness and Delight', words that were spoken with a commentary by John Summerson on a repeating gramophone record concealed behind a screen.

In Britain, the Modern Movement has been a moral and political battle for a share in shaping the environment and commanding the resources necessary to do so, against a background of reluctance and scepticism. The idea that 'modern' and 'good' are the same thing, while self-evidently right to some, is ultimately a subjective proposition. In a long-vanished dawn of Modernism, it was assumed that by avoiding certain errors, such as historic style, archaic construction methods or ornament, everything would turn out right. It took until the 1960s for this hope to be destroyed. We are still too close to the following decades to make a coherent story out of what happened next. For a country whose popular press has often enjoyed bashing modern architecture, we seem to have experienced an about-turn, so there are good reasons for claiming a victory for the white hats after their setback, yet the fields in which modern architecture is manifested are not unified, and what seems like success may be limited in its acceptance or long-term effect. Thus, for example, the things that matter most in architectural schools are often out of line with what concerns the architectural critics, and both are out of line with the more successful practitioners. The choice of finalists for the RIBA's annual Stirling Prize has virtually no impact on the most pressing problem of the time, the design of houses and the planning of new development. The richness and diversity of these different cultures are commendable, but the gaps between them undermine most generalizations that one tries to make.

Perhaps 'modern', an ambiguous word at best, is at the root of the problem, since it is no more than a reification of something that by its nature resists fixed definition. The conjunction of a temporal category (modern as in new) and a stylistic category (modern as a specific style of the twentieth century) worked at the beginning, but there was nothing

Louis Hellman, cartoon in *Architects' Journal* (20 June 1973).

in the logic of the situation to suggest that this represented any ultimate truth, and many commentators predicted drastic change in the near future. They might be surprised how little architectural ideas and arguments have changed since the 1930s. Either the ideas of that time, embodied in the work of the 'masters of modern architecture', were more potent even than was realized, or later generations have lacked the creativity and imagination to move very far away from them. Thus, paradoxically, Modernism early on became a period style that underwent a series of revivals and reworkings, in fact not unlike the history of jazz. When the early critics cemented the bond with morality (the separation of black and white), the whole issue was made irrationally emotive, and it is still almost impossible to have a calm examination of it.

In recognition that Britain is not the same thing as England, I make amends for any imbalance in the final chapter by examining the different histories of Modernism in other parts of the United Kingdom, before asking whether Britain or England has a 'special relationship' with Modernism. It is often assumed that British people are cautious, nostalgic, literal-minded and unwilling to discard pre-Modernist ways of ordering their surroundings. Superficial evidence suggests that we are not the only ones in this condition, but that the quality of 'average' building in many other European countries tends to be higher both in material and visual terms, even if it does not represent a Modernist's heaven. In other words, we do not seem to care very much about investing in architecture and urbanism of any kind, and have little consensus about quality. The social democracies of northern Europe seem to have managed to establish a better-designed public realm, owing to the higher status of design within their cultures, although we may be justifiably proud of our conservation of landscape and wildlife.

From the start, Modernism was viewed as a mission to convert the benighted, and inviting them, in the often-quoted words of W. H. Auden in 1930, to

> Harrow the house of the dead; look shining at
> New styles of architecture, a change of heart.

Since then the conversion process has been fitful, but nothing beats incomplete success as a motive for carrying on. Being a missionary might seem a rather old-fashioned and morally dubious activity in any other field today. The missionary does what he believes to be right, and if people do not like it, he will redouble his efforts. Louis Hellman's brilliant cartoons (several of them reproduced in this book) show how absurd the mission can appear at times. It changes shape and direction, but for me, the definition of Modernism could well be that of mission, of almost any kind. For this, as for the National Trust and the National Health Service, two other formative British organizations of the twentieth century, we may thank the inspiration of John Ruskin. An echo of Ruskin's *Seven Lamps of Architecture* (1849) may seem to have slipped into the chapter titles, while they also represent an extended version of Vitruvius' categories, known to English readers in their seventeenth-century formulation as 'commodity, firmness and delight'. While Ruskin, as an anti-industrialist advocate of handcrafts, may seem an odd grandfather for British Modernism, his presence in the way this narrative is structured will become apparent. My suggestion that British Modernism was at its most radical when aiming for such goals as compassion, happiness and conscience, rather than in its moments of material or purely aesthetic success, proposes Ruskinian priorities, and I do not think that these are frivolous or accidental issues.

Ruskin spent almost as much time on science as he did on art, and saw no division between them. This book has also tried to make connections between shifts in architecture and shifts in people's general understanding of the nature of the universe. Close correlation is seldom possible to prove, but I find the links easier to believe than the proposition that architecture, or even what is usually known as 'culture', are wholly autonomous fields driven by their own immutable logic alone.

In the generation before Ruskin, at the historical conjunction of moralized aesthetics and the progress of scientific thought, the theory of the Picturesque developed in England, proposing sensation in the face of nature as the basis for making and understanding art. This meant that rules were to be tested by subjectivity, rather than established by logic. It meant that opposites could be brought together without cancelling each other out. It has often been claimed that the Picturesque was the only original English contribution to aesthetics, and its effects have been profound. During the twentieth century, it provided plenty of grounds for controversy, and there is a current fashion among academics to condemn it. The Picturesque seems relevant, however, because of its concern with human sensations and responses, and its sensitivity to natural processes, in which it is not unlike the systems theory that entered architectural discourse in the 1950s and remains an ideological model and a practical tool today. Perhaps my approach to this task has been a Picturesque one, evoking a changing parade of images and characters, not easily reduced to simple generalizations, but operating quirkily and making up their own rules as they go along.

chapter one

Efficiency: From Modernity to Modernism

When did modern architecture in Britain begin? The country was not in step with the other developed nations where modern architecture emerged by stages between 1900 and 1920, and not until 1925 did actual built examples conforming to the definition of modern architecture become visible. It took at least five more years before a confident core of modern designers in Britain could be identified, and, in the opinion of many people, an influx of European refugees and émigrés was needed to make it happen.

When modern architecture 'arrived', many commentators claimed that it had been below the surface all the time. Georgian classicism shared many of its concerns with eliminating ornamental detailing, creating tidy and unified street pictures, and pushing new technology to provide buildings for transport and industry. During the period 1750–1820 a national English style developed, but, in the form of Georgian terraces and squares, it was not self-consciously English. A more immediate source was the Arts and Crafts Movement, which secularized the moral impulse of Victorian Gothic and turned it towards the improvement of society and the assistance of the underprivileged. Englishness was a conscious concern here, especially after 1900, and seems to have been linked to a spreading anxiety about Britain's economic performance in the world at large. This in turn triggered a new attitude to construction.

Military and economic challenges from abroad, above all from Germany, provided a climax to anxieties that had been growing since the 1880s. The historian Martin Wiener wrote: 'In every political camp the question was asked, what had gone wrong with England? Though answers varied, one answer that found wide support crossing party lines was "inefficiency".'[1] The call for 'efficiency' highlighted the uneasy combination of two attitudes, even in the same individual. The attitude broadly defined as 'Arts and Crafts' preferred older ways of building, resulting in buildings with a strong sense of locality, leading other countries to similar 'National Romantic' architectural movements. The alternative was to go international, an attitude associated with the 'Campaign for National

Daniel Burnham & Co. (job architect Francis Swales, with R. Frank Atkinson, engineer Sven Bylander), Selfridges, Oxford Street, London, under construction, 1910.

Efficiency' that was launched after the revelation at the outbreak of the Boer War in 1899 that many volunteers for the army had to be rejected on grounds of health.

The call for efficiency was answered with many solutions, combining old ideas of diligence and public service with new theories of mind, body and the physical world. It was a practical, not an aesthetic movement, with the aim of putting Britain back in the first rank of industrial progress and expanding the role of the state in most areas of life. Martin J. Wiener's classic account of the background to this movement, *English Culture and the Decline of the Industrial Spirit, 1850–1980* (1981), shows how rural and urban models of progress opposed each other, and Wiener is unequivocal in his condemnation of the romantic and backward-looking attitudes of the Arts and Crafts. By contrast, Frederick Taylor's Theory of Scientific Management and Henry Ford's development of the assembly line provided models for rethinking building methods during the first years of the twentieth century, and represented a new level of industrialism that attracted politicians with its promise of spreading material progress.

One of the fundamental justifications for modern architecture is its basis in new technology, one of the aspects of modernity that is normally assumed to lead to new formal solutions. It is, however, possible to adopt technology and disguise it in more familiar forms, which is broadly what happened in Britain between 1900 and 1930. The early histories of modern architecture viewed this as a serious error, believing that Modernism was, as Mies van der Rohe said, 'the spirit of the epoch translated into form', and that, allowing for slight variations, it was possible to know what this was, and dishonest and cowardly not to exercise this knowledge. In the history of ideas, the early twentieth century was notable for welcoming a number of theories that sharply divided right from wrong, and claimed a scientific basis for doing so. Ironically, the actual progress of science during this time, whether in physics or psychology, was away from such certainties, but architecture took a further fifty years to acknowledge and understand these changes and admit that reality is composed of difference and variation, which are not necessarily antagonistic to logic or principle.

It is thus tempting to adopt the language of the early Modernist histories, with their references to progress, 'looking forward' and 'leading to Modernism'. The first thirty years of the century make more sense if one does, but the danger has been that a ranking order of buildings emerges that depends entirely on their rating as 'pioneers', and tends to ignore other qualities, such as the skilled adaptation of classical models, or streetscape or organizational skill. By insisting that modernity and

Modernism are inseparable, more prominence is accorded to aesthetic factors than to actual innovation in engineering, unless the latter is correctly dressed. Pioneer hunting still has value, but only in our post-postmodernist age if stripped of its insistence on the one true path.

New Techniques: Modernity without Modernism

The career of Louis Gustave Mouchel is representative of the reluctance of British architecture and construction to accept technical innovation before 1900. Born in Cherbourg in 1852, Mouchel became a businessman in South Wales early in his life. In 1898 he became the agent for his compatriot François Hennebique's system of reinforced concrete, at the time that the provender mill for William Weaver and Company was under construction at Swansea (1897–8), the first multi-storeyed reinforced concrete building in Britain, for which workmen and materials were imported entirely from France. Mouchel learnt the techniques required for designing concrete, and set up an office in London in 1900 to license the Hennebique system, rapidly extending his network and supplying specialized design skills for British architects. Mouchel faced considerable prejudice in Britain, and the use of patent systems by 'pretentious foreigners' came under attack in 1907, shortly before his death.[2]

Concrete was not without well-placed supporters, however, and the Principal Surveyor to the Government Office of Works, Sir Henry Tanner, chaired a major committee on reinforced concrete at the RIBA in 1907, the year in which the Concrete Institute was founded. At a lecture at the Architectural Association (AA) in London in 1909, he warned his audience that architects 'would be relegated to interior decoration and external design by the reinforced concrete specialist, or, indeed, by the civil engi-

Weaver's Mill, Swansea, 1897. The building on the right is the first reinforced-concrete-framed structure in Britain, built by L. G. Mouchel, using the Hennebique system.

neer'[3]. In 1909 the fledgling architecture schools in Britain were actually moving away from experimental science and leaving consultants to design their concrete or steel structures. In the process that led to the establishment of the RIBA Board of Architectural Education in 1904, W. R. Lethaby advocated that 'a laboratory of building' should be attached to each school. This suggestion was overruled by the chairman, Reginald Blomfield, who was committed to promoting classical design in 'the grand manner', and the concept never instituted.[4] Among the exceptions were courses at the Brixton School of Building in south London, a school established in 1904 by the London County Council (LCC) under Lethaby's influence to bring architecture and building more closely together in the manner of a German *Technische Hochschule*; it was directed by Beresford Pite, an architect who as a teacher took a practical and constructional line, combined with a high level of artistic knowledge and taste.[5]

At the Liverpool School of Architecture, the energetic head, C. H. Reilly, was more concerned with the American approach, derived from the classicism of McKim, Mead and White, in which skill in handling conventional historical forms and complex axial plans was valued as evidence of professional ability, rather than any attempt to fuse new construction methods with new aesthetics. In terms of painting and theatre, Reilly's tastes were moderately progressive for his time, but he provides evidence of the way in which architecture followed a different course, with a preference for theatricality and 'dressing up'.[6] The atmosphere he created at Liverpool was intended to mix a Parisian Beaux-Arts Atelier with a bohemian artistic party, and it was a popular combination. In 1909, owing to the generosity of the local soap manufacturer Sir William Lever, Reilly was able to install the architecture school and the newly founded School of Civic Design in the eighteenth-century Bluecoat School, together with artists' studios and the 'Sandon Studios Club'.

Reilly designed relatively few buildings, and among his early works the only one to show constructional innovation was the church of St Barnabas, Shacklewell, London (1909–10), a simplified classical structure in brick with a concrete barrel-vaulted roof, of which Ian Nairn, writing in 1968, believed: 'England could so easily have stepped across to modern architecture from here, instead of relapsing into an eclectic fog.'[7] Reilly's preferences around this date would be better represented by the steel-framed Selfridges store on Oxford Street, nominally designed by the

Liverpool University School of Architecture studio in the Bluecoat School, c. 1910. At the rear of the room are Professors C. H. Reilly (Architecture, left) and S. D. Adshead (Civic Design, right).

leading Chicago architect Daniel Burnham, although actually the work of Francis Swales, a Canadian-born American studying in Europe. The whole project was described at the time as 'the American invasion of London'.[8] The steel itself was fabricated in Germany as an economy. Unlike the buildings in London by the Anglo-French partnership Mewès and Davis, which Reilly also admired, Selfridges could not have looked the way it did without the use of steel to create wide windows on the elevations, and, as Dan Cruickshank comments: 'the easy integration of new steel-frame and reinforced concrete construction with a traditionally detailed stone façade make Selfridges a spectacular example of the elegant synthesis of pioneering technology with appropriate history'.[9]

Taking advantage of the Office of Works exemption from building controls, Henry Tanner was able to use the Hennebique system when designing the King Edward Building of the General Post Office in London (1907–10), thereby reducing the cost by some £60,000 to £323,000, because of the economy possible on foundations. The publicly visible elevations of the building that survive are clad in conventional Edwardian Baroque masonry on the underlying concrete frame. The simplified rear elevations, which might be presented as more 'modern', have been destroyed.

Reinforced concrete does not just offer an alternative way of holding a building up, but also the potential for off-site prefabrication. This was originally developed for harbour works, where it avoided the need

John Brodie (City Engineer), prefabricated concrete flats in Eldon Street, Liverpool, under construction, 1904–5.

to form wet concrete below the waterline, and adapted in one notable example in Liverpool, where in 1904–5 John Brodie, the city engineer and a pioneer of electric tramways, as well as the inventor of the football goal net, made experiments in using large pre-cast panels of breeze concrete, incorporating waste material, for a block of flats in Eldon Street, including a flat roof for a children's playground. Brodie described his method as

> that of a dove-tailed box. Each of the four sides, the floor and ceiling of a room consisting of one concrete slab made in a mould at a depot . . . whence after maturing, it was conveyed behind a traction engine to the site and erected in position.[10]

Brodie saw this project as a prototype for cheap mass municipal housing, a thoroughly modern approach to a long-standing problem. In theory, by pre-casting the panels off-site, and cutting down on joinery and other trades, the result should have been cheap and serviceable, but the flats shared the fate of later prefabrication schemes that relied on economics of scale, and after exceeding their budget by 400 per cent were never repeated. The block was still in good condition when demolished in 1964. Brodie used the same system for a cottage in Letchworth, which still stands, and for municipal stables in the Liverpool suburb of Walton. The experiment was studied by an American architect, Grosvenor Atterbury, with results that were adopted in Europe after 1920. A further reason for the lack of widespread interest in Brodie's flats must have been their rather naive design, with mullioned windows in a vaguely Jacobean manner. He was an engineer, and not primarily concerned with matters of taste in new constructional forms, which architects themselves found hard to cope with. Given that Brodie was closely associated with Reilly in Liverpool, and also with Sir Edwin Lutyens in the layout of New Delhi in 1912, these influential figures did not lack the opportunity to hear about his work in this field, although they clearly did not consider it significant.

The Letchworth experiment was one of a number of attempts to provide cheap housing by industrialized methods before 1914. With existing models of transportable and demountable buildings, especially those for export overseas, the basic ideas were in place, while new products such as concrete blocks (which could be made on site by non-expert labour), expanded metal lathing and encased steel frames offered fireproofing, and thus removed the principal problem associated with timber and cast-iron structures. The relatively small scale of these constructions made this a more promising field for innovation, but the economics were still not compelling and no breakthrough was made.

For larger buildings during this period, reinforced concrete was less popular as a structural frame than steel. With the development of cheaper steel produced by the open-hearth method in the 1880s, its application for building was gradually appreciated by the construction industry, visibly in the Forth Rail Bridge of 1883–90, and invisibly in hotels, theatres and clubhouses in London and elsewhere. Steel buildings in which the structural forms of steel were more clearly visible are found, like their contemporary equivalents in concrete, outside the canon of 'polite' architecture and far from the influence of the RIBA in London. The Guinness Store House in Market Street, Dublin (1903–4), then part of the United Kingdom, still stands (unlike the demolished Weaver Building) in the register of 'pioneer' buildings, notable for the scale and complexity of its steel frame and the thinness of its admittedly rather conventional brick skin. This was permitted because it was not an inhabited building.

One field outside normal architectural interest in which steel was used was for football stadia, especially in the aftermath of a collapse of timber terracing at Ibrox Park, Glasgow, on 5 April 1902 with 25 deaths, in the presence of Archibald Leitch, the engineer who designed it in 1899. Leitch's career survived, and in 1906 he took out a patent for steel crush barriers, embedded in concrete terracing, which remained standard into the 1960s. The ability to build large-capacity stadia without further major structural disasters had a considerable effect on the development of football as the principal spectator sport for the working class in England and Scotland.

Both steel and reinforced concrete offered increased construction speeds, of which theatre designers in the 1890s took advantage. They could eliminate much of the mass masonry needed in solid load-bearing construction, and thus free up floor space within the building envelope. Building regulations based more on the need for fire protection than doubts about the strength of the materials were a hindrance to development in habitable buildings, rather than industrial structures. Even after the re-drafting of 1909, the London Building Act actually made modern methods more difficult to use than the earlier Act of 1894, which scarcely mentioned them.

Modern building services are less often considered than structure, and the first important example of a modern approach to air conditioning in the world was far from London, in Belfast, at the Royal Victoria Hospital, by the architects William Henman and Thomas Cooper (1900–02). Prior to this date, ventilation in hospital wards, considered a crucial issue since the time of Florence Nightingale, was achieved by a 'pavilion' plan, usually in the form of fingers off a central corridor. The use of a plenum or

forced-air system had been tried on a traditional plan at Birmingham in 1893, but at Belfast, where, as Reyner Banham noted, there was considerable local expertise in providing climatic conditioning for passenger ships, the wards were grouped in a single mass. As Banham describes, 'a set of steam engines driven by waste steam from the hospital laundry's boilers drove a pair of slow-turning engines on a common shaft in the engine house at the input end of the duct'.[11] With humidity control, the hospital can be claimed, in Banham's words, as 'the first major building to be air conditioned for human comfort'. The RIBA heard a report about it on completion, but the occasion seems to have been subject to a sort of filibuster operation that prevented a proper discussion, presumably owing to the threat implied by this novelty.

The industrial port cities, with their shipbuilding yards and foundries, were the natural cradle of modernity in the early twentieth century, in what Wyndham Lewis called 'ENGLAND, industrial island machine', while another writer referred to Glasgow as 'that mist-encircled, grim city of the

William Henman and Thomas Cooper, Royal Victoria Hospital, Belfast, 1900–02.

M. H. Baillie Scott, Blackwell, Windermere, Cumbria, 1900.

north which is filled with echoes of the terrible screech of the utilitarian, and haunted by the hideous eyes of thousands who make their God of gold'.[12] As Wiener indicates, the prosperous manufacturers moved out of the cities when they could, and commissioned houses that, by 1900, were likely to reflect traditional English values, as several previous generations had done before them. M. H. Baillie Scott's Blackwell, near

Edgar Wood,
Upmeads, Stafford,
1908.

Windermere (1900), was representative of the type, built as a holiday home for a Manchester brewer. These houses were admired by the German architect Hermann Muthesius in his book *Das Englische Haus* (1904) as 'an up-to-date national art – a cultural achievement for which England is certainly to be envied'.[13] It was houses of this type, rather than Brodie's cottage experiment, that provided the model for the Garden City style, as developed by Barry Parker and Raymond Unwin.

It was possible for individual architects to make a smooth transition from Arts and Crafts to proto-Modernism, as can be seen at Upmeads, Stafford (1908), where Edgar Wood adapted the flat concrete roofs that he and his associate J. H. Sellars had hitherto used for educational buildings. The design language of the elevations, more refined than any previous experiment in the domestic use of concrete, was a combination of neo-Tudor and neo-Georgian.[14] Although published at the time in striking photographs, it seems to have had little immediate impact, and Lawrence Weaver, generally an open-minded critic, while recognizing the advantage of a flat roof when an irregular plan outline was

H. P. Berlage, Holland House, Bury Street, City of London, 1914–15.

Charles Rennie Mackintosh, Glasgow School of Art, 1899–1910. This photograph of the library wing added in 1908–10 was published in Charles Marriott's *Modern English Architecture* (1924), one of the first to include this famous building in the canon of contemporary architecture.

desired, questioned the economy and utility of the idea.[15] For the time being, it represented a dead end.

From the nineteenth century onwards, a class distinction operated between 'commercial' architects, specializing in office and warehouse buildings, and others with a more general and supposedly more altruistic type of practice. 'Commercial' architects could make stylistic innovations, but the tendency among them and their clients was for conservatism, and around 1900 they settled comfortably into the Classical Revival cladding of steel-framed structures. Only occasionally do the backs or sides of these buildings, like the cast-iron panels on the Cotton Exchange in Liverpool by Matear and Simon (1905–6), show other possibilities. There was no desire to create a new or appropriate form of design for steel-framed buildings – as seen in the work of Louis Sullivan in northern cities of the U.S., and later in Vienna in the civil engineering and transport designs of Otto Wagner, or in Berlin in the Turbine Hall for AEG designed by Peter Behrens in 1909 – although it is believable that, in a different cultural climate, J. J. Burnet and others might have done so. Wagner attended the

RIBA's International Congress of Architects in 1906, but none of his buildings or those of the other architects mentioned was noticed in the press.[16] When the leading modern architect of the Netherlands, H. P. Berlage, designed Holland House in Bury Street, London EC3, in 1914, with a strong vertical emphasis on its steel frame and a richly decorated mosaic lobby, it too remained largely unnoticed, although the start of the First World War might have contributed to this neglect. Charles Rennie Mackintosh, now seen as an architect of equivalent stature to Wagner, was victim of the English prejudice against Art Nouveau as a decadent foreign style that threatened to corrupt the purity of native design. Scotland Street School of 1903–4 and the west wing of the Glasgow School of Art of 1908–9 show him moving towards a more abstract style in the same period that figures such as Behrens and Josef Hoffmann were adopting a simplified classicism in Germany and Austria. In Britain, the modernity of the steel frame usually led towards the conventional clarity of American classicism, as we have seen with Selfridges, or, in the case of Mackintosh's Glasgow antagonist and rival, Burnet, to a richly mannered style, which was common to other London architects such as J. J. Joass (another Glaswegian) and the young Charles Holden.

J. J. Burnet, Kodak Offices and Warehouse, Kingsway, London, 1909.

Burnet was one of the few architects who came anywhere near crossing the gap from classicism to proto-Modernism in the British Isles, although he had no conscious desire to be a Modernist in this sense.[17] Trained at the Ecole des Beaux-Arts in Paris, and perhaps the most considerable master of classicism of his generation, Burnet showed the influence of Chicago, a city he first visited in 1896, in his buildings in Glasgow, although at a smaller scale. After establishing a London office in 1904, Burnet curbed most of the inventiveness and freedom of his earlier work, although while he was working on the King Edward VII Galleries at the British Museum, he designed the Kodak Warehouse and Offices on Kingsway (1909), which was noticed at the time as a building where the steel construction, to some extent, could be read off the façade in the form of wider window spans and less surface depth than normal. For the Wallace-Scott Tailoring Institute at Cathcart, near Glasgow (1913–16), a model factory in a

Garden City setting, Burnet produced a building with no distinct period style, appropriate for industrial use but not, in his view, for a more 'polite' location.

When, in 1908, with a rare recognition of European events, the *Architectural Review* published two projects by Auguste Perret, the French master of the Modernist-classical balance, they had no immediate influence.[18] For the rest, Britain seemed largely to turn its back on Modernism, although not, as has been made clear, on modernity. Arguably, the latter was not only manifested in the amateurish aesthetics of engineers like Brodie, but in certain steel-framed buildings that march alongside the admiration of German architects, including Behrens and Mies van der Rohe, for Karl Friedrich Schinkel's austere reductions of classical form in the 1820s. Thus the early office buildings of Richardson & Gill in London are more or less forgotten as prototypes for what could be called 'another Modernism', because the architects discerned no separation between their aim of recapturing the design language of a hundred years earlier and their use of the latest building technology. The opportunity and the means to create modern architecture were present in Britain, but there was a lack of motivation to push more than the occasional architect past the 'comfort zone' of eclectic stylism.

Fitness for Purpose

Only in the years immediately prior to the First World War did the disparate architectural applications of the idea of efficiency begin to cohere in a vision of what might be described as a modern architecture of British origin. In hindsight, one wonders why even this stage took so long to happen, but the fact that the Arts and Crafts Movement was trying to get away from late Victorian borrowings from the styles of the world included an embrace of new styles as well as old, even though a prominent group of Arts and Crafts architects wrote a letter in 1901 to the *Magazine of Art* protesting about the gift of some French Art Nouveau furniture to the Victoria and Albert Museum, because it would corrupt students who needed to learn from first principles.[19] C. R. Ashbee, a leading figure in the Arts and Crafts, met Frank Lloyd Wright, still hardly known, in Chicago in 1900, but while admiring his work and arguing with him in a friendly way over the place of the machine in the future, Ashbee's mind was on things other than architecture, such as moving his Guild of Handicraft out of the East End and into the country.

The private house was often the place where experiments could be made, and even a single patron in Britain aware of Wright's work might have directed an architect onto this pathway, but Upmeads was as modern as houses ever got before 1914. The private houses of the European Modernists such as Peter Behrens, Mies van der Rohe, Le Corbusier and Gunnar Asplund were all more classical than modern before 1914, so Britain was less drastically out of step, but the energy present up to 1900 seems temporarily to have drained out of the country house and villa as experimental building types. This reflected a growing conservatism and anxiety among the house-building classes until the period around 1930, when small houses once more became the harbinger of the new wave of modern buildings.

In Edwardian Britain, W. R. Lethaby came closest to having a theory of modern architecture, based on a combination of French rationalist readings of history, a Ruskinian respect for workmanship and materials, and a distrust of facile imagery and decoration. This was despite his own mastery of historical styles, demonstrated when he was in the office of Norman Shaw. While Shaw lamented the perpetuation of eclecticism without doing much to change his ways, Lethaby aimed for a 'positive' architecture, based on reason. It was an open question what this would be, since it did not involve specific imagery. He wanted to divert architects' attention from individual buildings to the whole look of a city. Lethaby was one of a group of friends working in architecture, design and manufacture that visited the Deutsche Werkbund exhibition in Cologne in the fateful summer of 1914, where the experience of neatness and civic values, running a gamut from architecture to industrial design, inspired the group to found the Design and Industries Association (DIA) the following year. Lethaby felt that German designers had already moved to the position where British ones should be.

Lethaby shared a distrust of logic-driven theory with most of his contemporaries, including the rising classicist Sir Edwin Lutyens. The most cogent work of theory on the classical side, meanwhile, was *The Architecture of Humanism* by Geoffrey Scott, published in 1914 and partly devoted to the intellectual demolition of Lethaby and his heroes. Insofar as Scott's text suggests a particular type of architecture, it could be highly abstracted, although still based on Renaissance shapes, so that their preferences potentially intersected. The new shop for Heals on Tottenham Court Road by Smith and Brewer (1914–16) would satisfy both positions with its abstracted stone-clad steel frame, which created a dignified and rational street architecture without self-conscious 'period' detail. A more modern version of Lethaby's ideas can be glimpsed in the design for Dominion House (1913), a project conceived by the veteran Canadian businessman and patriot Lord Strathcona, to be built on the site later occupied by Bush House, Aldwych. It was designed by A. Randall Wells, a former associate of Lethaby in the construction of the church of All Saints, Brockhampton, in 1900,

Dunbar Smith and Cecil Brewer, Heal's, Tottenham Court Road, London. Perspective by R. Palmer Jones, 1914–16.

where concrete was used within a primitive rather than a Modernist design.

Dominion House was designed in reinforced concrete and, had it been built, it would have been the most significant example of proto-Modernism in Britain. As Nikolaus Pevsner commented, 'Wells inherited from Lethaby a sense of congruity between mediaeval methods for a still mediaeval job, and modern methods for a modern job.' While the mullions and transoms looked Tudor in origin, Pevsner considered 'the grid and the whole upward drive decidedly American'.[20] The design is remarkable for the proposed tall tower as much as for the wide expanses of glazing. It is equally surprising that a man of 93 should have commissioned such a progressive design to symbolize the British Empire, which was otherwise represented on the adjacent site by the Beaux-Arts classicism of Marshall Mackenzie's Australia House.

Hedging on the question of whether he actually liked 'the hardness, glare and brutality' of modern German cities (this was spoken during the

war), Lethaby concluded: 'I do, however, greatly admire the wonderful
efficiency and ambition of the Germans in city organisation'; and the DIA
welcomed the role of science and industry in refining design and univer-
salizing the spread of its products, thus bridging that gap between the two
cultures referred to earlier. Lethaby remained torn between his dislike of

resurgent eclecticism and doubts about the harshness of Modernism. One wonders what he made of the early Modernist icons of the Cologne Exhibition, the Model Factory by Gropius and the Glass Pavilion by Bruno Taut. His doubts strengthened over time, and it would be wrong to assume that the modern architecture he hoped for was the same as that which became current by 1930. In his last year, 1931, Lethaby wrote about Le Corbusier's phrase 'The house is a machine for living in':

> It is striking and really suggestive when judiciously interpreted, but some attempted applications seem only to be a new kind of whim works in a Corbusier 'style.' . . . The 'living in' should be the operative part of the saying. It would be a pity if, in addition to sham Gothic and sham Classic, we were to have sham modern as well.[21]

This comment was not simply conservative. By the time Lethaby said it, younger architects in Britain were worrying about the same thing, and finding themselves shifting further towards the soft materials and concepts of the Arts and Crafts.

In a lecture to the RIBA in 1921, Roger Fry, critic, painter and member of the Bloomsbury Group, who in 1909 had designed his own rather classical house at Guildford, made a greater allowance for aesthetics, declaring that as well as 'the beauty of a locomotive or a panther' (the type that the DIA favoured), there was 'Aesthetic beauty which results from the clear expression of an idea'.[22] He believed that the inherent weaknesses in English architectural thought ('vices' as he termed them) had been exacerbated by modern conditions, in other words that rather than modernity leading the English to Modernism, it had made it harder to attain. Fry's relatively modest call for a disinterested aesthetic study of architecture was followed by the architectural writers A. Trystan Edwards and Howard Robertson, both of whom were widely read by students, while *The Pleasures of Architecture* by Clough and Amabel Williams-Ellis was one of the few polemical books successfully aimed at the general reader.[23] Bloomsbury, in other ways a major force in inter-war culture, had little to offer for architecture, and no significant theorist followed Geoffrey Scott. There was a deficit in intelligent thought on architecture in the early Modernist period, apart from fragmentary occasional writings lacking a cohesive viewpoint adapted to the British background. Modernism therefore became an issue of partisanship, based on unsubstantiated assertions.

By a combination of curiosity about foreign activities, experiment among its members in their own commissioning of buildings, and promotion of a collection of related causes, the DIA nevertheless made a bridge to

Modernism. It fell short of becoming an avant-garde pressure group, retaining the Lethabite idea that self-conscious aestheticism was wrong. Thus, while some buildings of the 1920s associated with DIA members are the obvious first fruits of Modernism – such as the Silver End houses in Essex, which were inspired by New Ways at Northampton (1925), the house that Peter Behrens designed for Mackintosh's former patron W. J. Bassett-Lowke – others are more fence-sitting in their attitude to the obvious markers of the Modernist style, such as Charles Holden's Headquarters for the London Underground at 55 Broadway (1928).

After 1918: The Housing Crisis

At the end of the First World War, against a background of threatened revolution and with a shortage of conventional building materials and skills, the conditions existed for the delayed breakthrough from traditional to industrialized building methods. Central control by the government offered the possibility of the economies of scale that could benefit from technical research and experiment, bringing the whole machinery of efficiency to bear on the issue that social thinkers had so long wanted to address.[24] In Germany and the Netherlands, the conditions following the war gave the first major opportunities to emerging Modernist architects, but in Britain there was no avant-garde in waiting to translate technique into poetry. The exercise therefore became another example of modernity without Modernism. 'Architects, where is your vortex?' asked Wyndham Lewis, founder of the Vorticist movement, in 1919 – but he never got an answer.[25]

There were architects interested in the problem, such as S. D. Adshead, an associate of Charles Reilly, who in 1916 proposed a construction involving brick, concrete and a light steel frame, which was developed for post-war production as the 'Dorlonco' system by the Dorman Long steelworks. Although modern underneath, it was over-clad in the late Georgian style that Adshead favoured. Colin Davies comments:

S. D. Adshead, 'Dorlonco' houses at Dormanstown, Redcar, North Yorkshire, 1919.

it is hard now to reconstruct the logic of this form of construction. Its steel frame seems structurally redundant given the blockwork lining, and the cement render seemed doomed to fail, which it duly did in the years to come.[26]

In seeking unconventional building methods, Britain did not necessarily make more technical mistakes than other countries, but still failed to produce modern architecture by modern methods. Despite its shortcomings, the Dorlonco system was used for about 10,000 houses built by local authorities all over Britain.

It was people outside architecture who tended to find the idea of pre-fabrication most exciting. The Scottish industrialist William Weir was inspired by a meeting with Henry Ford to propose that he could erect 'tens of thousands of houses in blocks of 100 at £150 apiece, to consist of a couple of rooms with central heating, hot water, electric light, central laundry and a piece of land'.[27] Part of the attraction was that the building trades, with their union restrictions, could be outflanked by designing a standardized system suitable for unskilled labour. The Cabinet Secretary, Thomas Jones, recorded: 'there is no reason why we should not get tens of thousands of houses, ugly though they will be'.[28] This dilemma between productivity and beauty was naturally one that concerned even the most mechanistically minded architects. Some argued that pre-modern methods were just as appropriate for use in the crisis. The Ministry of Housing set up one experimental site at Acton in west London for industrialized housing, and another at Amesbury, Wiltshire, for houses using the traditional but then obsolete technique of rammed earth. These were not very widely adopted, although G. H. Skipper, an architect based in Norwich, used 'clay lump' in local authority housing schemes on the Norfolk borders, which endured into the 1990s. All the buildings of this type were in the almost universal Garden City cottage style. Concrete block is a material essentially similar to rammed earth

G. H. Skipper, housing at Garboldisham, Norfolk, 1920. The clay lump construction is seen at the time of demolition.

C.H.B. Quennell, house in Clockhouse Way, Braintree, Essex, 1919.

Crittall workmen demonstrating the strength of the 'Fenestra' joint, c.1907.

blocks such as those used by Skipper. Thus the handful of houses in the suburbs of Braintree, Essex, built with concrete blocks in 1919 by the architect C.H.B. Quennell, were not at the opposite end of the aesthetic spectrum, apart from their flat concrete roofs and metal windows supplied by the company that built the houses for its workers.

This was a local family business developed from ironmongery into the Crittall Manufacturing Company, and, at the end of the First World War, a major industrial concern in the area.[29] The story of Crittalls illustrates a typical DIA mixture of social concern and entrepreneurial flair. In 1905 the company bought the British patent rights for the 'Fenestra' design for steel windows from the Austrian engineer Karl Zucker. The design involved the use of a thinner metal section than before, formed by crossing over continuous frame elements, rather than cutting and jointing them at every intersection. This enabled the creation of much bigger windows, especially suitable for industrial premises. Crittall's younger son, W. F. Crittall, known as 'Pink', who had artistic aspirations, was set the task in 1908 of reducing the range of cross-sections from the wide and inefficient range then in use. His standardization exercise, so typical of the 'efficiency' mentality, boiled them down to one 'Universal section', which permitted casement windows to be manufactured by semi-skilled labour, while for the user glass could be replaced from inside without the need for scaffolding. Initially, these sections could be rolled only by mills in Germany, since none in Britain had the capacity. The third innovation was to use welding rather than more traditional jointing techniques.

Adjusting to the peacetime economy, Crittall was able to have his 'standard cottage window' adopted for government housing schemes, helped by the timber shortages of the time. He built a new factory in the country at Silver End and offered jobs to disabled war veterans, with housing available for company employees to rent. With houses at Silver End by Thomas Tait of Sir John Burnet and Partners completed in 1927, Britain acquired its first Modern Movement buildings, although more conservative Garden City houses and public buildings were in the majority at Silver End. Even so, the young American critic Henry-Russell Hitchcock, on the basis of photographs and drawings, compared them

'very favourably with the most advanced French, Dutch, and German work'.[30] Judged realistically against the European competition, however, Silver End scarcely deserves this status, although locally important.

1920s–1930s

What had become of the Efficiency campaign by the late 1920s? Government anxiety about progress in the building world led in 1917 to the foundation of the Building Research Station, although this research laboratory did not produce tangible results for some time. British architecture of the 1920s, continuing Edwardian themes of refined classicism and vernacular, deserves study, but only a few buildings obviously linked the Arts and Crafts to early Modernism. Prominent among them were the early Underground stations of Charles Holden on the southern extension of the Northern Line, commissioned by a DIA stalwart, Frank Pick. Starting with Westminster Station, which he remodelled in 1923, Holden established the basics of his future work for Pick, who in 1915 had exercised his first major piece of patronage in commissioning the sans-serif lettering still in use on the system from Edward Johnston, a protégé of Lethaby at the Central School of Arts and Crafts from the beginning of the century.

Holden's stations, like Johnston's lettering, were simpler and plainer than the earlier house styles of architecture on the Underground, relying on proportion and purity of form. To this extent they were classical, and both designers had a thorough if non-academic grounding in classical form. Holden saw the need to make his stations visually effective by day and night, with lofty booking halls through whose windows electric light could shine welcomingly. He developed a 'kit of parts' approach, helping to develop a corporate identity subtly rooted in a set of values that treated the travelling public with sympathy, while anxious not to over-excite them. The headquarters of the Underground over St James's Park Station, designed by Holden in 1928, was chiefly innovative on account of its adoption of a cruciform plan from hospital design, so as to avoid the use of light wells, and also in the controversial sculptures near street level commissioned from Jacob Epstein; but the form of the elevations, clad in Portland stone, was cautious and reticent, like Holden's later Senate House for London University. Neither the first set of Holden stations, designed in Portland stone for the southern section of the Northern Line in the mid-1920s, nor his more famous later stations on the Piccadilly Line from 1930 onwards can be called fully modern, in the sense of competing with the public service architecture then being created in Germany and the Netherlands, which Holden and Pick toured in 1930 in order to assess whether it had anything to offer them. In Germany, Pick felt that 'architecture has gone farther than that of any other country in its break with the past and the results cannot be said to be particularly satisfactory', sanctioning only a rather narrow path for Modernism between past and future.[31]

At the end of the 1920s several of the middle-aged architects who had been too young to be swept up fully in the Arts and Crafts Movement, and who exercised a generational reaction against its sometimes winsome simplicity, began to show a greater interest in Modernism in their work and pronouncements. They constitute a sort of 'lost generation', depleted by the First World War of a few major talents. Fated to be treated as marginal

Charles Holden,
Arnos Grove Station,
London, 1932.

33   Efficiency: From Modernity to Modernism

Elisabeth Scott
(Scott, Chesterton
and Shepherd),
Shakespeare
Memorial Theatre,
Stratford-upon-Avon,
Warwickshire,
1929–32.

figures in history, they nonetheless occupied many crucial positions in teaching and journalism and, most influentially, as competition assessors. They eased the long drawn-out transition from eclecticism, if only by making space for a younger generation who had not practised before the war.

One notable example was Robert Atkinson, a skilled eclectic designer who was Principal of the Architectural Association School in the early 1920s and selected Elisabeth Scott's scheme for the Shakespeare Memorial Theatre Competition in 1929. This plain brick mass stands solidly, as theatres with fly-towers must, over the River Avon, where other competitors were hoping to put something much more gestural and associational. Its virtues are partly negative ones, of not trying to upstage the surroundings. Inside, the north European equivalent of Art Deco, with marble wall claddings, stainless-steel chevrons and small pieces of mosaic, shows the popularity of Ragnar Östberg's Stockholm City Hall, a building easy to love but almost impossible to emulate.

Atkinson's colleague Howard Robertson, who with his partner John Murray Easton designed the Royal Horticultural Society New Hall in

Easton and Robertson,
Royal Horticultural
Society New Halls,
Vincent Square,
Westminster, 1928.

1927, was the most effective journalist in bringing Modernism in front of British architects in the second half of the 1920s, despite having been responsible for a strikingly un-modern British Pavilion at the Paris Exhibition of 1925, behind which Le Corbusier's Pavillon de l'Esprit Nouveau was concealed. As Atkinson's successor at the AA, Robertson looked tolerantly on students who, around 1929, began to 'go modern', usually as a result of reading Le Corbusier in their second or third year. The first wave to be thus affected joined Berthold Lubetkin in the formation of the Tecton Partnership in 1932. In contrast to the Modernist belief in an exclusive correlation between form, structure and function, Robertson believed that all styles could essentially be put on a single level by treating everything as a mixture of building construction and composition, with decoration added according to the requirements of the building type. By the 1930s, Easton and Robertson were starting to design flat-roofed buildings, usually in brick, with something of the Amsterdam School architecture of the early 1920s about them. Other architects in a similar bracket were G. Grey Wornum, winner of the competition for a new headquarters for the RIBA (1930–34), and H. S. Goodhart-Rendel, a complex figure suspected of dilettantism, who was an eclectic by conviction rather than opportunism, yet believed in the underlying logic of plan and construction. His position was unique, and although he made it apparent in copious writing and lecturing, few architects tried to join him. For some, one feels, Modernism represented an easy solution to the hard thinking required for understanding the complexity of combining form and content in architecture. The answer could be simply to leave the content out and focus on 'efficiency'.

Could architecture deal with ambivalence about modernity through a Modernism equivalent to that of Eliot and Joyce? Apart from the interiors of a house in Cambridge, Finella, created for a lecturer in English, Mansfield Forbes, in a richly themed poetic vein by a young Australian, Raymond McGrath, between 1927 and 1929, the direct evidence is not easy to find. The doctrine of efficiency had no time for inner contradiction. Therefore, when Le Corbusier's book of 1923, *Vers une architecture*, was published in translation in 1927 as *Towards a New Architecture*, it was seen (as Lethaby's comment reveals) as a text about the need for a mechanical approach to design and to life, even though it is now possible to read into it many more layers of meaning from Le Corbusier's richly stocked and divergent mind. His buildings themselves were equally seductive to those looking for inspiration, and beautifully presented in the photographs he carefully staged so that those who imitated them could be led intuitively into a Modernism with cultural depth. Le Corbusier's books (*Urbanisme* was translated in 1929 as *The City of Tomorrow*) were generally welcomed by reviewers, both inside and outside the architectural community. One may suspect that he represented, at the beginning, the latest Paris fashion, yet there was clearly a deeper appeal to the intellect and the senses, and it is hard to think of any other country where he had such a profound impact on the development of modern architecture, lasting even into the present. The influence of Walter Gropius, the Bauhaus school and German modern architecture generally is not so clearly identifiable, although Bruno Taut's *Modern Architecture* of 1929 introduced a wide range of German examples.[32]

The idea that there was an international community of modern architects was made visible in the foundation of CIAM (Congrès internationaux d'architecture moderne) in 1928. Howard Robertson attended the meeting of 1929 at Frankfurt on the Minimal Dwelling, but did not become a member; and it was only with the congress of 1933 on board the ss *Patris*, on the theme of 'The Functional City' and attended by Wells Coates as a representative of the newly founded MARS Group (and also by Ernö Goldfinger, soon to be resident in London), that the British involvement began. MARS stood for 'Modern Architectural Research', and Coates, with his scientific background, intended that actual research would result. When it did, it was more in the form of social survey work on housing than technical research, and from this point of view MARS was a failure, creating doubt in many minds as to the whole potential value of an approach dominated by science and technology.

The excited, multi-lingual and multi-factional world of the CIAM congresses contrasts with the more carefully stage-managed promotion of the 'International Style' in New York in 1932. This is now widely seen as the tipping point between the creative and highly politicized activities of individuals in a variety of countries, unconstrained by a 'party line', and the emergence of a Modernism suited to international corporate capitalism, and stripped of its political ideals. Henry-Russell Hitchcock, joint selector of the exhibition with Philip Johnson, was familiar with England, where, in common with Italy, Spain and Japan, 'modern architecture has only begun to appear'. They named Joseph Emberton, Frederick Etchells (a slightly dilettante architect responsible for the translation of Le Corbusier's books), Amyas Connell and Tait as representative figures. Emberton's Royal Corinthian Yacht Club at Burnham-

Joseph Emberton,
Royal Corinthian
Yacht Club, Burnham-
on-Crouch, Essex,
1930.

on-Crouch (1930) was illustrated in *The International Style*, a book that the Museum of Modern Art produced after the exhibition. CIAM and the exhibition occurred just ahead of Germany's transition to Nazism and the simultaneous exclusion of Modernism from Soviet architecture, which altered the ambitions of the whole movement. CIAM's ambition to comprehensively remodel all physical and social structures was deferred in most countries, even those without regimes overtly hostile to modern culture of all types.

First Fruits

In 1929 the historian and archaeologist Bernard Ashmole commissioned the young Connell, a New Zealand Rome Scholar, to build a house at Amersham in Buckinghamshire. It caused commotion before it was built, owing to local objections (the first of many to follow from the 1930s to the present), but on completion High and Over was a news sensation, with magazine articles including a favourable feature in *Country Life*, and a newsreel film. The design is fascinating in its slightly tentative approach to a new formal language of architecture, with a regular plan form, abstract decoration and a slight air of being built for an exhibition. Owing to the builder's inexperience, a frame structure with blockwork infill was used and rendered over with a smooth coat of cement (as were Le Corbusier's early villas), instead of the desired purist alternative of 'monolithic' reinforced concrete.

Connell's second house, in partnership with Basil Ward, also from New Zealand, played with asymmetry and irregularity. Built in Surrey for a 72-year-old accountant, Sir Arthur Lowes Dickinson, White House (as it is now called) was a true monolithic concrete construction. Ward later wrote:

> Connell conceived the idea of a monolithic reinforced-concrete structure, based on the 'Dom-ino' [the skeletal concrete house form devised by Le Corbusier in 1914] and, thereafter, we caused floors, walls (where these were required), columns, beams to be tied together to form a structural whole.[33]

This was seen by Ward as a total package, encompassing structure, use and aesthetics, each of which impacted on the other, with concrete as the means

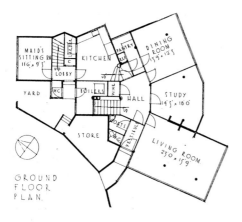

MAID'S SITTING RM 11'6 × 9'5

KITCHEN

DINING ROOM 17'9 × 12'5

YARD

WC

BOILERS

HALL

STUDY 14'5 × 18'0

STORE

LIVING ROOM 25'0 × 15'9

GROUND FLOOR PLAN.

Amyas Connell and Basil Ward, White House (originally New Farm), Haslemere, Hampshire, 1932.

Sir Owen Williams (architect and engineer), 'Wets' building, D10, Boots, Beeston, Nottingham, 1930, 'Curtain wall' design.

of uniting them. Joined in 1934 by Colin Lucas, an English-born architect who had already gained experience in using reinforced concrete, the firm of Connell, Ward and Lucas continued to experiment both aesthetically and structurally up to 1939. In 1956 Peter Smithson called them 'the nearest we had in England to first generation modern architects'.[34]

Owen Williams, an engineer specializing in concrete before the First World War and also interested in modern architecture, produced what might be called his 'breakthrough' building in 1930, and perhaps never surpassed it. This was his first design for Boots Pure Drug Company of Beeston, Nottinghamshire, which had temporarily been taken over by American owners. The 'Wets' building, known as D10, was a large concrete structure with a series of atria, planned for the production flow of pharmaceuticals and other products down to packaging floors and loading bays for despatch. It became modern architecture, rather than engineering, largely by virtue of its completely glazed exterior walls, the sublime length surpassing anything else of the sort done during the remainder of the decade. These were intended to be fully glazed as curtain walls. In the event, the floor

plates interrupted the glass in horizontal bands, slightly diminishing the effect.

Williams designed other buildings for industry, specializing in large spans and the deep basements needed for newspapers. His simplicity of approach made modern architecture seem easy, except for those with superfluous architectural knowledge to shed. He was an embodiment of the idea that engineers could effectively replace architects. Through Williams, Connell and a few others, concrete became established in Britain at the beginning of the 1930s as the supreme material for Modernism. Unlike Williams, Ove Arup, Danish by origin, was notable as an outstandingly sympathetic collaborator with architects who had not developed their own expertise, but who wished to go beyond conventional techniques. Without his help concrete buildings of the first Modernist generation in Britain would have been much cruder. His most famous collaboration was with Berthold Lubetkin, who came to London from Paris (and before that from Georgia, via a post-revolutionary education in Germany and Poland) at the end of 1931, and by forceful charm quickly found partners and jobs.

Lubetkin was the undoubted star of 1930s modern architecture in Britain, achieving a combination of social purpose and aesthetic athleticism, with a basis in applied research. On a family holiday visit to England in 1914, he had admired the 'trim confidence, harmony and balance' of a cricket match, the kind of thing that Lethaby wanted as a model for Modernism, contrasting it with 'the moribund fin de siècle world of creepy ornamentation'.[35] Lubetkin brought to modern architecture a depth of philosophical understanding previously lacking in England, belying the fear that too much thinking would spoil the architecture. He knew Russian Constructivism, and fed its influence into English-language publications at a time of enthusiasm for Russia as the great scientific society of the future among intellectuals, ironically just at the point when modern architecture there was being suppressed. His works, such as the Penguin Pool at London Zoo and the Highpoint Flats, are the best-known examples of 1930s Modernism, captivating as images, while rewarding further investigation into their constructional techniques and, at Highpoint, the detailed reconsideration of the equipment of daily life. Lubetkin made a less obvious but potentially more important shift within Modernist practice with the Finsbury

Lubetkin and Tecton, Highpoint One, Highgate, London, 1934–5.

DUCTS FOR POWER WIRING

ALL WIRING FOR ELECTRIC FITTINGS TAKEN
IN NEAT REMOVABLE SKIRTING · DUCTS ;
REPAIRS AND ADDITIONS QUICKLY & CHEAPLY
MADE. ALL CLINICAL EQUIPMENT EASILY CON-
NECTED

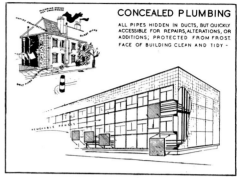

CONCEALED PLUMBING

ALL PIPES HIDDEN IN DUCTS, BUT QUICKLY
ACCESSIBLE FOR REPAIRS, ALTERATIONS, OR
ADDITIONS; PROTECTED FROM FROST.
FACE OF BUILDING CLEAN AND TIDY ·

Lubetkin and Tecton, Finsbury Health Centre, London, 1938. Drawings from a set prepared by the practice to explain the building to non-specialists.

Health Centre, where he designed the wings of the building, containing the medical areas, so that the services, water, heating and electric wiring – which Modernists usually buried in the concrete floor slab – were accessible for repair and change in panels beneath the windows. The move from relatively solid and massive buildings, especially those whose concrete began to cause problems even at an early date, towards lighter-weight structures pieced together from components was, at a relatively late stage in Modernism, a major acknowledgement of the difference between what actually was efficient, and that which merely looked as if it might be.

It has often been remarked that British Modernism depended largely on people who had come from elsewhere. While it might have been possible to have a completely home-grown Modernism in Britain (one thinks of Owen Williams, Joseph Emberton, Maxwell Fry or Frederick Gibberd, whose work, at its best, was scarcely inferior to the foreign arrivals), the émigré phenomenon is an inescapable part of the story and influenced the host architects, including those who went into partnership with the émigrés. From the end of 1933, refugees from Nazi Germany began to arrive in significant numbers, including three major architects, Erich Mendelsohn, Walter Gropius and Marcel Breuer, partnered for official purposes by Serge Chermayeff, Maxwell Fry and F.R.S. Yorke, respectively. Despite occasional xenophobia, these architects joined an already cosmopolitan intellectual and artistic scene in London, inhabited by figures such as Chermayeff, who was Russian by birth but English by education and naturalized at the time of his marriage.

The years 1930–31 laid the groundwork. Dmitri Mirsky wrote that the financial, political and social crisis following on from the Wall Street Crash

forced the intelligentsia of Great Britain to look face to face into historical realities from which there was no escaping . . . The

40

revival of interest in politics was accompanied by an increased need for a world view, for a system . . . a key to the chaos, the so puzzling confusion into which reality seemed to have moved.[36]

Le Corbusier appeared to offer such a key. A rapturous review in *The Listener*, the BBC's magazine, by the art critic Herbert Read early in 1931 set the tone for uncritical adulation of a city of towers, all air, sky and metaphysics, in which people are abstracted into distant tennis players. 'This is not a poet's vision; it is a practical scheme for which Le Corbusier can give you the working drawings and the estimated cost', Read finished his article, 'The cost is an immense economy. Why, then, not begin right now?'[37]

We can recognize the sense of impending crisis on all fronts in the personal account given by Maxwell Fry, a student at the Liverpool School under Reilly when classicism was still in full flood in the 1920s and apparently successful as an architect and planner, but suffering from an inner emptiness both in his professional and private life. He found encouragement in meetings of the DIA, 'the best available cutting edge at the time'. As the world economy threw all established patterns into doubt, Fry met the Canadian engineer Wells Coates, soon to become an architect himself, who pushed Fry further towards his leap to freedom. It happened, according to Fry's account, when looking at Devonshire House, Piccadilly, an American-style classical building by Reilly in partnership with Thomas Hastings, the New York architect to whom Fry had earlier been sent to learn up-to-date methods. 'I knew it all like a game played out', Fry wrote of the decoration on the building,

> That evening I sought out rolls of drawings treasured from those years of tutelage, and gazing at them, not without some fondness, I consigned them to the dustbin. Coming to my empty office in the morning I stretched paper on my board and at once set to work on the structure of a hypothetical block of working-class flats that would owe their economy to the balanced forces of what was well-known among engineers as a 'portal truss' in reinforced concrete.[38]

Modernism worked on a mixture of reason and emotion, and the combination of these was its great strength, at a time when ideas of efficiency were themselves highly emotive, owing to the rising sense of guilt among the more prosperous and educated population about the poor. The politicization that Mirsky describes took many forms to left and right, with modern architecture offering attractions to all of them.

As Fry's memory of the portal truss indicates, a specific construction form could take on the symbolism accorded by Victorians to the Gothic arch. Working-class flats enjoyed a brief period of architectural distinction at the beginning of the century in the work of the LCC, but it took foreign examples to show later architects that they could be the ultimate exemplars of the Modernist synthesis. In the earlier 1930s the idea of building high was especially exciting, because it had been associated with the wealthy and promised the extreme opposite of slum streets. The rather dour courtyards of the five-storey walk-up tenements, scarcely differing from Victorian Peabody Buildings, were still under construction in large numbers in the 1930s, especially by the LCC. These would go, to be replaced by the *Zeilenbau*, the parallel lines of scientifically spaced and oriented slab blocks advocated in Germany as housing funds began to tighten after 1930, and advocated by Gropius to CIAM in 1933. In his book of 1935, *The New Architecture and the Bauhaus*, he repeated the reasons for these forms, which duly began to appear in the planning of new

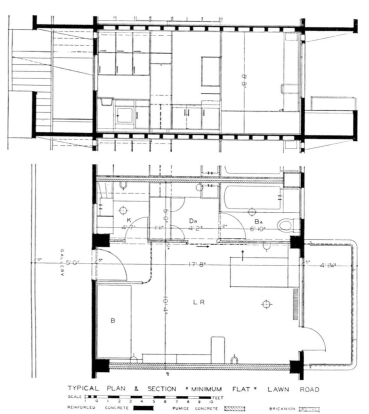

Wells Coates, Isokon Flats, Lawn Road, Hampstead, London, 1934. Plan and section of a standard 'minimum flat'.

housing in Britain in place of courtyards. During his residence in London, Gropius lived in the Isokon flats in Hampstead, a private development designed by Wells Coates for Jack Pritchard, an enthusiast for modern living and modern design. A small slab block with external access galleries, it would have seemed unremarkable in pre-Nazi Germany, but created a stir in sluggish London.

Flats were supposed to solve the dilemma of spreading suburbia, which was especially abhorrent to educated people, who imagined that the inhabitants lived pinched and incomplete lives. The Dudley Report of 1934 suggested that 'the cost of large-scale housing can be reduced by rationalized organization and carefully studied design to well below any level of cost yet achieved in this country'. Commenting on this in a letter to *The Times*, the quantity surveyor Cyril Sweett, the secretary of MARS, emphasized the labour-saving possibilities of central heating, hot water, fuel, and laundry and rubbish collection.[39] As demonstrated in the famous 'Frankfurt kitchen', the flat could become a domestic machine.

The Mopin system of lightweight steel framing filled with vibrated concrete (this made it set faster and without the danger of air pockets) employed at La Cité de la Muette, near Paris, by the architects Beaudoin & Lods, was applied in Britain at the Quarry Hill Flats, Leeds. This very large municipal development, completed in 1938, had waste chutes, a communal laundry and other amenities, all wrapped by one enclosing wall of housing on a hilltop slum-clearance site. Conventional labour and materials were not available to satisfy the whole house-building effort in Leeds, as Livett, the municipal architect, argued in justification of using Mopin, although the failure of the system in the 1970s was used as an excuse for their demolition.[40] Quarry Hill was extreme in its modernity but moderate in its Modernism, once more showing the lack of essential linkage between the two concepts.

Functionalism

With Modernism, the generalized concept of Efficiency was replaced in architecture in Britain with a widespread use of the word Functionalism. As Adrian Forty and others have noted, 'functional' can be used to translate three words used in German in the 1920s to define aspects of what was known as 'The New Building' (*Das Neues Bauen*): *sachlich*, *zweckmässig* and *fonctionell*.[41] These terms have individual and largely untranslatable meanings distinct from the English word, whose loss undoubtedly impoverished the potential of architectural criticism in Britain, while the word itself caught the popular imagination, to architects' dismay, although there is no evidence that the ultimate reduction

R.A.H. Livett, Quarry
Hill, Leeds, 1938. The
steel frame erected
as part of the 'Mopin'
system.

Quarry Hill completed.

of functionalism, by Gropius's successor at the Bauhaus, Hannes Meyer, 'function × economy = building', was known in Britain.

When the reception of Modernism in Britain during this period is discussed, it is usually the most adverse opinions that are quoted, such as those of Sir Reginald Blomfield in *Modernismus* (1934). As a representative of the 1880s generation, Blomfield could be expected to reject Modernism, but even a liberal intellectual such as Aldous Huxley, writing in 1930,

Economy of space in the morning room

'Economy of space', from W. Heath Robinson and K.R.G. Browne, *How to Live in a Flat* (1936).

admitted his dislike of Modernist rooms and furniture, 'to dine off an operating table, to loll in a dentist's chair – this is not my ideal of domestic bliss'.[42] A wider survey of the non-specialist press reveals many more balanced positions, critical of the majority of contemporary 'high design' architecture and the pattern of suburban development, two essentially unrelated aspects of the inter-war building world, but uncertain whether the alternative went too far. In *How to Live in a Flat* (1936), the illustrator William Heath Robinson, famous for imagining logical but unworkable machinery, conjured a vision of Edwardian ladies and gentlemen bewildered in a world of chromium-plated furniture and minimal dwellings. Other cartoons and comments presented the world of Modernism as equally outlandish.

A leader in *The Listener* in 1933 made a division between advocates of extreme and mechanistic functionalism on the one side and 'all those – not necessarily conservatives – who believe that architecture has internal laws of its own, independent of passing fashions or experimental mediums'. The writer wondered whether functionalism had become a heresy, since it was 'an exaggeration of one aspect of the truth insisted upon to the damage or denial of other and equally important truths'.[43] The belief that Modernism was meant to be uncomfortable was reinforced by the heated emotion of Nikolaus Pevsner's closing passage in *Pioneers of the Modern Movement from William Morris to Walter Gropius* (1936), characterizing the world of Gropius's architecture as 'a world of science and technique, of speed and danger, of hard struggles and no personal security'.[44] In fact, Gropius's message that the architect and artist needed to ameliorate the deadening effect of the machine left the door open for imagination and variety. In 1936 he built a timber house in Kent, one of many Modernist houses of that and subsequent years successfully to abandon concrete and steel, and his Impington Village College (1939) was built of load-bearing brick, a very different matter to the Bauhaus building. Modernism became trapped in its own rhetoric of efficiency, even when it had moved on to balance this with other factors, probably because efficiency was politically neutral and avoided the more contentious area of aesthetics. In the early 1930s the functionalist line was pushed to extremes in order to provide a principle by which modern architecture could be

T. P. Marwick,
Co-operative Society
Bread Street show-
room, Edinburgh,
1935.

distinguished from 'jazz modern', or Art Deco as it is now called.

The huge significance accorded to this distinction now seems difficult to understand. Buildings such as the Daily Express, Fleet Street (1930), by Owen Williams combine elements of sheep and goat (as the flashy American-style lobby inserted by Robert Atkinson would have been judged). The interiors at BBC Broadcasting House (1932) by Raymond McGrath and Serge Chermayeff were decorative in spirit, although with the crucial difference that the decoration was not 'applied'. After 1930 the primary architectural magazines, seeing themselves as leaders of taste, tended to exclude a large swathe of popular Modernism, including cinemas, that has subsequently been embraced by the public as the representative architecture of the inter-war years. The presumption was that true modern architecture would not come without a heroic struggle against the seductions of ornament. It was rare for firms working outside London to design genuinely modern buildings. In Yorkshire and Lancashire, the Co-operative Society, under W. A. Johnson, with a group of younger but more or less anonymous talents, produced stores in Huddersfield, Bradford and Southport that were admired in national magazines. Almost forgotten, but even more remarkable, is the Co-op's St Cuthbert's Showroom, Bread Street, Edinburgh, with one of the most complete curtain walls of glass on any British street before the 1950s. According to Charles McKean, this building 'provided an excellent advertisement by day and night for the goods within, satisfying the 1930s preoccupation with three-dimensionality'.[45] The only rival to this was Dunston 'B' Power Station, Gateshead, by the engineers Merz & McLellan (1930–31). This arguably went even further that Owen Williams's D10 building in translating engineering directly into modern architecture, for the turbine halls were surrounded by huge expanses of sheer glazing, as neatly capped at the top as the Bauhaus, with never a suspicion of ornament.[46]

During the 1930s many of the international Modernist avant-garde architects modified or abandoned their earlier insistence on engineering as an adequate analogy for architecture. Implying the subsidiary place of technique to poetry, Le Corbusier declared in 1930: 'Les techniques sont l'assiette même du lyrisme'. It soon became clear that functionalism did not work very well, and on this account, if no other, was ethically dubious,

46

especially in fields such as social housing. A new realism arose about adapting modern buildings to the uniquely stressful British climate, with its rapid alternation between freeze and thaw in the winter months. Contrary to the assumption that efficiency would always result from new techniques and products, it often seemed to come from the adaptation of old ones. At the same time, the idea of novelty remained strong in the imagination. In *Principles of Modern Building* (1938) by Richard Fitzmaurice of the Building Research Station, the subject of wall finishes was exhaustively researched, and the smooth white finishes beloved of Modernism were shown almost inevitably to deteriorate in the English climate.

This shift in design thinking was paralleled by a shift in understanding what science could do for architecture. The charismatic Communist crystallographer J. D. Bernal, fêted in the architectural community, showed that science had a deeper purpose of achieving rationality in society than just contributing to the invention of new technology. This could, of course, take varied forms, and utopian ideas remained alive in the urban planning that became CIAM's main mission during and after the Athens/ ss *Patris* congress of 1933. The MARS Plan for London, mainly by a young Tecton staff member, William Tatton-Brown, was the outcome of a struggle between a radial plan (which Tatton-Brown favoured) and a linear city on Russian utopian lines, favoured by the German émigré Arthur Korn. The 1938 MARS exhibition also showed 'The Concrete City of the Future', a model made to designs by Yorke and Breuer in 1936. If this was going to replace London, then at least one reviewer was happy with the status quo, writing that 'the new architecture seems to fail even more completely than

F.R.S. Yorke and
Marcel Breuer,
Concrete City of the
Future, 1936.

the "impressive" muddle of the Strand and Fleet Street'.[47] The difficulty of reconciling the Modernist call for a *tabula rasa*, even in historic cities, with the growing appreciation of their existing charms remained an insoluble puzzle for decades to come. Meanwhile, London began to display modern buildings, such as the Peter Jones store, that were deliberately 'contextual', showing the possibility of an amicable truce between old and new.

Prefabrication and Post-War Reconstruction

For many architects, the war became an opportunity to harness government finance for research and development beyond any peacetime levels, and prepare for reconstruction with new techniques adequate to the task. The emergency demanded a real attention to functionalism. 'Light and dry' construction techniques, bringing together coordinated products for rapid assembly, were well developed in Germany and advocated in Britain by Gropius. The idea of prefabrication, with its promise of rational progress in design through feedback to industry, controlled by the architect as sensitive technocrat, was especially compelling for designers. For common building types such as houses and flats, factory-made systems of building would obviate the need for 'architecture' of the conventional kind, while producing higher levels of comfort. The idea was present before the war, in designs by Leslie Martin and Sadie Speight among others, and in proposals made for evacuation camps, but it was overtaken by events in 1939, and the evacuees were billeted ad hoc wherever they were sent in the 'phoney war' that autumn.

Martin left his job as Head of Hull School of Architecture just before the war, and moved to London as principal assistant architect to the London Midland and Scottish Railways. Apart from war-damage repairs, he worked with one of the rising political figures of the younger generation, Richard Llewelyn-Davies, in devising rapid-assembly prefabricated station buildings. His attention was less on prefabrication as such and more on the potential of systematic analysis of various aspects of plan, section and construction that could generate forms at a broad conceptual level. Martin is acknowledged as a crucial figure in the history of British Modernism, his influence rising decade by decade until the 1960s. He supported younger architects, including James Stirling and the Smithsons, whose designs differed considerably from his own rational sobriety. Through his own practice and teaching he acquired many disciples. Both Martin and Llewelyn-Davies were influential in putting the idea of research into architectural education, thus upholding the pre-war ideal of progress though the combination of architecture and science.

In 1944 the Prime Minister, Winston Churchill, announced that he intended to build 500,000 temporary homes from steel, 'as a military operation', but this conflicted with a parallel promise to build permanent homes as well, and the figure was reduced to 150,000. Not for the last time, a politician quoted a large and arbitrary number to impress voters, without any idea whether it could actually be achieved. As at the end of the First World War, the deciding factor in favour of industrialism was less its association with the design potential or efficiency of manufacture, than the desire to avoid using regular building labour, which was not only insufficient for the task, but also prone to strikes and disruptions.

In America, by long tradition, houses were made from standardized timber components, so that the transition to off-site manufacture seemed a natural progression when the government began to intervene, creating timber cottages for the Tennessee Valley Authority, which were among the American examples promoted to the British public in *Homes by the Million* by Hugh Casson.[48] Aesthetically, the Arcon Pre-fab, designed by a small group of young Modernists, was the most elegant, with some of the accidental grace of Jean Prouvé's similar experiments in metal building in France. Technically, however, it was less developed than the anonymous AIROH house, made on the same production lines that had recently made Spitfire planes to win the Battle of Britain. The AIROH was, says Colin Davies, 'that rare thing in the history of the pre-fabricated house: a truly mass-produced product'.[49] It was, however, also more expensive than a permanent house.

It is not surprising to find costs, production methods and aesthetics coming apart from each other in the uncertain climate of improvisation during the closing stages of the war and the transition to peace. Although Prefabs were popular with the families who moved into them, the role of spearheading Modernism's penetration of mass culture was reserved for large-scale public housing in the 1950s and after. Similar to prefabs, but more conventional looking, were the permanent Demonstration Houses promoted by the government at Northolt, Middlesex, to develop partial alternatives to conventional building, using steel frames and a variety of cladding from metal sheets to concrete slabs and bricks. The British Iron and Steel Federation House of 1944, a comfortable design by Frederick Gibberd with vernacular overtones, was the only one to win architectural acclaim, and it was reproduced in large numbers.

The AIROH house prototype, exhibited by the Ministry of Works, 1944.

Frederick Gibberd,
The British Iron and
Steel Federation
House, 1944.
Prototype pair
erected at Northolt.

The school building programme after the war was a better example than the prefabs of the Gropius philosophy of architecture in action, indeed as good as any in the world. During the period of 1930s Modernism, schools tended to be 'half modern' under the local authority architects who designed them. Here, however, was a field suitable for a gently romanticized social architecture. Denis Clarke Hall's school at Richmond, Yorkshire, completed just as the war broke out, showed how Modernism could be a matter of fruit trees and cheerful colours as much as a brave new world of concrete or steel. In 1944 the 'Butler' Education Act prepared the way for a major rebuilding programme. Soon the rapidly rising birth rate, combined with growth in some residential areas, threatened to make existing school buildings unsustainable and made school building a political priority – and gave efficiency its finest hour.

The solution to this crisis that has become imprinted in history was the one developed in the architects' office of Hertfordshire County Council under the patronage of the Chief Education Officer John Newsom, and the architectural leadership of Stirrat Johnson-Marshall. With an eager team, the problem of rapid production to predictable budgets and timetables was analysed, and a solution found in liaison with the manufacturer, Hills of West Bromwich, who supplied a light steel frame system, based on modules that in simple repetition created standard classroom sizes. The frame not only worked in linear series, but also could be connected in any direction, allowing the plan forms to vary according to individual designers' interpretation of a site's special qualities or a refinement in teaching theory. It was clever, but unlike many prefabrication systems, not so clever as to limit practicability. In the minds of the designers, the effectiveness of the end product was dependent on a combination of factors, including the anonymity of the designer within a group and the sharing of research between all the parties involved. This was a moral ideal with a demonstrable outcome in an improved service to the public.

The Hertfordshire schools that began to be published in architectural magazines from 1946 had little resemblance to pre-war Modernist buildings, being less concerned with formality of exterior and more with creating interesting and colourful interior spaces, with outdoor planting

Architects' Co-Partnership, Margaret Wix Primary School, St Albans, c.1956, a typical Hertfordshire school.

and occasional pieces of modern sculpture. Where possible, items such as washbasins were redesigned, manufacturers being confident in future orders. What began in Hertfordshire spread to become a national system of building, refined over time by its inventors, such as the architect couple David and Mary Medd, who transferred to the architectural staff of the Ministry of Education. The Hills system was joined during the 1950s by CLASP (Consortium of Local Authorities Special Programme), which had many similar features, and continued into the 1970s, generating a whole university campus at York along the way.

Hertfordshire schools tamed technology from a devouring monster to a friendly servant. The people who designed them were keen on Lethaby, and one can imagine him returning the compliment. In this moment, the problem of reconciling function, social purpose and aesthetics seemed to reach equilibrium, although in the collectivism of a design group the impulse to excel could become dulled by routine over time. One response was to reinvigorate the poetics of architecture through a return to individualist creativity. Another was to attempt a return to a more rigorous functionalism through prefabrication. During the 1950s and '60s modern architects became split between these alternatives, occasionally crossing from one side to another.

Hertfordshire County Council (A.W.C. Barr), Templewood School, Welwyn Garden City, 1949.

chapter two

Compassion: Modern Architecture Builds the 'Just City'

In the Hertfordshire schools there was a balance between the technical aspects of Modernism and the humanist ones. The ethos of the schools was a nurturing one, in contrast to the sense of struggle and survival so prevalent in social thought at the beginning of the twentieth century. While the technical achievements of British Modernism were not insignificant, the application of creative and liberal social thinking to the design of buildings and cities was arguably Britain's most distinctive contribution to the Modern Movement worldwide. It is usually seen as something that coincided with the post-war welfare state, but, like that great change in social thinking, its roots go back much further, to the late nineteenth century, when the attractive, nature-conscious architecture of the middle classes was given to the poor as a sign of hope. Fascism had a substantial body of British sympathizers, so that during the 1930s, after modern architecture had taken root and begun to flourish, it was recruited along with the other arts to the cause of social democracy. Many architects were happy to moderate the harsh side of Modernism to show the benefits of a future as described by Louis MacNeice in the closing passages of *Autumn Journal* (1939):

> Where life is a choice of instruments and none
> Is debarred his natural music,
> Where the waters of life are free of the ice-blockade of hunger
> And thought is free as the sun . . . [1]

For poets of MacNeice's generation, including W. H. Auden and Stephen Spender, the early 1930s induced the same urgent feeling that dramatic change was required, for the sake of art and society alike, aided by Marx and Freud. Architecture shared these 'figureheads of our transition', as MacNeice called them, as well as the educated middle-class guilt about the condition of the working poor in Britain. From the Marxist abstractions of class and historical necessity, many of the young generation of cultural leaders in Britain moved towards a more tolerant and

Eric Mendelsohn and Serge Chermayeff, De La Warr Pavilion, Bexhill-on-Sea, East Sussex, 1935.

inclusive view of the future, tempered by age and experience, although the idealism lived on for many decades. In 1934 the American cultural critic and historian Lewis Mumford ended his book *Technics and Civilisation* with the opinion that 'it would be a gross mistake to seek wholly within the field of technics for an answer to all the problems that have been raised by technics'. What was needed was a 'rebuilding of the individual personality and the collective group, and the reorientation of all forms of thought and social activity towards life'.[2] In architecture and planning, subjects to which he devoted much of his time, Mumford saw the emergence of a 'biotechnic order . . . pointing to a civilisation in which the biological sciences will be freely applied to technology, and in which technology itself will be oriented toward the culture of life'.[3]

'The culture of life', the subject of MacNeice's passage, was an area in which Modernists intended to show their superiority to the rather tired, existing neo-Georgian norm of social architecture. If modern architecture were by its own definition architecture with a social purpose, then almost any examples would serve to illustrate the theme. Some were more carefully considered in this respect than others, while, conversely, it was possible to build social architecture that was not Modernist in looks, and is therefore unfairly struck out of the category. For example, the early flats built by the St Pancras Home Improvement Society, founded in 1923 by the charismatic Father Basil Jellicoe, a mission priest at St Mary's, Somers Town, near St Pancras station, were neo-Georgian, although good of their kind and ornamented with little pieces of sculpture or ceramic relief, with a strong focus on flower boxes, which distinguished them from dour Victorian tenements. Some of these flats can be seen in the background of a photograph showing General Sir Ian Hamilton (confusingly, the namesake of the Society's architect) setting fire to a pyre of rotten timbers from demolished terraces, surmounted by giant models of bedbugs, the curse of the slums, while Father Jellicoe looks on. This was only one of many publicity devices aimed at bringing in donations for the Society's work. Although the architecture was traditional, Jellicoe's fundraising techniques, involving a mobile cinema show, were not. The Trust engaged the first woman Chartered Surveyor in Britain, Irene Barclay.[4]

Quarry Hill Flats in Leeds was also inspired by a minister of religion turned local Labour politician, the Reverend Charles Jenkinson, carrying on the mission of late Victorian Christian socialism. A number of architects joined or sympathized with the Communist Party in the 1930s, despite the inconvenient fact that modern architecture was banned under Stalin, and revived academic classicism took its place.[5]

Left-wing attitudes accompanied a shift in the architect's own role from gentleman practitioner to employee of a public organization.

54

General Sir Ian Hamilton sets fire to a ceremonial bonfire of rotten timber and giant models of rat, flea and bug, to promote the work of the St Pancras Housing Society, January 1931.

Writing in 1942, John Summerson related this to the discovery of Modernism in the 1920s, which itself led to

> a wider conception of what architecture is, of its relation to siting, to town-planning and thus to sociology, and more remotely to politics: then, from politics back to sociology, and the sociological position of the architect himself.[6]

The Association of Architects, Surveyors and Technical Assistants (AASTA) was formed to be effectively a trade union for architects of the type that Summerson described, working for local authorities or for organizations such as the Miners' Welfare Commission and the Scottish Special Housing Association. He believed that the political situation of the 1930s infused it with vitality so that it 'came to fill the role . . . proposed by the MARS Group, but which that round-table of architectural highbrows was too supine and introvert to perform'. The professional status of architects was more clearly defined in the Architects' Registration Act passed in 1938.

Sweden demonstrated the links between Social Democracy and Modernism by turning to the former in 1932 after the corrupt conservative regime of the 1920s reached its nadir and the army shot five strikers, and to the latter in 1930 at the Stockholm Exhibition, where Gunnar Asplund, Sven Markelius and the theorist Gregor Paulsson revealed a change of heart, explaining it in a lengthy manifesto, *acceptera* ('Accept!') in 1931. Keynsian economic policies succeeded in generating employment and the foundations of a Social Democratic welfare state, defined in the word *folkhemmet* ('the people's home'), in which people of all conditions would be cared for. In Sweden, expenditure on children's education and health was seen as investment in human capital, and this exposed the callousness and ultimate inefficiency of Britain's tight-fisted welfare provision.

The new thinking of the 1930s was that compassion was a precondition for efficiency, not a hindrance. Another political model observed with interest from Britain was that of America under Franklin D. Roosevelt's New Deal. The project that caught the imagination of architects and planners most strongly was the Tennessee Valley Authority, one of the New Deal showpieces, which involved coordinated control of natural resources, relocation of population as well as prefabricated housing, reflecting Lewis Mumford's ideas of regional reconstruction.

A Modern Architecture of Compassion?

Ignorance and poverty were barriers to health, as was the mind–body split introduced by mechanist thinking and the social conventions against showing the body, especially for women. The generation after the First World War began to overcome some of these problems, and Modernism offered an appropriate architecture of compassion because it too was stripped down, effacing the signs of history and class and connecting with sunlight and nature, especially in the still-polluted industrial cities.

Often, the buildings were one-off solutions, owing to the absence of consistent financial provision. Most exceptional in its novelty of approach was the Pioneer Health Centre in Peckham in south-east London, established in 1926 in rented premises by two doctors. It proposed a radical alternative to health care in this poor but stable community, based on prevention rather than cure, and linked to the structure of the family rather than the individual. In 1935 the Centre opened its purpose-built headquarters, designed by Owen Williams. The concrete frame structure enabled the flat roof to be used for roller skating and provided visual transparency inside, so that members seeing swimming or other activities done by people like themselves would be encouraged to join in. In place of the industrial order of production there was 'a sort of anarchy' deliberately fostered by the organizers, which was seen as 'the first condition in any experiment in human applied biology'.[7] It is a sad

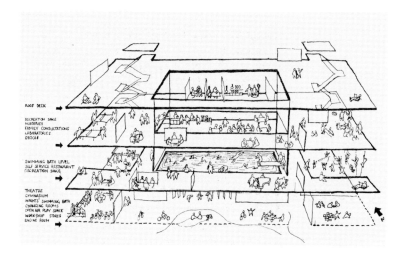

Sir Owen Williams, Pioneer Health Centre, Peckham, London, 1935. This cut-away drawing dates from 1951, shortly before the closure of the Centre.

reflection on the limits of the post-war welfare state that the Centre was shut down in 1951, rather than being emulated all over the country. The building was admired by Walter Gropius, not only as the best of the new architecture in Britain, but also 'the only one that he found interesting'.[8] Jack Donaldson, who as a young man decided to give most of his money to fund the Centre, was also the client for the Wood House, Shipbourne, designed by Gropius.

The Finsbury Health Centre, opened in 1938 and designed by Lubetkin and Tecton, operated in a different way, chiefly as a TB screening centre and clinic. As well as its intelligent approach to making building services accessible, it presented a familiar image of a public building, with a central entrance surmounted by the borough coat of arms and neo-Victorian lettering, and a symmetrical layout. It showed Lubetkin's rapid shift from 'white Modernism' to the use of colours and textures. The combination of imagery as well as certain formal devices within the design was recognizable in post-war architecture, especially the Royal Festival Hall of 1951.

Most social and architectural experiments had to be carried out by private trusts or voluntary bodies, limiting their scope but avoiding the danger of bureaucratic ossification of architecture. Even where public money was used, it required an uncommon patron somewhere in the organization concerned for modern architecture to be the outcome. This was the case with the De La Warr Pavilion at Bexhill-on-Sea, Sussex, by Mendelsohn and Chermayeff, which was the result of an architectural competition assessed by Thomas Tait and promoted by the mayor, the 9th Earl De La Warr, who was the chief local landowner and also a

W. E. Lescaze,
boarding house for
Dartington School,
Devon, 1934.

member of Ramsay MacDonald's cabinet. The amenities were standard
for a municipal seaside theatre, with a restaurant, although a public
library and reading room represented a higher cultural aspiration, not
unlike the combination in a Soviet Workers' Club. The architecture was
exceptional, offering space, light and a lift to the spirits. There was a conservative faction in the town that resented the style of the building and
contested the money spent on it, but the building was completed without any major compromise and opened in 1935, by the Duke and Duchess
of York, the future George VI and Queen Elizabeth.

   'The sun is one of our emotive nouns' wrote Auden in 1938, and liberation through physical activity in the open air was learnt by the British
from working-class Germany in the 1920s, as well as from the international rich on the Côte d'Azur. Many municipalities built open-air
swimming baths or 'lidos' from 1928 onwards, the date when central
funding became available for the purpose. They came in a variety of
architectural styles, including various forms of Modernism. None was

H. Vicars Lobb, Youth
Hostel, Holmbury St
Mary, Surrey, 1935.

G. Philip Bell, Yacht Club, Strangford Lough, Co. Down, Northern Ireland, 1938.

designed by leading architects. They were most often the work of borough engineers, but the basic requirements produced accidental beauty. Other outdoor leisure pursuits were embodied in Modernist buildings, such as sailing in the Royal Corinthian Yacht Club by Emberton, or the forgotten little yacht club on Strangford Lough in Ulster by G. Philip Bell. The Youth Hostels Association, founded in 1930, began to commission new buildings, including the Modernist brick hostel at Holmbury St Mary, Surrey, by H. Vicars Lobb, which was originally furnished with Aalto chairs.[9] An exhibition on Health, Sport and Fitness held at the RIBA in 1938 reflected a government campaign for what the RIBA president of the time described as 'fitter, flatter Britons' in the form of the Physical Training and Recreation Act of 1937. The exhibition showed a number of Continental examples (including many from Germany and Italy, where fitness formed part of the Fascist programme), which put the meanness of British provisions to shame. The architectural historian Christopher Hussey, reviewing it in *Country Life*, advocated a more active use of the countryside for leisure as a corollary to its preservation, but noted that in Sweden sports provision was funded by a tax on football pools. Meanwhile, an editorial in the DIA's *Trend* magazine commented on 'the curious irony that here where the open air was loved for itself (Wordsworth, Constable) and where games are a religion, green spaces are still a world away from thousands who need them most – the children of the slums'.[10]

The feeling that urban mass culture was a danger to people's better instincts led Henry Morris, the young Education Officer of Cambridgeshire County Council, to invent the idea of the Village Colleges in 1923, completing the first building in 1930 at Sawston. A Village College was a local school with additional facilities, such as meeting rooms and a public lending library for use by the adult population in the evenings. It was a simple idea for getting maximum use from one set of facilities, but also asserted that farm labourers and their wives could and should have somewhere to go in their leisure time other than the pub. The county architect, S. E. Urwin, designed Sawston in a neo-Georgian style, but was urged by Morris to adopt a modern style for the next two colleges, at Bottisham (1937) and Linton (1938). The final one of the

Walter Gropius and Maxwell Fry, Impington Village College, Cambridge, 1937–9. The model shows an unexecuted gymnasium.

pre-war series was Impington, designed by Walter Gropius and executed to a tight budget after his departure to the USA in 1937 by Jack Howe, a young assistant in the office of Maxwell Fry. Other local authority architects made a contribution comparable to Urwin's, such as W. T. Curtis, designer of many brick schools in Middlesex to accommodate the rising population of the suburbs. A small number of local authorities, such as the West Riding of Yorkshire, commissioned modern buildings, either from outside architects such as Oliver Hill (Whitwood Mere, Castleford, 1939) and Burnet, Tait and Lorne. Invariably, the commissions came from a young and persuasive officer on the council staff.

Britain had many theorists of alternative education, some of whom opened schools in existing buildings, lacking the funds to build new. The only school to employ modern architecture in quantity was Dartington, part of a project of rural reconstruction by Dorothy and Leonard Elmhirst, endowed with the American fortune she had inherited, and run by Leonard in emulation of the poet Rabindranath Tagore's community of Santinikatan in Bengal. Beginning in 1926, radical arts, ecological recovery and scientific efficiency were brought together in the luscious Devon countryside, in buildings ranging from a medieval royal great house, through late Arts and Crafts to Modernism, which arrived almost by accident in 1932 in the luggage of the new headmaster of Dartington School, the educational experiment that was one of the manifold activities. W. B. Curry had worked in a school near Philadelphia designed by the Swiss Modernist William Lescaze, and persuaded Dartington to employ him for a number of years. A set of fine 'International Style' buildings resulted.

The Miners' Welfare Commission was set up in 1921, and through its architecture aimed to provide the miner and his family 'with fuller

opportunities for recreation both of body and mind, with a brighter social life, and generally with a healthier and sweeter environment than the nature of his occupation can otherwise offer to him'.[11] Pithead baths were a priority, enabling miners to change out of working clothes and avoid the daily ritual of a tub in front of the kitchen fire after work. The Commission initially used the designs of a retired naval commander, B. T. Coote, but after 1925 J. H. Forshaw, one of a new breed of public architects, was employed to lead a MWC architects' branch, and 345 pithead baths were built between 1928 and 1939. Like Curtis in Middlesex, or Harold Rowbotham, who designed park buildings for the LCC, they found that the Dutch brick style of W. M. Dudok, architect of Hilversum New Town, suited their purposes of representing progress rather than revolution. The style involved clear interlocking volumes with horizontal bands of windows, contrasted with points of vertical emphasis around towers or staircases. Although not at the cutting edge of style, these buildings, resulting from research and teamwork, brought the tangible benefits of Modernism to a group of workers whose living conditions were typical of unreformed Victorian capitalism. Since the virtual collapse of the British coal industry in the 1980s, few remain standing.

A whirlpool bath at a pithead bath building provided by the Miners' Welfare Commission.

Charles Holden's work for Frank Pick and the London Underground has been mentioned already, but its missionary context deserves more exploration. In a fascinating analysis, the American historian Michael Saler has linked Pick's tastes and motives for social improvement back to the Arts and Crafts Movement, and more specifically to his Nonconformist background in York. From the example of Pick and the Underground, Saler has generalized a 'medi-aeval modernist' style in distinction to a more avant-garde Modernism of the 1930s, defined by its iconography, which retained traditional symbolism in a modern style. There is certainly something in the unpretentiousness of these buildings, and their inclusion within a complete programme of public service design, that extends more widely in the ethos of English Modernism both before and after the war. Although the writings of Ruskin were deeply unfashionable between the wars, his effect on linking the aesthetic, social and spiritual remained a deep underlying influence.

In 1939 Nikolaus Pevsner wrote:

> it would be wrong to assume that there are no British architects of strong personality who have contributed new and independent solutions to the international modern style. There are several – just as there are certain modern themes specially developed or even created in England, e.g. the planned trading estate, the pit-head bath or the health centre.[12]

John Summerson in 1942 predicted 'a regression from the most advanced outposts reached by, say, Tecton Maxwell Fry or Wells Coates' and that instead,

> interest will centre in evolving a type of design incorporating many accepted formulas of planning and finish, but more flexible than anything which there could have been before the onset of the 'modern' movement between the wars.[13]

In a book review of 1940, Tim Bennett, a brilliant young architect killed in 1942, looked forward to an even greater convergence between architectural style and popular taste in a Modernist vernacular, with words that Lethaby might have used: 'We can look forward to a time when architecture will again be fine building, just as old manors and churches were "fine" cottages and barns.'[14]

An even wider pluralism was evident in an exercise conducted early in 1939 to ask 50 public figures to choose their favourite six modern buildings.[15] The outcome failed to follow obvious preferences for one sub-section of modern architecture rather than another, so that most respondents mixed the more traditional examples, such as Battersea Power Station (11 votes) with more obviously modern ones, such as Peter Jones (highest score with 15 votes). A few completely traditional buildings, such as the Jockey Club at Newmarket by Albert Richardson and the church of St Philip, Cosham, by Ninian Comper, received at least one vote, the latter being the choice of John Betjeman, the poet who worked on the *Architectural Review* between 1930 and 1935, later becoming a national figure responsible for opening English eyes to buildings and the environment. Comper was at odds with the modern world, as Betjeman also increasingly became, but was an original artist and a profound thinker.[16] Modern architecture appealed to educated people, but even among these it remained a minority taste. By the time of the war, some supporters had doubts about the chances of it becoming popular in its existing form. John Summerson, who wrote much of the caption copy for the MARS Group's exhibition at the beginning of 1938, confessed in a letter to the painter Ben Nicholson in 1940: 'I think modern architecture will have to beat a retreat, simply because the public can't understand it, never will, and hates it like poison.'[17] Unwilling to commit to any alternative, Summerson concealed his ambivalent feeling.

Garden Cities – Horizontal or Vertical?

When 1930s Modernists in Britain thought about planning new cities, they experienced less sense of a violent break with the past than was the case with architectural style. The great English contribution to European Modernism was the Garden City, not for its architecture, which was no more modern than simplified Arts and Crafts, but for the concept of a planned settlement in which grass and trees played a significant role and industry was carefully zoned away from housing. Before the First World War, the architect of New Frankfurt, Ernst May, worked for the leading designer of the Garden City movement, Raymond Unwin, and the influence could easily be traced in his work. In the 1930s Unwin himself became one of the figures of the older generation sympathetic to Modernism.

What had begun so promisingly in the planning and construction of the first garden suburbs and the Town Planning Act of 1909, the first of its kind, had gone terribly wrong by the 1930s, but governments seemed unable to correct it through further legislation. The historian Alan Jackson attributed the dismal result to lack of central government time and willpower, lack of properly qualified planning advisers at a local level, and lack of coordination between local authorities.[18] For the left, private enterprise in a free market was bound to lower cultural standards and only the collaboration of intellectuals with the state could be trusted to deliver efficiency and fair shares to all. The romantic right (along with a section of the left) deplored the suburbanization of England, which was besmirching the country and upsetting social hierarchies.

The despised suburban semi-detached villa (a paired grouping of houses symmetrical about a party wall) effected an extraordinary transfor-

Mrs Elsy Borders with her family outside 'Insanity', 81 Kingsway, Coney Hall, Kent, 1939.

mation in British social class. It went further towards solving the slum problem than any direct government intervention, but the cost in amenity and aesthetics was a high one, and the original and much more principled Garden City movement was blamed for producing 'a hermaphrodite, sterile, imbecile, a monster, abhorrent, loathsome to the Nature which he worships'.[19] The more politically minded saw these houses as the expression of impotent individualism, expressed in their minute differentiation and compartmentalization of outdoor space, detracting from the spirit of community. The Architects' and Technicians' Organisation (ATO, into which AASTA was absorbed in 1941) was set up 'to help people on housing estates who were having problems over repairs or faulty construction', including the most famous, Mrs Elsy Borders, who trained as a lawyer to defend her case against a jerry builder in south-east London. The public sector alternative, municipal 'cottage estates' in places such as Becontree, Essex, and Wythenshawe, Manchester, were architecturally sober but dull because of the lack of such basic urban amenities as shops and markets.

By the end of the 1930s a growing section of architectural opinion saw suburbs as a wasted opportunity to create towns more on the lines of English tradition, usually interpreted as a Georgian palimpsest overlaid on medieval street plans. The received idea of Modernism as a mathematical grid had little to offer in this respect, and a new alliance between Modernism and history began to emerge in Britain. The new housing estates in Germany by May and others from the mid-1920s showed the lesson of open space and controlled growth interpreted not in vernacular cottage architecture, but in a mixture of terraced houses and medium-rise flats, not so far removed from the semi, but symbolic of community rather than individualism. British schemes such as Quarry Hill, Leeds, aimed to recreate this feeling of a large, embracing, neutral background of architecture, although the central space at Quarry Hill was never landscaped to match Taut's Hufeisen or horseshoe of flats at Britz.

Writing in 1974, Alison Ravetz summarized the arguments of the time in favour of flats under the headings of economics and social

Photomontage of slab block of flats on the site of Blenheim Palace, created in 1935 for an article by W. A. Eden in the *Architectural Review*.

exigency – the wastefulness of leaving inner urban sites underdeveloped; technical innovation; social idealism; Continental example; fine architecture; and the preservation of rural land.[20] The mathematics of density appeared to favour height, giving the promised benefit of open space. The enthusiasm for flats of the type proposed by Le Corbusier was driven by the desperate feeling of the early 1930s, encouraging solutions that went against traditional habits almost for their own sake in order to acknowledge the need for radical change. A theoretical proposal of 1935 showed a slab block occupying the site of Blenheim Palace, and therefore doing no damage to the landscape, contrasted with a scatter of low-density low-rise dwellings. These images subtly helped to insert the large housing slab within a cultural tradition of English landscape design, promising to the worker the amenities of a duke, although the Danish writer Steen Eiler Rasmussen warned the British against adopting these inferior standards of housing and abandoning their own traditions.[21]

The incentive to build flats grew stronger during the course of the 1930s. The Housing Act of 1930 offered a subsidy from central government funds to local authorities based on the number of people displaced, which increased for buildings more than three storeys in height. Suburban cottage estates were still eligible for subsidy until 1933, when Sir Hilton Young, the Health Minister of the coalition (National) government, reserved the subsidy exclusively for flats. The Dudley Report on Slum Clearance of 1934 anticipated the use of much taller flats, and in the comment of Lewis Silkin as Chairman of the LCC Housing Committee we hear an anticipation of post-war confidence in high rise. He believed that though the public

> might be prejudiced in favour of five storey as against ten storey blocks, the question should be viewed with an open mind and it might be found advisable to build higher than they at present contemplated.[22]

The Housing Act of 1935 accelerated the rate of slum clearance by offering higher subsidies for a limited term of three years, producing what Alison Ravetz calls 'the great quinquennium' of flat building. The take-up rate for building flats varied considerably from one place to another, although by 1939, Ravetz argues, there was a wider acceptance from many different groups of the idea of living in flats.

The acceptance of flats, never more than grudging, reflected a lack of imagination or will to do anything different. London was still restricted by its Building Regulations to 80 feet of habitable height, usually making six or seven storeys. For cheaper flats, five storeys was the maximum practicable height without the additional cost of lifts. The models of the future of working-class housing were more often from the private sector, including Wells Coates's Isokon (1934), Lubetkin's and Tecton's Highpoint (1935) and Frederick Gibberd's Pullman Court (1935). Where flats by elite modern architects were actually for the working class, they were mainly supported by some form of subsidy, as with Maxwell Fry's Sassoon House, Peckham (1934), which was funded by a private benefactor, or the industrial sponsorship of his Kensal House (1936). Longer established housing charities, such as the Guinness Trust and the Four Per Cent Industrial Dwellings Company, also employed modern, if less newsworthy, architects on some of their schemes.[23]

Kensal House was the most effective of the Modernist blocks in its inclusion of shared social facilities of a type offered in some Continental schemes, owing to the involvement of the housing consultant Elizabeth Denby, who gave Fry his earlier opportunity at Sassoon House after his

E. Maxwell Fry, with housing consultant Elizabeth Denby, Kensal House Flats, North Kensington, London, 1937.

epiphany of the portal truss. From experience in housing management rather than architecture, she could see beyond the abstraction of community to the reality. Kensal House was commissioned by the Gas Light and Coke Company, whose initial interest was to improve the design of gas-fired domestic appliances, until Denby persuaded them to develop a derelict industrial site in North Kensington, her main area of activity, as a full-scale demonstration of modern living, and Fry put himself forward for the commission. Aided by the topography of the site, which made it difficult for the ground level to be inhabited, there was a communal room, a workshop for men and, the greatest coup of all, a nursery school introduced as an addition to the brief in the round shape of a former gasholder on the site. Equally important, however, was the desire to ease the woman's work at home in cooking and laundry by a more thoughtful design of spaces and equipment. Denby referred to the scheme as an 'urban village', and wrote about the delight with which many of the residents had responded to the new opportunities for gardening and maintenance.[24] She insisted that when one resident constructed an elaborate trellis on his balcony, seemingly at odds with the modern aesthetic, others should be allowed to do the same. Kensal House appeared in the form of a model in the pioneering documentary film *Housing Problems* (1935), in tacit contrast to an LCC block, which

Elizabeth Denby, The All-Europe House, as displayed at the *Daily Mail Ideal Home Exhibition*, 1939.

was efficient but soulless. On completion, a separate film showed it in action, while the Ascot Water Heater Company produced a lavish book on flats, in which it occupied centre stage.

Denby joined with architects and activists, many of them women, in a series of exhibitions, under the title *New Homes for Old*, between 1931 and 1938. The campaign shifted from persuading authorities simply to take responsibility for housing to arguments about the most appropriate forms of provision. In 1934 the Housing Centre was formed by voluntary activists, mostly women, among them the architect Judith Ledeboer, who made a link with members of the MARS Group and the ATO. They were critical of 'the erection of human cages, which are a mockery of housing', as they described the standard walk-up tenement blocks normally provided by local authorities, which had almost no amenities, no connection with a wider neighbourhood and no visual graces.[25] Denby was uneasy with the whole notion that flats would become the universal housing form of the future, suggesting that there was a position beyond the 'choice between two impractical and unnecessary extremes' represented by Garden Cities and flats.[26] 'The rows of terrace cottages built in Regency days, with a small garden in front and a long one behind', she explained at the RIBA in 1936, 'were built at a density of 50 or 60 dwellings to the acre. That is the density at which we are now building flats.'[27] This solution fell between the subsidy provisions of the government, and Denby was patronizingly put down by Lewis Silkin, who could not imagine altering the ministerial norms. In the conclusion to her book *Europe Re-housed* (1938), however, Denby proposed that social housing should ideally merge invisibly into the urban texture through a mixture of rehabilitation and new-build infill, with an end to 'zoning snobberies' more typical of the European city or the pre-industrial British city. Clean and quiet industries should be readmitted. 'This would encourage a welcome return to "street architecture" in Britain', she believed.[28] In the same year, students at the Architectural Association, working under Max Lock, later an important planner, took the bold step of interviewing the potential clients for new housing in Ocean Street, Stepney, with the help of the left-wing group Mass-Observation. This was a LCC redevelopment area where two-storey terraces

Preparation of the MARS Group display on Bethnal Green for the New Homes for Old Group, shown at the Building Trades Exhibition, Olympia, London, 1934.

were destined to be replaced with standard flats, as the subsidy regulations required. They discovered that the majority of residents would prefer replacement houses, and furthermore that overall density would be unaffected if these were provided. Although this exercise received some attention at the time, the methodology and the outcome were largely forgotten in the post-war years.

Denby seems in retrospect an increasingly significant figure. She stood almost alone in her capacity to assess the actual situation in housing, unaffected by dogma, and thus to move beyond the cruder models of technological progress that appealed so strongly to architects. F. R. Yerbury, long-serving secretary of the AA, recognized her special contribution:

> she obviously does not belong to that scientifically-minded school of thought which would teach people how to live. Rather, one imagines, she would help them to live in a more comfortable and richer way than they had been able to do so before.[29]

The Romantic Turn in Modern Architecture

It is becoming more widely recognized how much Modernism of the 1930s differed from that of the 1920s, turning from the active to the contemplative mode, and more concerned to heal than to destroy.[30] Marcel Breuer, arriving in London in 1935, published an important text, 'Where Do We Stand?', in the *Architectural Review* in April (it was originally delivered to the Swiss Werkbund in Zurich the previous year).[31] He registered his own desire to go beyond mechanistic forms to a more intuitive way of designing, and pointed to a more varied range of possibilities within Modernism. The freedom to experiment and run the full range of expression had become for him 'the real gauge of our strength'.

Breuer's thoughts matched the rural, contemplative image of Britain that emerged in response to the crisis at the beginning of the decade. Interest revived in the eighteenth-century landscape and the Picturesque eclecticism of the Regency, seen afresh through Modernist trends in poetry and painting, especially Surrealism. The *Architectural Review* was keen to promote this self-referential and educated type of Modernism, which was potentially less alienating for the public than the 'high' Modernism of the previous decade.

Timber was a crucial material and Serge Chermayeff's house at Bentley Wood, completed in 1938, was one of several modern timber houses of the time, remaining the most celebrated example of a perfect balance between Modernism and the English tradition of rapport with nature. Breuer made his contribution in the Gane Show House at the Royal West

Marcel Breuer, pavilion
for A. E. Gane Ltd at
the Royal West of
England Show, 1936.

of England Show in 1935, presenting a mixture of rough-stone walling, much of it built on the curve (allowing a thin wall to stand without buttressing), with large panes of glass and plywood inside. Lubetkin's enriched palette of materials at the Finsbury Health Centre has been mentioned, and Maxwell Fry later recorded his search just before the war for 'something richer and more satisfying than reinforced concrete, and not so much for the structure as for the finish'. The results can be seen in a student hostel in North Gower Street, London (1939), where Fry

> used brick to give texture: rough red brick, and shiny, blue-glazed tiles, set in contrast to a highly finished façade of sliding metal windows alternating with opaque, vitreous-glass panels, so that the two sets of surfaces – the metallic and the organic – should set up a lively conversation within the framework of the whole.[32]

J. M. Richards, writing for a popular audience of Penguin readers in 1940, saw regionalism in architecture as a form of progress, and not confined to England:

E. Maxwell Fry, Cecil
Residential Hostel for
Women, North Gower
Street, St Pancras,
London, 1939.

Countries have their own different temperaments and ideals, and
different climates, habits and raw materials. They also have a past,
and the national culture of which their modern architecture is
part is not separable from its roots, even if it were desirable that it
should be. So, as modern architecture matures, a new differentiation according to national characteristics is inevitable – not on
the basis of the racial exclusiveness of Nazism, and not so clear
or distinct as would have been the case many years ago . . . As
mankind is still organised into nations – biologically as well as
politically – a permanently international architecture would not
even be produced by literal functionalism.[33]

The appeal to biology was part of the romantic trend, operating on
the level of popular science writing, in which mechanistic models for
understanding the world were being replaced by holistic ones. During
and after the war, the separate profession of landscape architecture in
Britain began to have an effect, combining scientific understanding of

the land with a humanist understanding of how the environment had been shaped historically. At the end of the war, books by the landscape architects Brenda Colvin (*Land and Landscape*, 1948) and Sylvia Crowe (*Tomorrow's Landscape*, 1956) offered architects a fresh way of understanding the relationship of buildings to other human interventions in the landscape. As Colvin wrote:

> human life at the present stage of evolution becomes so artificial that we seem easily to forget that man is just part of the rest of nature and that, in spite of his immense powers of adaptation and his ability to create new conditions, he is still utterly dependent on such things as weather, soil and plants for his very existence.[34]

Landscape and planting became a fully integrated aspect of the best modern architecture in the post-war decades, so that it is hard to recall how much needed to be learnt. Switzerland, Germany, the Scandinavian countries and America all offered examples of designed landscapes that worked with modern architecture, often unobtrusively, as in Holger Blom's famous linear park on the shore of Lake Malaren in Stockholm. Where early Modernist architecture might seem to involve mostly looking up into the sky, the next phase included much attention to what was beneath one's feet. Geoffrey Jellicoe, who taught at the AA in the early 1930s and encouraged modern design, made this a feature of his studio discussions. Frederick Gibberd took over from him as head of the school during the war, and led many major post-war practitioners such as Powell & Moya, Leonard Manasseh and Neville Conder to think less of the building form in itself and more about the spaces between buildings. Jellicoe, Gibberd and other architects such as Peter Shepheard developed a dual practice designing buildings and open spaces of various kinds after the war, from small urban parks and gardens to the settings for large industries, including power stations. Many other architects had a sideline in planting trees and shrubs around their buildings to model the space and develop atmosphere. Thus the often rather bald presentation of modern architecture changed to a situation where the building form was deliberately lost over time in leaves and shadows. The tendency was to revert to apparently 'traditional' materials for paving and other hard landscape works, such as cobbled borders to paths, but these could equally be seen as modern in a timeless sense.

Planning and Wartime Reconstruction

The war gave the cause of the revised modern architecture and planning its great opportunity, which was met in the new spirit of anti-extremist tolerance. As Sonya Rose has written,

> as early as 1939, and gathering strength as the war progressed, there was a growing almost millenarian belief that a new Britain would rise up from the ruins of war. This would be a Britain not only with rebuilt cities and towns, but a Britain that was socially transformed.[35]

Thus the social direction of Modernism in the 1930s already set a path that was followed into the 1950s.

In 1940, with the outcome of the war still extremely uncertain, the architect Ralph Tubbs, a pre-war assistant to Ernö Goldfinger, organized the exhibition *Living in Cities* for the '1940 Council' and the British Institute of Adult Education, one of the first of many exhibitions that were circulated to show servicemen and other war workers what they could hope for after the war. Penguin Books produced an attractive companion volume, whose penultimate page, titled 'Some Misconceptions', indicated the shift away from functionalism by this date:

> That modern architecture ignores tradition
> That modern architecture means flat roofs and white concrete walls
> That architects are trying to impose an international style
> That planners want everyone to live in flats
> That the modern planner's idea of the city of to-morrow is a city of skyscrapers
> That 'garden cities' are a solution to the town-planning problems of to-day.[36]

The last item reflected the new concern to regenerate existing cities, already partially cleared by bombs in many cases, retaining a real commitment to urbanity. The popular left-wing illustrated weekly *Picture Post* devoted the first issue of 1941 to 'A Plan for Britain', with an article on planning and architecture by Maxwell Fry, with 'before' and 'after' illustrations of a typical industrial town, remodelled as a Corbusian idyll of slab blocks among greenery, similar to the endpapers of Tubbs's book, which were not wholly reassuring in respect of the 'misconceptions' quoted. 'The town of the future can well be a place of open spaces diversified and dignified by building and interlaced by traffic ways for vehicles

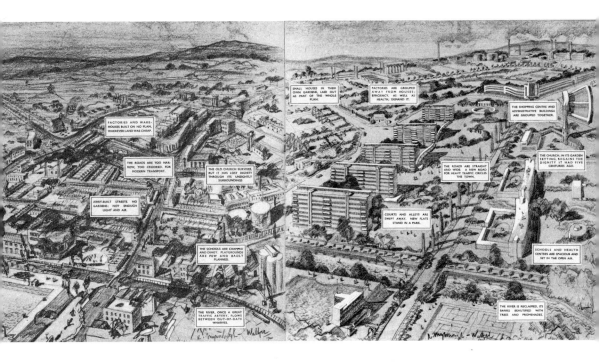

Within the illustration:

FACTORIES AND WARE-HOUSES BUILT ON NO PLAN, WHEREVER LAND WAS CHEAP.

THE ROADS ARE TOO NAR-ROW, TOO CROOKED, FOR MODERN TRANSPORT.

THE OLD CHURCH SURVIVES, BUT IT HAS LOST DIGNITY THROUGH ITS UNSIGHTLY SURROUNDINGS!

JERRY-BUILT STREETS. NO GARDENS; NOT ENOUGH LIGHT AND AIR.

THE SCHOOLS ARE CRAMPED AND DINGY. PLAYGROUNDS ARE FEW AND BADLY PLANNED.

THE RIVER, ONCE A GREAT TRAFFIC ARTERY, FLOWS BETWEEN OUT-OF-DATE WHARVES.

SMALL HOUSES IN THEIR OWN GARDENS, LAID OUT AS PART OF THE 'WHOLE PLAN.

FACTORIES ARE GROUPED AWAY FROM HOUSES; EFFICIENCY, AS WELL AS HEALTH, DEMAND IT.

THE SHOPPING CENTRE AND ADMINISTRATIVE BUILDINGS ARE GROUPED TOGETHER.

THE ROADS ARE STRAIGHT AND WIDE. A NEW ROAD FOR HEAVY TRAFFIC CIRCLES THE TOWN.

THE CHURCH, IN ITS GARDEN SETTING, REGAINS THE DIGNITY IT HAD FIVE CENTURIES AGO.

COURTS AND ALLEYS ARE SWEPT AWAY. NEW FLATS STAND IN A PARK.

SCHOOLS AND HEALTH CENTRES ARE SPACIOUS AND SET IN THE OPEN AIR.

THE RIVER IS RECLAIMED, ITS BANKS BEAUTIFIED WITH TREES AND PROMENADES.

R. Myerscough-Walker, 'A Plan for Britain', *Picture Post*, 14 January 1941.

and walkers', Fry wrote, adding: 'I have often thought that parts of Cambridge might set the standard.'[37]

When the bombs began to fall, the architect and planner William Holford, the young former head of Civic Design at Liverpool, was recruited to a new 'Reconstruction Group'. In a letter of 1942, he explained how the political pressures constrained action:

> Government holds, in this tightly packed and ancient island, an uneasy balance between public and private interest, but has not solved the difficulty of promoting development itself – in which I include good architecture, public works, national parks and reservations, even a first class road system.[38]

These were tasks requiring new legislation and administration. Despite hesitations, a Ministry of Town and Country Planning was created in November 1942, against a background of growing optimism about the outcome of the war, helped by the entry of the Americans and Russians as allies of Britain.

Heavy bombing in Coventry in November 1940 allowed a pre-war re-planning scheme for the congested medieval centre to proceed, under

Basil Spence, Coventry Cathedral, 1951–62.

Donald Gibson (City Architect), plan for the reconstruction of Coventry city centre after bombing, 1941.

Donald Gibson, one of the new type of official architect planners who had arrived in his post before the war and was impatient to reject the cautious and conservative ideas of his seniors. Gibson's new scheme involved a new shopping centre, all pedestrianized on two levels, placed on axis with the spire of the bombed cathedral, encircled by a ring road, and containing such groups of historic buildings as had survived amid the new trees and grass. Beyond the ring road, Gibson and his team planned new residential neighbourhoods, and although the architecture was mostly rather pedestrian too, Basil Spence's picturesquely sited new cathedral, won in competition in 1951, added zest to the mixture – and Gibson considered it a major achievement to have avoided having a Gothic design by Giles Gilbert Scott.

One of the chief concerns for Holford and his team who transferred to the new ministry was the location of industry, a problem emphasized by the seemingly terminal unemployment in many areas where traditional heavy industries such as steel and shipbuilding had virtually ceased. Research and legislation in the 1930s established a principle that government aid was needed to bring new industries into such areas, and the wartime Barlow Report set a new policy framework for creating benign and rational relationships between population, landscape and employment.

Brynmawr, a small and remote town in the Welsh Valleys, was typical of the places the Barlow Report intended to help. During the 1930s it was

Cyril Mardall (Sjöström), Community Centre, Brynmawr, Gwent, Wales (unexecuted), c. 1939.

already known through the independent action of a group of Quakers, who established new light industries. One member of this group, Lord Forrester, an electrical engineer and industrialist, also had an interest in architecture, and commissioned pre-war projects (unbuilt) for prefabricated timber housing and a civic centre from Cyril Sjöström (later known as Cyril Mardall) in a light Scandinavian style. During the war, Forrester commissioned a group of former AA students, formed into the Architects Co-Operative Partnership, to build a large factory, the Brynmawr Rubber Factory (1947–51; demolished 2001), which represented an emotional commitment to create an exceptional if not wholly

Architects Co-Operative Partnership (consulting engineer Ove Arup and Partners), Brynmawr Rubber Factory, Gwent, Wales (demolished), 1947–51.

appropriate building. These architects aimed, through an anonymous group practice, to avoid the egotism of the earlier generation and, like architects in public service, to become part of a shared movement based on research and openness to experiment.

The Barlow Report was followed by the Scott Report on Land Utilisation in Rural Areas (1942), anticipating new building in the country in the form of enlargement of existing villages and the enhancement of their community facilities. The report included a section on planning, recommending avoidance of historical styles but at the same time an abstract sympathy for materials and context. Formally planned towns and villages from the eighteenth century were upheld as exemplars to dispel fears of incongruity.[39] Paired to the Scott Report was the Uthwatt Report, in some ways the most radical of these three foundation stones of post-war planning, in that it recommended that the increased value accruing from developed land should be returned to the community, and that development rights should effectively be nationalized by a restriction to existing uses, unless permission was granted otherwise.

In 1943 Fry's new personal and professional partner, Jane Drew (they married in 1942), organized an exhibition *Rebuilding Britain*, based on the work of the RIBA reconstruction committee, which was shown at the National Gallery before touring. It represented the united front of Modernist architecture and planning, broadly on CIAM lines with an emphasis on separate zones for different activities, but with plenty of un-frightening examples of recent buildings with pitched roofs and small-paned windows, and pairings to suggest the continuity between Georgian and modern. The New Towns policy was anticipated, in the recommendation that no single city should be allowed to grow beyond a certain size. There was a naive confidence in the predictability of the future, and in unlimited supplies of energy and materials, as seen in the revised wartime version of the 1937 MARS plan that was proposed as a basis for London. Rural planning and modernization assumed a new importance, and new green belts around cities were expected to provide fresh food in the future. In common with almost all Modernist thinking of this time, the value of densely built, historic cities was forgotten, even though writers, artists and photographers were discovering it anew. Thus Lionel Brett, a young architect of the time, wrote in response to the Royal Academy's Beaux-Arts plan of 1943:

From *Rebuilding Britain*, 1944.

We still have too many dingy old schools with depressing asphalt playgrounds. No wonder some children don't enjoy lessons. Sunlight, fresh air and bright surroundings can make a lot of difference. The school above is at Zürich.

Peter Jones, a big store in Sloane Square. The front is all glass, and it looks very bright and pleasant, and can be kept clean even in the dirty London atmosphere.

78

LONDON NEEDS A NEW PLAN NOW

the lover of London would find his mysteries gone. By mysteries I do not mean slums or smoke or traffic blocks, but the curving line, the sheepy park, the piled-up asymmetrical silhouette, the secret alley and the silent square. Parisian vistas are not in this tradition.[40]

The inability to see London for what it could be when only gently modernized was the legacy of generations of demonizing the slums, for which the overarching solution was deemed to be a low density of population. How low became the only question. For the County of London Plan (1943), Patrick Abercrombie suggested 136 persons per acre as a desirable norm for the reconstruction of built-up areas, an apparently random figure. For Frederick Osborn, this was too many, and he worked hard to ensure that the Greater London Plan (1945) lowered the number to 100, and proposed eight or ten new towns well outside the existing limits of London, combined with a cessation of suburban building by setting up a green belt. Moving through the East End of London today, with its patchwork of surviving narrow streets and its 'rationally' placed but visually incoherent slab blocks and 'mixed development', interspersed with large and seemingly superfluous open spaces and a few surviving historic churches and pubs, one experiences the results of 1940s thinking in action, and it seems a very inept way to make a city.

Installing an exhibition of the County of London plan, 1944.

Abercrombie applied the concept of 'neighbourhood planning' to existing areas, and Shoreditch was drawn and modelled in detail to show the effect of creating schools and other public facilities in the centre of an area bounded by major roads. Since population had been declining in central London since the Second World War, this trend was accepted as proper and good, because the remaining residents could stretch into new space, while the New Towns took the emigrants. The reintroduction of nature into the city was a major theme, with new parks projected in areas that were poorly served, and the River Lea turned into a linear park. Today, we may think that there are limits to extending urban nature before it interferes with urbanity and ease of movement, and that 'neighbourhoods' conceived in this fashion can become ghettos of social exclusion, cut off by major roads. As Abercrombie showed in his plan for Plymouth, where he wanted to maintain the oldest part of the city, the Barbican, as a historic centre, he was sympathetic to the accidental poetry of urban development, although the Plymouth plan equally shows how clumsily he hoped to improve it. Local opposition to the Plymouth plan at the end of the war inspired the young director Jill Craigie to make a film, half fact and half fiction, about the people of the city and the planner coming among them, finishing with a rousing march of the young through the ruins of the old in favour of new houses, schools and pools.[41]

Thus the war ended, with high hopes and nearly ten more years of hardship ahead. The provisions of the welfare state, offering health care

Still from the closing sequence of *The Way We Live*, director Jill Craigie, 1945.

and education from national taxation, 'free at the point of delivery', were mostly in place by the time of the 1945 elections, in which Jill Craigie's future husband, Michael Foot, later a leader of the Labour Party, whom she met while making her film, was elected to the seat of Devonport Dockyard. He served under Clement Attlee in the administration that also introduced in 1947 the Town and Country Planning Act, which put into legislative form the modified recommendations of Barlow, Scott and Uthwatt. These included provision for the protection of historic buildings by 'listing' without compensation to owners, and a presumption against the development of any land unless it was provided for in local planning documents. By nationalizing development rights, the government came close to actually nationalizing land.

New Empiricism

In June 1947 the Swedish architect Sven Backström wrote a text to accompany publication in the *Architectural Review* of three new Swedish houses, under the title 'The New Empiricism', a name that stuck as a description of the new form of Modernism.[42] The image in the article of Sven Markelius's apparently informal bungalow near Stockholm, with a back view of his daughter standing naked on the grass, was a sufficient summary of the 'positive and life-assenting in architecture' to which Backström referred. The published plan of the house lovingly included the canopy of each birch tree, and the shallow pitched roof with a deep overhang, a feature just beginning to enter Modernism before the war, set a pattern that was functionally more reliable and socially more acceptable than the flat roof for housing after 1945.

Frederick Gibberd, housing at Somerford Road, Hackney, London, 1947.

Sweden, which had remained relatively unaffected by the war, was a popular destination for architects who picked up the new and unpretentious forms of modern architecture, landscape and planning. These values were found in housing at Somerford Road, Hackney (1947), by Frederick Gibberd, a 'mixed development' of flats and houses, linked by pedestrian pathways and sensitively landscaped, one of the early projects at a time when all building was still heavily restricted. Among Gibberd's friends were Herbert Tayler and David Green, who found themselves in Lowestoft during the war, and went on to build more than 700

houses in the remote Loddon district of Norfolk, up to the early 1970s. These all had shallow pitched roofs, overhanging eaves and small decorative details, combined with sensitivity to the rise and fall of the site and the gardening ambitions of the residents. In Tayler's words:

> We realised that having broken away from the international modern stuff, functional style if you like, that people lacked decoration and enjoyment in the look of the houses and so we introduced all sorts of colours, different colours for each house, brick patterns, dates . . . Everybody liked it, people do like decoration.[43]

The New Empiricism corresponded to the dominant mood of relief at the end of the war, and suited the patchwork effects demanded by erratic supplies of materials. Domesticity of any kind was welcome for a while, and even the despised suburbs began to look charming in the eyes of J. M. Richards, whose book, *The Castles on the Ground* (1946), struck at the roots of Modernist belief in a way he could scarcely have imagined ten years previously. It was a poetic reverie, but also a serious acknowledgement that the lifestyle choice of the majority of English people might not deserve the disdain poured on it by the architectural community. Without sanctioning the cruder forms of inter-war suburb, Richards made the case for the independent life that could be achieved in these surroundings. To succeed, he wrote, the Modern Movement 'must keep in touch at all costs with the people it serves, and . . . the needs of suburban dwellers, as expressed in the architectural style they have evolved for themselves, is something it cannot afford to misunderstand'.[44]

Since the MARS Group was strong in numbers and organizing ability at the end of the war, it was asked to organize two of the renewed series of CIAM conferences (1947 and 1951) at which the agenda reflected the change of mood in British architecture, with the themes of 'Architecture in Relation to the Common Man' and 'The Heart of the City'. The conference of 1951 coincided with the Festival of Britain, an event involving many of the younger MARS members in designing temporary exhibition pavilions on the South Bank in London, where a heavily bombed site gave a long-sought opportunity to extend the cultural and ceremonial centre of the capital across the river. The exhibition layout demonstrated the principles of Townscape, a visual philosophy of informal composition developed in the *Architectural Review* by the editor, Hubert de Cronin Hastings, and a brilliant architect draughtsman, formerly with Tecton, Gordon Cullen. This was the culmination of a decade spent investigating the doctrine of the Picturesque that Hastings and Pevsner, who carried out the research under Hastings's direction and encouragement, both considered the key to understanding the English genius in the past and projecting it into a compassionate Modernist future, through the layout strategies of the late Georgian and Regency periods, rather than the direct imitation of that phase of architecture.

Of the eight topics through which Nikolaus Pevsner chose in 1955 to illustrate his radio lectures on 'The Englishness of English Art', the last was 'The Genius of the Place', a phrase made famous in 1731 by the poet Alexander Pope to describe how to avoid the aridity of the French or Dutch formal garden styles. Pevsner connected the English delight in nature and gardening to the mildness of the climate, adding that 'this eminently English style is also due to that English quality of tolerance, of "every case on its own merit"'.[45] The picturesque rather than formal approach to Modernism, Pevsner believed, was the quality that 'has much to teach the Continent and America'. In his analysis, Britain (or at least England) had arrived at Modernism through a sort of back door that had been standing open in history all the while, short-circuiting the more laborious journey made by other nations.

The conditions of the South Bank exhibition site, intersected by Hungerford Bridge, made it difficult to use a conventional symmetrical exhibition layout, apart from the Concourse that extended from Waterloo Station to the Skylon on the river bank, but in any case informality was preferred by the Director of Architecture, Hugh Casson, as a political statement and as a more valuable model for urban renewal in the near future. Out of the repertory of pre-war Modernism, a team of architects developed architectural strategies for the exhibition buildings that integrated the work of painters and sculptors, displayed engineering

The Concourse, South Bank Exhibition, Festival of Britain, London, 1951 (fountains designed by H. T. Cadbury-Brown, with the sea and ships pavilion by Basil Spence beyond).

in a playful spirit, using as much bright colour as possible, and creating a general feeling of uplift both literal and metaphysical.[46] Although the site had only one tree at the beginning, mature trees were brought in, and informal landscape and planting played an important role. The Royal Festival Hall, offered by the LCC as its contribution to the site and as a permanent symphony hall for London, reflected the rise in popularity of the serious arts during the war, especially classical music and ballet. It was an achievement to build anything on this scale under such difficult conditions, and the result was held to be highly satisfactory, despite later problems with over-engineered acoustics. In line with the ethos of the time, it was a team effort, involving Robert Matthew, Leslie Martin and Peter Moro, a former assistant of Lubetkin. More recently, the Festival Hall has been 'reinvented' as 'the People's Palace', and its ability to include all types of people at all times of day within the capacious foyer spaces understood as part of the original intention, although at first it operated in a more conventional manner.

84

Robert Matthew and
Leslie Martin with
Peter Moro, Royal
Festival Hall, London,
1947–51.

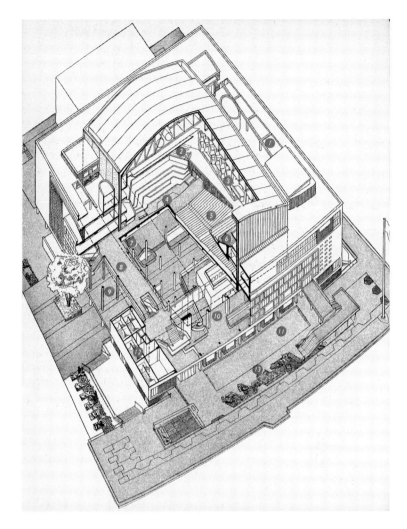

All the content of the exhibitions was related to Britain in different ways, providing a mixture of self-scrutiny and mild self-celebration. It was certainly hoped that visitors would learn new ways to enjoy themselves, with modern design doing what it could to encourage a light heart and an open attitude. The Festival was anti-militaristic and, as Casson said in a film made shortly after the event, 'nobody was taught to hate anything'.[47] In contrast to earlier national exhibitions at Wembley in 1924 and Glasgow in 1938, it said almost nothing about the British Empire, which at the end of the war mutated into the British Commonwealth of Nations. Whatever the deficiencies of the project as serious modern architecture, it proved popular and its rapid demolition (apart from the permanent Royal Festival Hall and a handful of other buildings) in October 1951, under the newly returned Conservative government of Winston Churchill, was widely regretted.

In the East End of London, the 'Live Architecture Exhibition' came in two parts. The Lansbury Estate was a demonstration of the rebuilding of a small urban core and neighbourhood, according to Abercrombie's principles, master planned by Frederick Gibberd, who designed the Chrisp Street Market as a junction of two pedestrian streets with shops beneath arcades, more like the sort of city square one might meet in a small European town than anything previously known in London or most parts of Britain. Terraces of houses and low-rise flats continued the theme in yellow London brick, with schools, churches, a Festival pub and a clock tower, which visitors in 1951 could ascend to see Lansbury laid out like an architectural model beneath them. Gibberd made the Town Hall at Harlow New Town (the fledgling town was included in the CIAM round of visits) into a similar 'Outlook Tower', following the pattern set by Patrick Geddes for gaining civic consciousness by looking down from above. If Lansbury with its small windows and pitched roofs making variations on London models was the architecture of compassion, it was a very quiet revolution.

The New Towns were a direct continuation of the Garden City movement of the beginning of the century, too obviously so for Colin Boyne, technical editor of the *Architects' Journal*, who wrote in 1955: 'they have achieved very little more than Letchworth or Welwyn achieved twenty years ago'.[48] As Summerson wrote: 'there was a reluctance to think out the architectural problems of the new towns with the intensity which was being devoted to urban problems'.[49] Their architecture aimed to please, and as a result was rather bland, even if the spaces were agreeable.

Frederick Gibberd,
Chrisp Street Market,
Lansbury Estate,
London, 1951.

86

Frederick Gibberd
(architect and planner),
model for centre,
Harlow New Town,
Essex, 1948.

The amount of green space began to seem like an overreaction to the slums, and the different neighbourhoods, all planned with precision according to the latest research, felt too distant from the commercial centre and from each other.

In 1951 the post-war reconstruction campaign was still struggling to survive the withdrawal of American loans that in 1947 had hindered the full development of the welfare state. Older social patterns and older forms of architecture began to assert themselves under the Conservative government, while the Cold War destroyed whatever fragile consensus existed between the worlds of capitalism and communism, when American forces were sent to fight in Korea in 1950, followed by conscripted British troops in 1951. The pain of the transition to a post-imperial stage reached a climax for Britain with the Suez Crisis in 1956. By later twentieth-century standards, as well as by comparison with the 1930s, Britain during the 1950s showed unbelievable levels of commitment to social spending, public sector employment and public ownership of resources, coming close to the realization of a British *Folkshemmet*. It was undertaken, however, without the equivalent commitment to change that was achieved by the post-war Swedish political system. The qualities of lightness, colour and even pattern that developed out of this time of doubt and danger were discarded when the mood changed, but they still help to explain how, despite the gap between modern architecture and the public, bridges can be built.

chapter three

Poetics: The Moral Dilemma of Modern Aesthetics

British architecture has never specialized in theory, and around 1951 the closest it came was the Revived Picturesque, an anti-theoretical theory at best. Modernism had arrived, but did not know where to go next. As has happened in the past, the theory followed behind the stylistic change as a post-hoc remedy and explanation. John Summerson wrote in 1956:

> throughout the 30s principles were almost taken for granted – swallowed one might say in slogan form – while the idiom was assiduously acquired . . . but already in 1951 there was a perceptible hostility to whatever was idiomatic and a tendency to go in search of principles.[1]

What was found was not a fully reasoned theory, but a mixture of different types of prejudice and analogy, which I have chosen to call 'poetics' since it was also, according to the origin of the word, a way of getting things done.

Architects who followed the path of compassion, even to a relatively small extent, were accused by their younger peers of betraying true Modernism by making it too easy and therefore dull. The Festival of Britain was condemned as a bad joke before it had even finished by young artists and architects in the bar of the Institute of Contemporary Art. A young architect, Colin St John Wilson, writing regularly in *The Observer* from early in 1951, commented on the 'extraordinary effeminacy' of the Lansbury Estate:

> an architecture of 'cold feet' . . . symptomatic of that post-war loss of nerve which, from a sense of guilt towards the scientific methods and machines that have been used for destruction, reacts with a split-minded desire to retreat into a world of cosiness.[2]

Sheffield City Architects' Department (J. L. Womersley, with Ivor Smith and Jack Lynn), Park Hill, Sheffield, 1957–61.

Wilson's views were typical of the new generation, usually characterized as New Brutalists, who are examined in more detail at the end of this chapter. For the first time in the history of Modernism in Britain, there was a

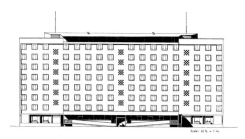 

Scale : 32 ft. = 1 in.   Scale : 32 ft. = 1 in.

Lubetkin and Tecton,
Spa Green Flats,
Finsbury, London,
1943–50.

battle of styles within the movement, a signal that the enemy outside, in the form of traditional styles, was nearly defeated, so that the luxury of infighting was now available. In the sharp new critical climate, *Architectural Design* published in 1951 the German critic Julius Posener's article 'Knots in the Master's Carpet', criticizing Lubetkin's elevations for his first major block of council flats at Spa Green, Islington, where he had indeed derived his two-dimensional patterning from his knowledge of oriental kilims.[3] Even before the war, Highpoint II, the 1938 block adjacent to the flats of 1935, was criticized for 'formalism'. When Lubetkin was appointed to design the new town of Peterlee in County Durham in 1949, he announced that he would avoid 'picturesque gimmicks or trivialities' as out of keeping with the serious and dangerous lives of the miners for whom it was intended. It seems unlikely that he would have kept this promise had his designs been carried out. Lubetkin's career tailed off in the 1950s in disillusion and anger, although he left behind in the North-East two architects, Gordon Ryder and Peter Yates, who showed in a scintillating set of regional projects where Lubetkin's work might have led on to.

When Denys Lasdun picked up the completion of the Hallfield Estate in Paddington, London, from Lubetkin's dissolution of the Tecton partnership in 1949, he retained the patterned façades that were already part of the design, and was pitied rather than criticized by Reyner Banham for 'belonging to the party of order at a time when the Modern Movement is having one of its periodic leanings in the other direction'[4] Lasdun made a decisive break from pattern-making in the Hallfield School, which is based on plan forms and larger elements, without surface decoration; and then in some housing projects in Bethnal Green between 1952 and 1957 he broke up the monolithic block of housing into a 'cluster' tower, a form that he hoped would achieve the aim of 'association' when residents stopped for a chat on the open walkways between their flats. Within a short time, it was recognized as 'a social failure though a sculptural triumph'.[5]

There were a few major monumental buildings completed in the years immediately following the Festival, despite continuing building

David Aberdeen,
Congress House,
Great Russell Street,
London, 1951–7.

Ernö Goldfinger and
Colin Penn, offices of
the *Daily Worker*,
Farringdon, London,
1949.

restrictions, such as Congress House, Great Russell Street (1955), by David Aberdeen, a skilled interpretation of the idiom of Le Corbusier, previously unknown in the streets of London. The curves of its side elevation could be contrasted with the rather dour but practical offices of the *Daily Worker*, the Communist newspaper, reconstructed by Ernö Goldfinger on a bombsite in Farringdon Road. Goldfinger resisted the picturesque, despite skilfully fitting his terrace of houses in Hampstead of 1938–9 into a London street. With his personal contacts with such masters as Auguste Perret and Adolf Loos, he was a link to the first principles of the first generation of Modernism, and lived by them rather than by 'idiom'. As his pre-war assistant H. T. Cadbury-Brown wrote, 'Goldfinger's importance as an architect in England derives from his steadfast aim to create a rational and vernacular answer to architectural problems.'[6] Until the second half of the 1950s, Goldfinger had no large projects, but then received major commissions for commercial offices and housing.

Cadbury-Brown himself, belonging to the same generation as Lasdun, revealed an individual approach tailored to the conditions of

each job within a small practice, culminating in scale and civic importance with the Royal College of Art in Kensington Gore, next to the
Albert Hall, with a strong sculptural form and dark tonality. The critic
Ian Nairn described it as 'the "angry" style completely justified, yet still
angry or whatever is the exact opposite of complacent'.[7] Yet the mass and
siting of the tall Darwin Building, containing workshops and studios,
were carefully calculated to respond to the group of Victorian buildings
around it. Sensitivity of this kind was a legacy of the 1930s Modernists,
including Chermayeff, Goldfinger and Lubetkin, who valued the architect's role in contributing to urban identity by enhancing the existing
situation. By the mid-1950s Italian post-war architects had extended
the range of examples, and Ernesto Rogers wrote in *Italy Builds* (1955):
'functionalism is not only the finest means of expressing every construction according to its specific character, but also of adapting every building to the problems of its site and its cultural situation'. He believed that,
rather than being a contradiction of pre-war rationalism, the post-war
interest in context showed 'the same principles . . . going deeper, according to the same unchanging method'.[8] The eclecticism and mannerism
that this attitude promoted, apparently so subversive towards a pure
ideal of Modernism, was duly criticized in Britain as a retreat from
modern architecture, an 'infantile regression', a revival of Art Nouveau.[9]
Consequently, some of the best modern architecture of the 1950s and '60s
that avoided strict Puritanism (such as the work of Patrick Gwynne) has
not been considered as part of the mainstream.

The side stream of contextual modernism took many forms, including the sensitive insertions in Oxford and Cambridge made by Powell &
Moya (Brasenose, Oxford, 1960–61, and St John's, Cambridge, 1963–67).
They represent what is now called 'Situated Modernism', a middle way
betwen the simplifications of high modernism and the reactionaries
opposed to it.[10] As we have seen, this tendency was already well developed in Britain by the 1930s, although apparently misunderstood and
forgotten. Recognition of the continuity between, say, Maxwell Fry's
work of the late 1930s, Powell & Moya, the Smithsons and the designs of
Ahrends, Burton & Koralek, in terms of materials, shaping of outdoor
space, requires a view of the path of history different from the one that
is generally understood.

As architects with a pre-war reputation, Lubetkin and Goldfinger
were in danger of becoming figures of the past. Lasdun, their junior by
more than ten years, was closer to the post-war generation of Powell and
Moya, whose Churchill Gardens Flats, won in competition in 1946,
showed an alternative treatment of a brief similar to Hallfield. Churchill
Gardens looked austere, 'more in the tradition of the early contemporary

architects than any other scheme of recent years', as one commentator suggested, but was also gentle and unassertive, despite its size.[11] Chamberlin, Powell & Bon, winners of the competition for housing at Golden Lane on the edge of the City in 1951, used coloured panels typical of the period. Their smaller jobs in the 1950s, such as Bousfield Primary School, Kensington, and the Cooper Tabor Seed Warehouse, Witham, both of 1955, are characterized by a kind of romantic jollity that does not compromise the directness of their conceptual approach.

Similarly positioned between 'Contemporary' (the phrase used for various kinds of 'soft' Modernism) and Brutalism was the private sector housing designed by Eric Lyons for the development company SPAN, starting in the years 1954–6 at Parkleys, in the sedate west London suburb of Ham, and continued in Blackheath from 1956 into the 1980s. The politeness of the tile hanging and white-painted boarding, set in well-maintained landscape, was appropriate to the middle-class professional clientele. Lyons insisted that he had learnt important principles during a brief pre-war spell working under Walter Gropius in the 1930s. Arguably these details were secondary, and SPAN projects were at least as modern as the *Siedlungen* of Berlin or Zurich in their combination of rigour, a little charm and a lot of foliage.

The influence of Mies van der Rohe's American buildings began to appear as a new strand of British Modernism, for example in Gatwick Airport (1957), by Yorke Rosenberg Mardall, with its clear grid of steel, 'a Swiss watch of a building' as Nairn described it. This represented a generational shift, not only within the firm, but among buildings repre-

Eric Lyons for SPAN Developments, The Keep, Blackheath Park, London, 1958.

Yorke Rosenberg
Mardall, The Pier,
Gatwick Airport,
West Sussex, 1957.

senting national prestige.[12] Kenneth Frampton recalled more recently that it 'had revolutionised overnight the performance level of British corporate practice'.[13] Banham approved with only minor reservations, admiring a dominant and appropriate concern with movement, and an absence of self-conscious 'architecture' that made Gatwick seem part of the ascendant New Brutalist trend.[14] The project was developed under Yorke's supervision by two young assistants, Brian Henderson and David Allford. Although he had been a pre-war pioneer of New Empiricism, Yorke seemed happy to be drawn in to the new wave, which was also a return to his Modernist roots. He was friendly with several pre-war Czech Modernists, such as Havlicek and Honzig, who were stylistically very rigorous, and chose one of their pupils, Eugene Rosenberg, as a partner following the latter's escape from Czechoslovakia and wartime internment as an enemy alien.

Gatwick showed the new concern with curtain-wall systems that seems utterly characteristic of the 1950s, and was linked not only to schools, but also to commercial office architecture. In this market, developers, now willing to forego Neo-classical or Georgian elevations, found that a Miesian wall was not only in line with a new image of Britain as an international economy, but also offered the optimum net to gross space ratio to the developer. For the permissible development envelope on any given site, the thickness of the wall represented the profit margin, and the thinner it was, the higher the rentable floor area on the inside. While many practices kept clear of commercial work as a matter of moral if not political principle, Gollins, Melvin and Ward were among the artistically esteemed who showed that 'good modern architecture' was not incompatible with developers' values. To begin with, it was a gentlemanly game, as seen in the pair of five-storey blocks facing each other in New Cavendish Street, London, of 1955 and 1957. Then Castrol

Gollins, Melvin and Ward, Castrol House, Marylebone Road, London, 1959.

House in Marylebone Road (1960), by the same firm, gave London its first equivalent of Lever House in New York – the classic podium-and-slab development of 1953 by Skidmore, Owings and Merrill – signalling a new brashness and scale.

Leslie Martin preferred to design as a member of a team and, after leaving the LCC in 1956 to become Professor of Architecture at Cambridge, assembled a 'studio' (rather than an office), including Colin St John Wilson, who also taught in the school, and Patrick Hodgkinson. Both were members of London avant-garde architectural circles, and Wilson's extension to the School of Architecture demonstrated Corbusian construction and an obsession with geometrical relationships, a theme that young architects discovered with zest from the art historian Rudolf Wittkower's book *Architectural Principles in the Age of Humanism* in the early 1950s. A modern application of mathematical relationships was promoted by Le Corbusier in two books describing his *Modulor* published in 1948 and 1955. Harvey Court for Gonville and

Caius College (1960–62), developed by Wilson and Hodgkinson from a Martin concept, was too polite to be Brutalist, yet as defiantly non-picturesque as it could be, with a dominant use of brick and a severe geometric grid, set in a garden but avoiding too much interaction with it.

After the Brynmawr factory, Architects Co-Partnership (their revised, less politicized title) specialized in schools. Using the Hills and later the CLASP systems, they achieved a high level of rigour. Later, at Dunelm House, the student union at Durham University (1961–5), they made an excursion into concrete 'crumble', to use the preferred phrase for a building with a multiple form rather than a single volume, and at the University of Essex (1962–5) moved more thoroughly into what by then had been marked out as Brutalist territory. At the same time, ACP developed a line in sensitive infill for historic settings, such as St John's College, Oxford (1958), and St Paul's Cathedral Choir School, London (1963–4), where the use of Portland stone cladding added weight and respectability.

Sir Leslie Martin with Colin A. St John Wilson and Patrick Hodgkinson, Harvey Court, Gonville and Caius College, Cambridge, 1960–62.

Architects' Co-Partnership, Dunelm House (Students' Union), Durham, 1965.

Alison and Peter Smithson, Smithdon Secondary School, Hunstanton, Norfolk, 1949–52.

Enter New Brutalism

From these examples, we can see that the generation between the first founders of inter-war Modernism and the New Brutalists did not remain stuck in the Festival idiom, and that historical accounts that jump straight between these events risk omitting many of the buildings that were most discussed at the time. Even so, the temptation to tell the story of Brutalism according to its own traditions cannot be resisted, and is equally part of the mythology of Modernism in Britain. This is how it begins. Peter and Alison Smithson met as students at Durham University School of Architecture and were married in 1949. The following year, while both still in their twenties, they won the competition for a new secondary school at Hunstanton in Norfolk. While the Smithsons' competition statement referred to 'a close study of educational needs', it combined these with 'purely formal requirements', without enlarging on what these were, but apparently in deliberate provocation of what the earlier generation of functionalists had condemned as 'formalism'.[15]

The plan was virtually symmetrical, in contrast to the prevailing anti-axiality, and included courtyards, a feature that existing Modernists thought they had eradicated. The aesthetic defined in the term 'as found' prevailed, with glass set against steel without subframes, in defiance of thermal prudence. Plumbing and other services were exposed to view, almost as a form of decoration. According to generation or taste, architects of the time loved Hunstanton or loathed it. Even the choice of heavy steel (rather than the thin austerity sections of Hills) was provocative in its extravagance, causing delayed completion by fourteen months, owing to steel shortages during the Korean War. The School architects following the Hertfordshire system were, by contrast, devoted to issues of practicality that the Smithsons blithely ignored in the pursuit of artistic perfection. The Smithsons, who were the first major architects for several decades to commit themselves regularly to print, wrote that 'only a person familiar with the pathetic figure of English functionalism supported since the war on a crutch of pseudo-science can understand why it was necessary to make such an obvious statement and design such a didactic building', hitting straight at the rationale of the Hertfordshire achievement.[16] As the *Architectural Review* commented, this attitude reflected 'a peculiar ruthlessness – overriding gentlemen's agreements and routine solutions – which pervades the whole design from original conception to finished details'.[17]

The point of the New Brutalists, the name the Smithsons acquired around 1953 that became a label for a whole generation and style, was to provoke the establishment, yet both the Smithsons, appearing on the scene as the clever but disruptive children of a Modern Movement that thought it had settled down for a conformist middle age, justified their rebellion with a rare innate sense of architecture and a personal manner in which arrogance was combined with a vulnerable kind of directness. In a world in which women architects were still a rarity, Alison displayed poise and self-confidence. She was famous for making all her own clothes, in an infinite succession of surprising styles that anticipated the 1960s repertory of Mary Quant.

The term 'New Brutalism' began as an in-joke, but the Smithsons' reaction to the 'over-refinement and dry academic-abstract geometries lurking in the International Style' was in earnest.[18] The label was first applied in print to a house design of 1952 by the Smithsons for a small central London site, of which they wrote: 'It is necessary to create an architecture of reality . . . an art concerned with the natural order, the poetic relationship between living things and environment.'[19] It was like a plain industrial warehouse, but also a knowing reference to Le Corbusier's latest exercise in primitivism, the Maisons Jaoul near Paris, completed in 1953, for, as they later remarked, 'Mies is great but Corb communicates.'[20]

The spirit of New Brutalism, cultivated by a complex overlapping crowd of friends and rivals in architecture and the other arts, soon began to set the tone for London architecture more widely. Some practices with a pre-war ancestry rebuilt their reputations in the 1950s and '60s through giving young assistants their head to produce buildings in the new style. Edward Lyons and Lawrence Israel, who had worked as a respectable but far from cutting-edge practice before the war, first added

a new partner with strong design skills, Tom Ellis, and then attracted at different periods James Stirling, James Gowan, David Gray, John Miller, Alan Colquhoun, Neave Brown and several more assistants and associates who took up the challenge of a tougher and more eloquent architecture, and went on to make independent names for themselves. The partners were fully involved in the design of buildings such as Trescobeas School, Falmouth (1955–7), a single Corbusian mass of rough concrete structure, and the Old Vic Theatre Annexe, London (1958), on which Miller and Colquhoun worked before going into partnership. These were certainly tougher meat than ACP's Miesian Risinghill School, Islington (1962), or Castrol House, or even than Lasdun's Hallfield.[21] Their toughness comes from a typically Brutalist mixture of materials and forms, with a tendency to exaggerate functional elements of a design to produce a sense of alienation rather than conformity.

After the success of John Osborne's play *Look Back in Anger* at the Royal Court in 1956, the phrase 'Angry Young Man' was adapted to fit any other sign of youthful rebellion. Discussing whether New Brutalists were the angry young men of architecture, Banham analysed the conditions that inhibited young architects from 'singing the blues out loud', such as the importance of patronage within the profession (meaning that it was suicidal to rock the boat too much), the indifference of the public and the active hostility of planners and mortgage lenders to any extreme forms of architecture. There were scandals inside the architectural establishment, he hinted, around which a powerful conspiracy of silence had been built, making it almost impossible for young architects to put their generalized sense of anger to good purpose in their own field. These conditions favoured gradual change at best, and for these reasons Banham believed that the concept of Brutalism 'was tamed from a violent revolutionary outburst to a fashionable vernacular'.[22]

Similar movements of revolt against politeness and gentility occurred at different moments in the other arts. In painting, the showing in 1945 of Francis Bacon's *Three Figures at the Base of a Crucifixion* was a challenge to purist abstraction and even to the romantic use of twisted thorns and bombed ruins that was Graham Sutherland's wartime repertory. In sculpture, the phrase 'the Geometry of Fear' was coined by Herbert Read in 1952, and included among its protagonists Eduardo Paolozzi and William Turnbull, both of whom were part of the Independent Group and New Brutalist circles. Poetry followed slightly later, with A. Alvarez subtitling his preface to the Penguin anthology *The New Poetry* in 1962, 'Beyond the Gentility Principle'. Some of the anti-gentility leading up to the 'angry young' movement was a genuine expression of new entrants into a cultural field apparently dominated by a comfortable middle-class establishment. The mediation of culture in print and broadcasting gave way to new voices, such as Banham's, proclaiming 'outsider' status in content and style.

Ethic or Aesthetic?

According to an early Smithson utterance, Brutalism was 'an ethic not an aesthetic'. On this basis, there were two Brutalisms. One of them, the 'ethic', was a personal, almost subjective matter, and hence limited perhaps to the Smithsons alone, and Banham as their prophet. In their view, few others measured up to their standards. Banham questioned whether the aesthetic had triumphed over the much more elusive idea of an ethic.[23] The need to have one ethic for the benefit of people and a different one for design was a perennial avant-garde problem, and the people ethic was the more readily sacrificed.

James Stirling and James Gowan tried to reject the Brutalist label in relation to their first major work, the Langham House Close, known as Ham Common Flats (1958). Although they moved among the same interconnected circles as the Smithsons, they represented a different approach, in which the aesthetic, although seldom explicitly declared, was almost everything, and the ethic merely a means to reach the aesthetic. Superficially, their flats resemble the Maisons Jaoul, about which Stirling wrote in the *Architectural Review* in September 1955, with the combination of brick and concrete and the use of an inverted L-shaped window, but they are much neater in construction than Le Corbusier's

James Stirling and
James Gowan,
Langham House
Close, Ham Common,
Surrey, 1958.

James Stirling and
James Gowan,
Department of
Engineering,
Leicester University,
1959–63.

deliberately rustic response to a Paris suburb. 'Their work is not "styled"
but pure and full of harmony as we found it in constructivism', wrote
Arthur Korn, an émigré veteran of the 1920s Berlin avant-garde.[24] Fore-
armed by a reference to 'more protest than is needed' from Nairn, Mark
Girouard, later to become Stirling's biographer, found them, by contrast,
'exquisite, reticent, beautifully scaled, delicate, totally inoffensive (in the
nasty sense of the word), buildings which really were a pleasure and a
delight to look at'.[25]

With the Engineering Building at Leicester University (1959–63), the last
major project executed before the partnership split up, Stirling and Gowan
hit harder. The vigorous articulation of the different parts of the brief combined an apparently impeccable argument from function to form with a
more overt reference to Constructivism, but far enough removed to avoid
pastiche. While relatively small in size, it achieved a heroic sense of scale,
and, like all Stirling's work, it posed well for the camera, especially at night.

It was more sensational even than Hunstanton, and even more irritating and puzzling to some of the older generation.

In 1959 Gowan, writing about the reform of architectural education, stated:

> it is becoming apparent that architecture, mainly due to economic pressure, is becoming multi-aesthetic; that is, not one style but a number of styles, each appropriate to the particular problem, are developing.[26]

This was reasonable and liberating, giving permission to think again about style, without the constraints of a single style, nor yet the doctrine of association that led down the primrose path to picturesque eclecticism. Reviewing the Leicester building, Banham noted the shock value, causing more staid followers of Modernism to half hope that it would not actually function as intended, and thus demonstrate the wrongness of its 'formalism'.[27] Despite some technical problems, they were disappointed. What was more shocking about Stirling was his revelation that architecture was a deadly serious game about form, and not much about anything else. With the superficially similar History Faculty and Library in Cambridge (1964–8), completed without Gowan, the context was especially savoury for a Brutalist, in that its neighbour was Casson and Conder's polite and slightly historicized Arts Faculty buildings, with their spaces calculated in terms of the dimensions of Cambridge college courts, and their materials and weathering informed by tradition.

Douglas Stephen (1923–1991) was another crucial member of the London Brutalist scene, not famous for any single work, but a provider of design opportunities to some of his contemporaries who were developing academic careers, such as Robert Maxwell and Kenneth Frampton. His Centre Heights building at Swiss Cottage (with Panos Koulermos) of 1959–62 was an early example of Brutalism in a commercial development, along with the work designed by Rodney Gordon in the office of Owen Luder, such as Eros House, Catford (1962–3).

The Independent Group and Team 10

The Institute of Contemporary Arts was founded in 1946 by survivors of the inter-war avant-garde, led by Roland Penrose and Herbert Read. The Smithsons' friend, the artist and photographer Nigel Henderson, organized the exhibition *Growth and Form* there in 1951 with the sculptor Eduardo Paolozzi and the artist Richard Hamilton. The exhibition,

which went beyond the pre-war interest in the application of scientific ideas for useful purposes to an interest in the imagery that science could generate for the imagination, and a series of exhibitions involving these and other figures, led from the legacy of pre-war Surrealism to Pop Art. *A Parallel of Life and Art* (1953), in which the Smithsons were active collaborators, dipped deeper into the well of imagery and imagination, dissolving rational connections and categories in favour of intuitive visual logic in a 'cave of images'.[28] Soon after the exhibition proposal was made in April 1952, Banham, who joined the staff of the *Architectural Review* around the same time, was invited by the ICA to convene the 'young independent group', whose name has become attached to the Parallel of Life and Art, and whose members went on to become a significant avant-garde network in London.

The next exhibition devised by members of the Independent Group was held at the Whitechapel Art Gallery. *This is Tomorrow* was the brain-

this is tomorrow whitechapel art gallery

aug. 9 - sept 9 1956

Poster by Richard
Hamilton for the *This
is Tomorrow* exhibi-
tion, Whitechapel
Art Gallery, London,
1956 (reproducing
Hamilton's collage
*Just What Is It That
Makes Today's Homes
So Different, So
Appealing?*).

child of Theo Crosby, architect and technical editor of *Architectural Design* and
editor of the 'little magazine' *uppercase*.
He imposed a format of collaborations
between architects, engineers and artists to
create separate sections of the exhibition,
displaying the divergent interests of the
core group. The 'Art Brut' aspects of the
Independent Group were evident in *Patio
and Pavilion*, a collaboration between the
Smithsons, Henderson and Paolozzi. A
simple timber shed was placed in a space
suggestive of an urban backyard, possibly
following a nuclear catastrophe, but also,
perhaps, indicating the future treasures of
a consumer society, represented on the exhibition poster by Hamilton's famous
collage *Just What Is It That Makes Today's
Homes So Different, So Appealing?* All this
was mixed incongruously with the survivors of English Constructivism, such as
Victor Pasmore, who was involved as an
artist in trying to give some visual interest
to new housing in Peterlee, having been
drawn to rescuing it from post-Lubetkin banality.

The links that had begun to form among the younger members of
MARS at the CIAM congress in 1951 were cemented at the congress of
1953 at Aix-en-Provence. This was attended unofficially by crowds of
students who camped in tents in the courtyard of the Ecole des Arts et
Métiers and concluded proceedings by organizing a striptease on the
roof of the Unité d'Habitation, which acted as the chief architectural
focus. The Smithsons produced a striking 'grille' as the basis of their
presentation, using Nigel Henderson's photos of children playing in
the streets of Bethnal Green to explain their idea of 'association'. Le
Corbusier proposed that the founders of CIAM should begin to hand
over to a younger generation, although in reality he was reluctant to
let go, and Team 10 – formed chiefly by the British (Smithsons, John
Voelker, William and Gillian Howell) and Dutch (Jaap Bakema, Aldo van
Eyck, Haan) groups, with the addition of a Frenchman (George Candilis)
and a French-based American (Shadrach Woods) – represented those
who wanted to take over. Later members were the Italian Giancarlo de
Carlo and Ralph Erskine, who although British by birth practised in

Alison and Peter
Smithson, Dubrovnik
Scroll and Valley
Section Grid, for
CIAM X at Dubrovnik,
1956.

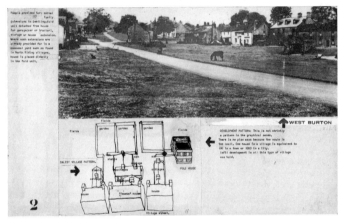

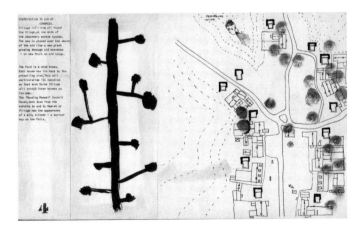

Sweden. Through Team 10, the New Brutalist avant-garde found an international platform and alliances for discussions of urbanism as a wider extension of architecture. These individuals, in Voelker's words, 'were all trying to find a means through which this attitude could become an approach and in consequence a positive force in urbanism'.[29] It sounds imprecise, and it was.

Although the CIAM of the Athens Charter was supposed to be the opposite of what Team 10 stood for, they were not always so far removed in their use of sweeping universal concepts. Against the 'four functions' of 'Habiter, Travailler, Circuler, Cultiver l'Esprit et le Corps' named in the Athens Charter, the Doorn Manifesto, drafted by the group in 1954, proposed 'villages, towns, cities', a classification based on the Valley Section of the Scottish pioneer planner Patrick Geddes, and therefore supposing a rather old-fashioned organization of economic production in relation to landscape. One outcome in 1954 was a plan based on the village of West Burton in Yorkshire, where 'the new is placed over the old like a new plant growing through old branches – or new fruit on old twigs'.[30] At the tenth CIAM congress, held at Dubrovnik in 1955, the Smithsons used this as one of the starting points for their 'grille', on the theme of village housing. The compact huddles of vernacular houses in stone-built northern English villages effaced the dreary reality of New Towns or semi-detached suburbs, but were by now a world away from Mies. In 1967 the Smithsons explained their scheme of 'infill' as directly inspired by the 'complete

Alison and Peter
Smithson, Robin Hood
Gardens, Poplar,
London, 1966–72.

image system where every piece was correspondingly new in a new system of relationships', which they had found in the early 1950s in the work of Jackson Pollock or Paolozzi.[31]

The principles behind this scheme appear with hindsight as an inspired insight into a persisting problem of appropriate but modern village housing, but apart from the single house for the engineer Derek Sugden at Watford (1955–6), the Smithsons never had an opportunity to put such a scheme into action, unlike Giancarlo de Carlo, who developed a new language for Italian villages. The closest equivalent was the village of Rushbrooke in Suffolk designed by John Weeks and Michael Huckstepp for Lord Rothschild in 1957, with monopitched roofs on white painted walls, shyly concealing their front doors behind screen walls that link one house to another. To a commission from the jazz musician Humphrey Lyttelton, Voelcker built a house at Arkley, Hertfordshire (1957), in the form of a three-sided courtyard with inward sloping roofs, a typical Brutalist solution to screen out a suburban site.

Kenneth Frampton has discussed the lack of logical connection between the Smithsons' admiration for the bye-law streets of Bethnal Green (as captured in Henderson's photographs) and their attempt to reconstitute them as 'streets in the sky' in their proposal for the Golden Lane housing competition in 1951. On what grounds could they admire the street layouts and squares of Georgian and Victorian London, while declaring, without much further investigation, that these forms were no longer applicable under modern conditions, while living in pre-1900 terrace houses themselves? Their stream of new ideas in urbanism and architecture, mostly in the form of competition projects, was nonetheless influential internationally. In the scheme for Sheffield University (1955), movement through the site rather than merely between buildings generated a new relationship between architecture and planning. The winner, a cool slab and tower by Gollins Melvin Ward, was aiming to solve a different set of problems.

Team 10 went on fighting against CIAM until its destruction in 1959. Despite internal conflicts of their own, the members continued to meet into the 1980s. When the cruder forms of Modernist housing in Britain were perceived to have failed at the end of the 1960s, Ralph Erskine, admittedly rather a fringe member of Team 10, built the Byker Development in Newcastle upon Tyne (1973–80), a scheme that demonstrated

McMorran & Whitby,
Holloway Estate,
Parkhurst Road,
Camden, London,
c. 1960.

LCC Architects,
Highbury Quadrant
Estate, Islington,
London, 1954.

the principles of mixed use and indefinite form as means of creating a new sense of authentic place, with a strong emphasis on pedestrian pathways. By contrast, the Robin Hood Gardens scheme in Poplar by the Smithsons (1966–72), which faced some of the same problems and opportunities in terms of a site close to a busy road, was by their own admission a disappointing realization of so many years thought about housing design, even though it created a magical outdoor space overlooking the Thames, between two snaking slab blocks.

London County Council Housing

During the war, the LCC's Valuer's Department took over responsibility for housing, implementing the construction of old plans for gallery-access flats until 1949, when architects were able to reclaim the task. A job in housing or schools at the LCC soon became the way that many of the best architects of the next thirty years began their career. 'Far from being shackled by bureaucratic caution', wrote Banham in 1965, 'LCC architects were free to leap on every passing stylistic bandwagon and even roll a few of their own.'[32] Everything after 1949 was more or less modern, but conflict developed between some members of the rapidly growing Housing Division, who favoured a gentle, picturesque approach, and others who had links with New Brutalism. The architectural conservatives (who were confusingly furthest to the left politically) liked using brick, pitched roofs and what was derisively called 'People's Detailing'. They did not go so far towards Georgian classicism as Donald McMorran (the assessor for the Golden Lane competition), who designed a number of schemes for the City of London, demonstrating that this way of working need not be stale and soulless.[33] The conservatives of the left were aware of their continuity with the Arts and Crafts Movement and its importance for the earliest LCC housing in the 1890s. David Gregory-Jones, one of the leading members of this group, lived for a while at William Morris's Red House in Bexleyheath, after it was bought by two other LCC architects, Edward Hollamby and Dick Toms.[34] The Highbury Quadrant Estate in Islington (1954) is representative of their work. Since so many of them were Communist Party members or supporters, a palpable change of style took place after 1956, when the Soviet president Nikita Krushchev repudiated the conservative style of Stalinism in favour of something more modern.

LCC Architects, Alton Estate, Roehampton, Wandsworth, London: in the foreground Alton East, 1952–5, in the background, Alton West, 1954–8.

The middle position following the principles of mixed-development high- and low-rise housing set in a park-like landscape was popular in Sweden, in new towns such as Välingby.[35] This approach suited the LCC sites that bordered open land, offering fine existing trees from the gardens

of older houses equally as ornament and as obstruction to gridded plan schemes. At Roehampton, this form of moderate 'soft' Modernism resulted in 'point blocks' of moderate height on a hilltop site, and two-storey brick-built houses. That was 'Alton East', whose ancestry was traced by Pevsner back to an English reinterpretation of Modernist housing by Gropius and Fry at St Leonard's Hill, Windsor, and thence to a generously landscaped AA scheme of 1938 for extending the town of Faringdon.[36] 'Alton West', developed slightly later, displayed the third, 'hard' option, developed by a team led by Colin Lucas, who was received into the LCC as a hero of the 1930s Modernist battlefield, with the involvement of Bill Howell and his future partners John Killick and John Partridge. Colin St John Wilson was another member, working on the development of the 12-foot-wide maisonettes that constituted the housing units in the five parallel slab blocks on the crest of the hill, in homage to Le Corbusier's Unité d'Habitation, completed in 1957. Modern sculpture punctuates the parkland at intervals, recreating the arcadian feeling of a Capability Brown park.

Similar buildings arose on other London sites with less leafy fore-grounds. Compared with the pre-war building-code restrictions, it became administratively easier to build tall housing after 1950, and Alton West included square tower blocks of seven storeys. Although this is the feature most associated with post-war housing in Britain as a whole, it was scarcely an issue before 1958, when it began to be driven by a complex set of overlapping political, planning and economic motives. Team 10 members were more inclined to favour lower-rise solutions to match their concept of enclosing urban form.

As with the 'victories' of Team 10 and the Independent Group over the older generation, it is hard after fifty years to understand why so much heat was generated over choices between methods that, in hindsight in a case such as Roehampton, seem to offer relatively minor differences compared to the much wider range of possibilities that we can now imagine. The answer must therefore lie in the significance of the image, which was so important during this period – the Roehampton maisonettes looked impressive in photographs, even though, owing to planning pressure, they were reoriented and pushed off the crest of the hill in order to be less conspicuous. The typical local authority office, rather than grounding architects in reality, as was hoped when campaigned for in the late 1930s, seems in the case of the LCC, at least, to have distanced them even further from a sense of accountability for their actions. The liberalism of Leslie Martin's oversight of the department (until his departure to Cambridge) was a kind of benign anarchy operating within an extremely rigid bureaucracy, heightening the sense of unreality.

Access deck at
Park Hill, Sheffield,
1957–61.

Streets in the Sky

In 1962 a young architect, Jack Lynn, described most English high rise as 'bungalows stacked one above the other . . . [like] tidy solutions of a storage problem'.[37] Park Hill in Sheffield, on which he worked with Ivor Smith under the council architect, J. L. Womersly, tried to find a better way to create high density with a sense of place. It came closer to the Team 10 idea of making the residential building an indistinguishable part of the urban plan, rather than something slotted into an abstract scheme. The high rise and high density of Park Hill coexisted in Sheffield, as in London, with a more arcadian (or suburban) development, so that a range of housing options were available, but for a city where much of the industry and employment was still located in the centre, Park Hill had advantages. The 995 dwellings were positioned on a hillside previously occupied by crime-ridden slum terraces. Smith emphasized the distinctive nature of the English street 'approachable from either end and off which every house was entered directly through its own front door', and felt that this was crucial to 'our national independence of character and at the same time with community structure'.[38] Here was a plain explanation for not imitating the internal access corridors of the Unité and opting instead, without apparently noticing the difference, for a form that can never really be a street, if only because front doors do not face each other, although it was a proud claim that the milk float, another feature of English daily life, could drive off the hillside onto the decks to deliver the 'pinta' to the doorsteps, where the inhabitants, to the architects' delight, ornamented their thresholds with personalized pieces of coloured lino.

The street decks at Park Hill emphasized the new focus on circulation spaces and routes as a means of recovering the sense of community within this otherwise forbidding mass of structure. The combination of tough and homely was typical of a new sense of northern identity, far removed from the lush pastures of Roehampton. Here, as in other industrial northern cities with Labour councils, psephology influenced housing form, encouraging councils to provide high-quality housing to keep their voting supporters living within the city's electoral boundaries.

On completion of the flats in 1961, commentators believed from the evidence of their eyes that the decks 'worked' and that, in Banham's words:

> toddlers play on them; teens mend bikes, keep dates, swap gossip on them, teds occasionally brawl; heroic Sheffield grans sit, legs akimbo, at the street-deck door, backed by spectacular tableaux of floral wall-paper and aspidistras in Art-Nouveau pots on spindly wooden stands.[39]

By 1972, in a much altered architectural climate, Robert Maxwell was far less sure, and after stating the good intentions all round, admitted:

> we must wonder whether they constitute a human environment for ordinary people. Like Regency terraces in Bath or Bristol, they produce magnificent skylines. Unlike the Regency terraces, however, they were not freely chosen by the people who went to live in them.[40]

In the short term, at any rate, Park Hill looked like a possible shape for the future, and the medium-rise deck-access complex was widely adopted in the 1960s as an alternative to the high-rise tower that might avoid some of the more obvious social problems without sacrificing high density, although in the event both were capable of spectacular failure.

History and Theory

Colin Rowe was a new type of figure on the architectural scene. One of his contemporaries at the Liverpool School of Architecture, Robert Maxwell, has written: 'He could imbue the present with an excitement derived from past moments of creation, and students were often sent to the library to check out the plan of a Palladian villa before drawing up their plan for a secondary school.'[41] Nothing like his essay 'The Mathematics of the Ideal Villa' in the *Architectural Review* in 1947 had ever been published, and Rowe's parallel analysis of Palladio's Villa Malcontenta and Le Corbusier's Villa Stein at Garches remains a tour de force of lateral thinking. 'Mannerism in Modern Architecture'(1950) was almost equally influential in its time, drawing recent and remote pasts closer together, in defiance of Hegel's theory of 'the spirit of the age' and the concomitant of evolutionary progress that dominated most versions of history. Rowe's approach had much in common with that of the émigré philosopher Karl Popper.

In Rowe's writing and teaching, classical architecture was revealed as deeper than Geoffrey Scott imagined in *The Architecture of Humanism*, the book of 1914 that his doctoral supervisor Rudolf Wittkower set out to refute. Wittkower's own large-format pictorial survey, *British Art and the Mediterranean* (with Fritz Saxl), of 1948 was equally important, and a favourite browsing book for another Liverpool contemporary, James Stirling. Among the examples from all the arts, from prehistory to the 1930s, the neo-Palladian architecture of the 1720s, disdained by historians up to the Second World War, stands out in its geometric clarity, as revealed by European eyes. Rowe's influence led to a more general understanding of the abstract formal aspects of architecture, which, if not entirely absent from inter-war Modernism, were certainly not consciously stated at the time. If one is looking for Modernist analogues to Palladian villas, then Colin Lucas's Greenside, Wentworth (1937), is a strong candidate, with its tripartite ordering of elevations in both vertical and horizontal directions. James Gowan's minute house at Cowes on the Isle of Wight (1958) shows the new significance accorded to plan form in its set of simple rectangular divisions, with an axially symmetrical footprint.

When history was seen as a source of examples that could be translated abstractly into modern form, it had considerable potential for contributing to the revival of architectural imagery. New illustrated books, such as the Pelican History of Art series, made the latest scholarship accessible; and in a way that could not have been imaginable in the 1930s, whole areas of the past, including the history of the Modern Movement itself, were opened up for heated discussion at the evening lecture meetings of the RIBA, or at the AA.

Maguire & Murray,
St Paul's, Bow
Common, Tower
Hamlets, London,
1958–60.

Church Design

The popular historian A.J.P. Taylor closed the decade by declaring 'Belief is over. That was the keynote of the Fifties . . . a wonderful decade with all the old nonsense being shovelled underground.'[42] This was not actually true, and the decade saw an increase in church attendance, and a growth in construction in all denominations. Was religion a curiosity for study, or could it become relevant to the future of Modernism? The

Gillespie, Kidd & Coia, St Paul, Glenrothes, Fife, 1956–7.

Gillespie, Kidd & Coia, St Peter's College, Cardross, Argyll, 1957–68, photographed in 1994 in a ruinous condition that has grown progressively more severe, despite the protection of 'A' grade listing, since the buildings were abandoned in 1987.

'liturgical movement' in church design in Germany and France originated before the war, and Le Corbusier's pilgrimage chapel at Ronchamp, opened in 1958, was one of its products, shocking to those who imagined Modernism as something fundamentally secular. Stirling, who wrote on it for the *Architectural Review*, found it disturbingly 'contemporary' in its applied art.[43] The liking of Team 10 members for anthropology led to increased awareness of building customs and superstitions, 'the doorstep, the street, the kraal, the longhouse, people carrying a whole roof to put over their house etc', as Voelcker wrote in 1965.[44] The Smithsons and Colin St John Wilson (the son of an Anglican bishop) were among the entrants in the competition for Coventry Cathedral, with large undivided spaces for worship owing nothing to Anglican tradition. The first church to carry some of these ideas into practice was St Paul, Bow Common, designed in the years 1958–60 by Robert Maguire and Keith Murray, members of The New Churches Research Group, another of whose members, Peter Hammond, published the manifesto of their thinking, *Liturgy and Architecture*, in 1960.

St Paul demonstrated New Brutalist principles to perfection, with its attention to the quality of space for movement of people within its square plan based on early Christian tradition, achieved with relatively cheap materials 'honestly' displayed, although enriched with mosaic. The liturgical thinking behind it went back to the Christian Socialism of Conrad Noel, the 'Red Priest' of Thaxted, in the 1920s, and the open area of the floor was a deliberate reference to Thaxted without the need for Gothic detail. When Coventry Cathedral opened in 1962, the public flocked to see it, but critics preferred Maguire's and Murray's more austere approach.

Some of the most radical and adventurous new churches of the 1950s and '60s were built in Scotland by Gillespie, Kidd & Coia, a Glasgow firm with a long history, latterly directed by Jack Coia, a stylistically

labile Glaswegian of Italian extraction who had established firm connections with the Roman Catholic diocese before the war. A young architect, Isi Metzstein, a refugee from pre-war Berlin, was joined in 1953 by Andrew MacMillan; they were allowed to have their way with the design of buildings, and the results were seen in the church of St Paul, Glenrothes (1954), which was strongly influenced by modern German churches in its focus on effects of light and space rather than decoration and association. Coia acted almost entirely as the man who got the commissions (his office was strategically next door to the Catholic Diocese headquarters) and his assistants went on to produce a stream of churches and other buildings, working with a verve and freedom scarcely comparable south of the border, culminating in the Seminary of St Paul at Cardross, a massive single building based on an ingenious cross-section, reminiscent in some respects of Le Corbusier's monastery of La Tourette.

H. A. Mealand (City Planning Officer) and Sir Leslie Martin (LCC), 'Route XI', London Wall, City of London, 1955; office blocks by various architects.

'Good morning America, how are you?'

In 1953 the London correspondent of *Newsweek* estimated that one out of every three Englishmen was more or less antagonistic to anything that came from America, 'from Buicks to businessmen'.[45] Like it or not, the United States, having won the war alongside the British, was an unavoidable influence in the post-war period, from the promotion of freedom through modern art to jazz, television cartoons and comic books. The guardians of British culture from F. R. Leavis before the war to Richard Hoggart and Raymond Williams after it found all this alarming.[46] America, still expensive and difficult for British people to visit, was exciting because it was different, and Independent Group members demonstrated their freedom by collecting comics and incorporating them in their art. This enthusiasm was the sweet coating on a serious interest in the architect's role in mass communication, something to which pre-war Modernism had given little thought. Until well into the

1950s, the taste-makers of architecture and design despised streamlining as an earlier generation despised Art Deco, but the new imagery represented a different kind of modernity altogether. IG member John McHale, who came back from the States in 1955 with a suitcase full of precious comics, recognized that advertisements, film stars and rock and roll musicians all constituted a new type of high-speed 'expendable ikon' to replace 'totems, masks, a ritual dance, a poem or a cathedral', which in the past had provided 'useable images', and which the Modernists thought they had abolished.[47]

For the 'Machine-made America' issue of the *Architectural Review* in May 1957 McHale designed a cover collage of 'infra-grilled steak, pre-mixed cake, dream kitchens, dream-cars, machine-tools, power-mixers, parkways, harbours, tickertape, spark-plugs and electronics'. This was intended to show how 'in terms of quantity, the US is now the homeland of the modern movement, and quantity, backed by wealth, industry and technical skill, is the prerequisite of architectural quality today'.[48] The pages on individual architects were tellingly arranged in descending order of age, beginning with Mies (Frank Lloyd Wright was omitted 'at his own request'). In 1955 the LCC instigated a development scheme for a new street, London Wall, alias Route 11, flanked by six tall, sheer, glass-

Denys Lasdun and Partners, Royal College of Physicians, Outer Circle, Regent's Park, London, 1960–64.

clad slabs in echelon, similar in effect to the controversial redevelopment of the Hötorget in Stockholm under Sven Markelius (1946–66), with its 'five trumpet blasts'. Glass curtain walls and their detailing, famous in 'Machine-made America', celebrated 'the first time in the history of the modern movement that a common vocabulary of form, pattern and proportion is becoming acceptable to architect, builder and client and public'.[49]

London Wall was devised to include a complete network of upper-level pedestrian walkways, a version of the idea that occupied Team 10 members in the later 1950s as a solution to the problem of increasing motor traffic on narrow European city streets, rather than the grids of American downtowns. The 'Pedway' aimed to create a more vital and active zone at the upper level, with the inclusion of shops and kiosks. In Team 10 schemes, such as the 'Berlin Haupstadt' competition entered by the Smithsons with Peter Sigmund (1957–8), the pedestrian network was more complex, overlaying the grid of streets with a figure more like an Abstract Expressionist doodle, indicating desire lines between points. None of these systems was ever completed to the point where their viability could be properly assessed.

A completely different impulse came from Louis Kahn, whose message of formal austerity and massive structure linked to ideas of universal cultural meanings was inspiring, not least because it reasserted the architect's irreplaceable skill, not as a technician but as a poet. The kind of monumentality that Kahn's Yale University Art Gallery (1955) portrayed was close in character to the refined version of Brutalism developed by Denys Lasdun in the second half of the 1950s, which culminated in what he considered his 'breakthrough' building, the Royal College of Physicians in Regent's Park (1959–65). The brief, for large ceremonial spaces, and the relatively generous budget enabled Lasdun, in the phrase he applied to architecture in general, to 'oscillate between reason and feeling'.[50] Lasdun's building is eminently programmatic, but it is much more than this, as implied in his view of the design process as 'a shift from the notion of "organisation" to "organism"' and even 'a microcosm of the city'.[51] Kahn's planning ideas, represented in his scheme for Philadelphia (1953), resembled his buildings in attempting to 'find expression from the order of movement', equally a long-term feature of Le Corbusier's designs. This approach was increasingly reflected in Lasdun's work, and influential on the Smithsons, who were also transfixed by American culture, in the development of a theory of the significance of 'the spaces in between'.[52]

The Royal College of Physicians, in common with early Brutalism in general, seemed quintessentially European in its appeal to timeless values

Alison and
Peter Smithson,
The Economist Group,
St James's Street,
Westminster, London,
1962–4.

120

and apparently irreconcilable with consumer culture, although the emphasis on an atrium space in the college was similar in intention to Victor Gruen's designs for both open and covered multi-storey shopping centres with their own parking, a building type as yet scarcely visible in Europe, shown in the 'Machine-made America' issue of the *Architectural Review*. The Smithsons' 'House of the Future' for the Ideal Home Exhibition in 1956 was one response in a populist context, and an attempt to win the market for mass-produced homes by space-age seduction. As Banham wrote, they 'tried to design a house that society would want badly enough to make mass-production feasible – smart, slick, styled-up, mechanically advanced, gimmicky and expendable, like a car'.[53] It made a good exhibition piece and, like most attempts to see into the future, combined a mixture of accurate foresight and wild miscalculation. The project ended there.

The Smithsons' architectural journey acquired upward mobility with the *Economist* complex in St James's Street, the heart of the revived establishment of gentlemen's clubs and traditional luxury shops, far removed from American mass culture. Sir Geoffrey Crowther, who had developed the modern reputation of this long-established magazine, wanted a tenth-floor penthouse flat. To achieve this within the 'plot ratio' of 5:1, dictating that what was taken in upward thrust of buildings must be given back in terms of lower-level construction on the same site, a larger site was acquired, and the Smithsons were invited, at Leslie Martin's suggestion, along with a more conventional firm, George, Trew & Dunn, to submit proposals. The Smithsons' alternative to a slab-and-podium scheme was accepted in 1960, and the building was completed in 1964. The tall tower stands away from St James's Street, onto which a smaller corner building fronts with polite scale. A third separate building in the opposite corner completes the family of objects, with Boodles Club as an elderly guest tucked in to complete the table, but attention is deliberately directed towards the raised plaza (a name favoured in the USA). Seldom can so small a space have been invested with such a weight of architectural meaning. In London, where the spaces between buildings have tended to be accidental, it had a special significance in reversing the order of figure and ground, and as a short cut it offers a pleasing progression, recognized by Gordon Cullen, who reviewed it for the *Architectural Review*, as a perfect demonstration of the principles of Townscape, the aesthetic despised by the Brutalists. Banham criticized it for excessive conformity to its surroundings and the cladding of roach-bed Portland Stone, writing that 'the Established solutions – even the modern ones – are bankrupt, and we need a new set of principles, not a new set of conventions'.[54] Nairn asked how a space like this was actually going to acquire life.[55] All the Smithsons' good intentions achieved little more real urban activity than the later notorious Paternoster Square, the Economist Building's down-market City cousin, filling the bomb site to the north of St Paul's Cathedral. The American critic Peter Blake criticized the 'papier mâché Portland Stone', but Brian Henderson recalls that it was the first London building he did not feel ashamed to take American visitors to admire, and Alvin Boyarsky, a Canadian pupil of Colin Rowe, considered it 'a time bomb ticking away for the moment when it can exert, by its explosive example, a direction for the rebuilding and infilling of a city such as London'.[56]

By the time that Banham's book on *The New Brutalism* was published in 1966, much of the architecture across the world by the Smithsons' contemporaries, often described as 'the third generation', could be connected to the moves made in the 1950s by a small splinter group in Britain. 'It was', he wrote,

> an extraordinarily exciting period in the evolution of ideas in Britain, both in the portable arts and in architecture – one of those unrepeatable episodes whose importance is discernible even at the time, although their full consequence cannot be appreciated until much later.[57]

Was the Economist Building actually the ticking bomb of New Brutalism's demise at the moment when it seemed to have succeeded? Could their visions of social improvement really work on such an apparently shallow grounding, however urgently and wittily delivered in words? In 1957 Peter Smithson revealed how, in a typical CIAM scheme, 'the whole social structure is treated almost as an art gambit which can be moved about rather than being a serious matter for the people who actually have to live there', but was their alternative, politely islanded in the heart of Establishment London, more than a pleasant diversion?[58]

Opinions differed. Robin Middleton, reviewing Banham's book in *Architectural Design*, believed that the Economist Building was 'a perfectly logical outcome of Brutalist doctrine' and that 'Brutalism marches on'.[59] To a large extent, he was right, partly because Brutalism can be extended to cover so many things – the right to be difficult in pursuit of architecture as an art, truth to materials, social engagement and regional character – all of which have assumed increasing importance since the 1950s. In the early twenty-first century, projects like the Sugden House and the Economist Building continue to inspire young architects concerned with such questions.

chapter four

Production: White Heat and Burnout

In 1959, eight years after Winston Churchill had supplanted the post-war Labour Government of Clement Attlee, the Conservative Party continued in power with its fourth successive general election victory. The returning Prime Minister, Harold Macmillan, an Edwardian and a First World War veteran, managed to display not only the skills of political survival but also the ability to ride the currents of change in society. Although Britain experienced less economic growth during the 1950s than the defeated countries of France, Germany, Italy and Japan, the growth was at least continuous, putting into the distance the economic swings of the inter-war years and enabling Macmillan to make his famous statement, at a public meeting on 20 July 1957, that 'most of our people have never had it so good'. In 1959 *Queen*, a fashion magazine owned by a privileged young rebel, Joscelyn Stevens (later Rector of the Royal College of Art and Chairman of English Heritage), published an issue to celebrate the arrival of a consumer boom, as if in preparation for something new on the horizon.

This chapter recapitulates aspects of the 1950s from a different angle to the previous one, that of architectural production rather than thinking, and carries the story into the 1960s. While few people heard or understood the arguments about architectural theory between New Brutalists and New Empiricists, millions were affected by the new housing, office buildings, urban renewal schemes and roads that delivered the long-awaited modern age. Since the end of the war, despite the continuing threat posed by the Communist bloc, and the consequent heavy investment in military manpower and hardware, the increase in material progress in the West bred a new confidence about the need for modernity in Britain, including the freedom to exercise consumer choice.

Internationally, Britain had very little weight left to swing, as became clear when Macmillan's predecessor, Anthony Eden, was forced to capitulate over the Suez crisis in 1956 because the American president, Dwight Eisenhower, refused to support the Anglo-French military intervention in the canal zone, and threatened economic sanctions.

Sir Basil Spence and Partners (J. S. Bonnington), Sunderland Civic Centre, Co. Durham, 1970–73.

New worries soon occurred. Even though Stalin, Britain's and America's wartime ally and peacetime adversary, died in 1953, the Soviet suppression of the independent Communist regime in Hungary in 1956 showed that little had substantially changed behind the Iron Curtain. On 13 August 1961 the DDR leader, Walter Ulbricht, began building the Berlin Wall overnight to stem the flow of emigration to the newly prosperous Federal Republic. In 1962 Nikita Krushchev and John F. Kennedy were facing each other down with nuclear weapons as the gaming counters in the Cuba Missile Crisis. Britain was America's client in its attempt to remain among the nuclear powers, and the Aldermaston Marches were organized annually between 1958 and 1965 by the Campaign for Nuclear Disarmament (CND) and its Committee of 100, gaining 100,000 supporters in Trafalgar Square at the end of March 1965.

International tension continued to mount in the 1960s. Mao Zedong's China was a closed and hostile society, fear of which drew the United States into covert and then overt engagement in Indo-China, where American policy was committed to halting the spread of Chinese Communist influence, known as 'the domino effect'. The start of the Vietnam War is officially dated 1965, and although the Labour Prime Minister, Harold Wilson, resisted Lyndon Johnson's attempts to draw Britain into military engagement, the impact of the war on American society became increasingly disturbing in Britain, a process that culminated in the Grosvenor Square riots outside the US Embassy in 1968. The Middle East, where Britain maintained post-imperial links with Israel and the oil-producing rival states of Iraq and Iran, showed how the location of oil reserves underlay international politics throughout the postwar period. In Britain's own backyard, the unfinished history of Irish independence returned with a vengeance after 1966 with the start of 'the troubles' in Ulster and their seemingly endless continuation.

In the domestic politics of Britain, the simple diagram of the decade is one of alternation between Conservative (1951–64) and Labour (returned twice in 1964 and again in 1966) governments, and then a reversion to Conservative in 1970. In the 1950s the relative consensus existing between the two major parties was symbolized in the imaginary figure of 'Mr Butskell', created by the *Economist* in 1954, who combined aspects of the Conservative Chancellor of the Exchequer and would-be leader, Rab Butler, and his Labour predecessor, Hugh Gaitskell. Butler was influential in framing the Education Act of 1944 that set a new pattern for expanded state education, locally administered, developing from a three-tier system to include what was seen as a more inclusive model in the Comprehensive School, the first 300 of which were opened by 1964. Gaitskell died young in 1963, making way for Wilson as a younger leader, skilled in economic manipulations and keen to present Labour as a party of scientific and social transformation, a kind of consumerist sequel to Atlee. Images of modern architecture formed a natural backdrop for his vision of Britain's future.

The Town and Country Planning Act of 1947 followed the recommendations of the wartime Uthwatt Committee by imposing a tax of 100 per cent on the increase in value through development, a charge known as 'betterment'. This unprecedented measure could have changed the face of post-war Britain by diverting the profits of development to the state, but it was alien to Conservative thinking, and, in a generally popular move, Macmillan deleted this part of the Act in 1953 on the grounds that 'betterment' was difficult to understand and administer. This allowed the business of development to proceed as usual, with the difference that local authorities were required to draw up local development plans and refuse to grant permissions for new buildings or uses that varied from the plans or the existing uses. This remained effectively a nationalization of land, and a rather arbitrary check to development. Building licences were a wartime measure to direct scarce resources into government projects. In peacetime they continued to restrain private construction, until abolished by Macmillan in 1954 as a further part of what he called his 'bonfire of controls'.

The altruistic but arduous period of government-led post-war reconstruction, limping rather than striding since the withdrawal of American Marshall Aid in 1947, was ended. Churchill's order to clear the Festival buildings from the South Bank site immediately the exhibition closed in October 1951 was a symbolic gesture of rupture with the Atlee government's paternalistic vision. After 1954 all kinds of building work grew exponentially in a new condition of dualism, in which the state still commissioned more than at any previous time, while a boom in commercial property development soon began. The backlog of reconstruction and rehousing dated back to the Depression years, and many reasonable people seem to have expected a complete renewal of the built environment, bar a few historic relics. Until the mid-1960s, therefore, there was a widespread presumption that any kind of development, if not necessarily modern architecture itself, was bound to be good.

The relaxation of controls was necessary if only because, as part of their election strategy in 1950, the Conservative Party Conference had made a commitment to build 300,000 houses per year. As H.C.G. Matthew comments, 'This was difficult to achieve, and implied possible distortion of industrial investment, an increase in inflation, and even some effect on supplies for rearmament and the Korean war.'[1] Macmillan was appointed Minister of Local Government and Planning and enjoyed

Louis Hellman, cartoon
in *Architects' Journal*
(22 November 1967).

the sense of heroism that this commitment conferred on his role. Already in 1952, nearly 240,000 new houses were built with the encouragement of government subsidies, a figure that rose to nearly 350,000, representing a mixture of public and private sector, by 1954, when the controls were scrapped.

Compared to the semi-derelict condition of Britain at the end of the war, the changes were palpable. At the same time, expectations rose. The phenomenon that the American economist J. K. Galbraith described in his book *The Affluent Society* (1958), with its consumerist attitude, was beginning to emerge in Britain after nearly two decades of short supplies, high income tax, lack of entrepreneurial imagination and flair, and absence of consumer credit. Class division was reinforced by the differing abilities to find personal expression through spending and acquisition, until the dam broke and everyone could join in. When Macmillan handed over his role in 1955, two years before succeeding Anthony Eden as Prime Minister, the government was already reducing subsidies as an economy measure. The problems associated with the supply of public housing could therefore be traced back to the diminishing means available for satisfying rising expectations.

Housing: Going Up

With the release of height restrictions in the early 1950s, Britain experienced one of the forms of modern architecture that held especial potency in the public mind. The story of the 1960s could be told as one of rise and fall, of hope and disillusion, relating to tall buildings of all kinds, whether for offices, hospitals, housing or even, in the case of Essex, university accommodation. High rise is the aspect of 1960s housing that is remembered above all others. Given the number of reasons for not making tall buildings for residential use in the public sector, it is necessary to assume that there was some deeper compulsion than mere novelty to realize the vision of a city of towers, up to forty years after Le Corbusier had first woven his spell. Perhaps pent-up frustration with a Modern Movement that had developed through the twenty years between 1930 and 1950 without being allowed to pass through this experimental phase provides some explanation. Between the Scylla of dense low-rise urban streets, from which politicians were still able to win votes by promising to release 'the people', and the Charybdis of Subtopia and suburban sprawl, which threatened so many values dear to the political and artistic establishment, the high rise set amid greenery was a form of get-out clause. Britain was keen to shed the image of its past, and high rise signalled progress in unambiguous terms to observers overseas. The means

and the opportunities were present, and combined to create a critical mass sufficient to give this form of housing a self-propelling impetus.

Catching up on the backlog of housing and accommodating the 'baby boom' was a problem for every country after the Second World War. The memory of the British experience has remained one of shame and regret, tempered with explanations and excuses and occasional denials that there was ever anything wrong with high-rise housing. The wisdom of Elizabeth Denby, noted in chapter Two, failed to penetrate the consciousness of architects and planners deeply enough to prevent what have subsequently been seen as self-reinforcing mistakes that resulted from a wilful dissociation between people and their physical environment. As Lionel Brett said in 1961, the affluent society posed 'the great philosophical question that haunts the architect's subconscious – the flashpoint at which Architecture and Politics meet: "Should people have what they want, or what they ought to want?"'[2] Architects believed they ought to want high-rise flats. The people soon began to think differently.

There is an argument, put forward by Stefan Muthesius and Miles Glendinning in *Tower Block* (1994), that architects were marginal to the high-rise housing process, however much they hoped for engagement in it through the construction industry and work with local authorities, and however much they took the blame for disasters later on. Writing in 1974, E. W. Cooney saw 'evidence of enthusiasm among architects at one time and, later, a good deal of doubt and disillusionment'.[3] High rise could take the form of slabs or towers. Slab blocks appeared most frequently in pre-war drawings and in early post-war building schemes such as Churchill Gardens, and they never ceased to be a significant element in most housing schemes. Another form of the early 1950s was the Y-plan, usually found in rather undistinguished architectural form, with the major

Frederick Gibberd,
The Lawn, Mark Hall
Moors, Harlow, Essex,
1950–51.

LLC Architects
Department (Colin
Lucas), Oakland
Court, Ackroyden
Estate, Wimbledon
Park, London,
1950–54.

exception of Skinner, Bailey and Lubetkin's Bevin Court, Islington (1951–4), which is on a grander scale and contains at its centre the most magnificent staircase in the whole of British flat building.

Towers had a special attraction for architects, however, and at Harlow Frederick Gibberd's The Lawn (1950–51) was, at ten storeys, a novelty justified by the wish to retain seven oak trees, which would have been felled in the course of a standard low-rise development. Gibberd also wanted to create variety in the New Town, and The Lawn reflected similar 'point blocks' in the Stockholm suburbs. At the Ackroydon Estate, Wimbledon (1950–54), Oakland Court and other LCC blocks were eleven storeys high, and the plan form was a T shape, which pioneered the use of internally ventilated bathrooms, a change that gave architects the freedom to arrange flats more compactly in slender towers. The LCC was partly able to pursue its own course because, unlike other local authorities, its financial borrowing was approved directly by an annual Bill in Parliament, rather than through individual government departments.[4]

Mixed development, as demonstrated by Gibberd at Harlow, corresponded to the picturesque interpretation of Modernism, and offered a more flexible range of accommodation, with larger houses with gardens for families and high rise for those without children, who would appreciate the light, fresh air (a significant consideration before the Clean Air Act of 1962), views and privacy, giving 'more pleasure to more people . . . a new kind of space, surprise views', as Frederick Gibberd said at an RIBA Symposium on high flats in February 1955; or as Herbert Tayler of Tayler and Green put it, an escape from 'a uniform pinkish grey hell' of standard post-war housing.[5] Both parts of the Alton Estate at Roehampton were mixed development, for which Sweden offered examples. Most of the early LCC high-rise blocks were on the edge of parkland, which allowed them 'breathing space' and offered rewarding views for the residents. Holford promoted the same arguments for inner London, attempting in vain to 'break the height barrier' in schemes for which he was a planning consultant at St Paul's and Piccadilly Circus.

High residential buildings remained more expensive than houses (twice as much per unit in some cases), but in 1955 speakers at the RIBA Symposium were keen to find ways to bring down the costs and justify their increasing use, aesthetically, economically and in terms of population density. They expressed concern about the loss of agricultural land if lower densities were adopted, not only in terms of loss of amenity, but also in terms of the adverse balance of payments resulting from increased food imports. Biodiversity and ecosystems were as yet unfamiliar concepts in architectural and planning circles, but the Conservatives were the party of farming and landowners, whose interests they were bound to uphold. Where new housing replaced existing slums, the original population might have to be rehoused in the same area, since the New Towns programme was slowing down, for similar reasons of saving farmland. New Town growth required the relocation of industry, as the Barlow Report hoped to encourage, but despite incentives many industries preferred to stay in the cities, rather than risk losing their existing workforce, for whom new housing had to be provided.

By 1958 government enthusiasm for height was tempered by a general desire to pull back from the whole public housing programme, which had always been anomalous for a Conservative administration. By 1956 the 'emergency' had been going on for ten years and the sense of urgency was declining.[6] New housing starts dipped after 1957, but rising population, loss of existing stock through slum clearance and the increase in the number of separate households contributed to a new awareness of crisis, with late Victorian streets of rented terraced 'bye-law' housing acquiring the name 'twilight zones'.[7] In the dying days of Macmillan's successor, Alec Douglas-Home, the Housing Act of 1964 authorized local authorities to intervene and improve conditions in the private rented sector, a sensitive subject after the posthumous exposure (in relation to the Profumo affair) of the notorious landlord Peter Rachman, whose activities had sparked the Notting Hill race riots of 1958. The Housing Corporation, an intermediary funding body between government and housing providers, is one of the 1964 Act's lasting legacies. The graph of new housing began to rise again, and the incoming Labour Government of Harold Wilson, not to be outdone, set a target of 500,000 new homes per year by 1970. This fitted Wilson's famous promise to 'forge a new Britain in the white heat of the technological revolution'. The pre-election rhetoric combined images of technological expertise with those of social liberation, and high-rise flats offered a perfect manifestation of the linkage.

Only after Wilson's return with a stronger majority in 1966 (the year of *Cathy Come Home*, a television drama exposing the still-appalling conditions of private rented housing) did house building begin to take off, despite the worsening economic situation that drove local authorities harder to find cheap ways of building. Between 1966 and 1968 there was a boom in medium rise (five to nine storeys), because seemingly by accident the government was permitting almost unrestricted subsidies. In 1964 the government set up the National Building Agency under the former LCC architect A. W. Cleeve Barr, specifically to review 'systems building' techniques from some 400 alternatives developed by eager contractors. The involvement of architects in these systems was limited to the layout of blocks and the choice of cladding panels, but many shared the excitement about finally leaping forward from the long-derided inefficiencies of site labour. This transition reopened the breach between mechanist and humanist philosophies, between efficiency and compassion. It was not that each necessarily excluded the other. The Hertfordshire schools showed how system building could be humanized, but the poetic transformation made by New Brutalism gave encouragement to architects who wanted to achieve a striking or existentially alienating effect of repetition and bleakness in the name of economy.

It did not matter whether or not this effect was genuinely cheap. In a form of accountancy suited to the short-term aims of politicians, 'First cost', the capital sum expended to produce the building, was usually the only measure, with operation costs and future maintenance ignored. As with the pre-war enthusiasm for efficiency, value was calculated from a balance sheet, but was also read back from the visual form, in which 'frills', such as the landscaping and careful adaptation to site demonstrated by RMJM at the CLASP-built York University, could look like waste when applied to housing.

Sam Bunton, Red Road Flats, Glasgow, 1962.

The very tallest flats, which attracted especial criticism for this reason, were not system-built. Red Road, Glasgow (1962–9), a group of 27–31-storey towers by Sam Bunton, an architect with a love for American ideas and methods, was steel-framed and covered in asbestos sheet; it was the highest social housing in Europe at the time. Bunton declared that 'housing today isn't domestic architecture – it's public building. You mustn't expect airs and graces.'[8] Red Road's London equivalent was the 31-storey Trellick Tower (1967), built for the LCC's successor body, the Greater London Council (GLC), by Ernö Goldfinger as the crown of the mixed-development Cheltenham Estate in North Kensington. The tallest-ever London housing block, it is robustly built using concrete poured on site rather than prefabricated and has felicities of design that could be expected from an architect of Goldfinger's training and background. It was a bespoke building, in the LCC tradition, not a mass-market product, but for many years the difference seemed insignificant.

The Gorbals area south of the River Clyde in Glasgow was a notorious slum, and although its stone-built tenements might, in the following decade, have been saved for rehabilitation, there was no alternative in the 1960s mind to clearing buildings and streets together and starting again. Robert Matthew contributed a mixed development of towers and lower blocks between 1958 and 1964, while Basil Spence's 'Hutchesontown C' (Queen Elizabeth Square) development (1961–6) was the more architecturally striking, a version of Le Corbusier's Unité d'Habitation, borrowing an earlier Corbusian idea of 'hanging gardens' to create elevated open spaces between flats. Exacerbated by the harsh climate and construction faults, the good points of the flats were overweighed by the problems. As the job architect said,

> What we did not realise when we were building things of this nature is that they involve very high maintenance cost. And that cost was impossible for the local authority to deal with.[9]

The problems were considered so intractable that the 'Queenies', as the blocks were known, were demolished, amid much publicity, in 1993.

Despite extensive use of prefabrication, encouraged by government subsidies for tall buildings, high flats never competed in cost with

Newham Borough Council (using the Larsen-Nielsen system), Ronan Point, Freemason's Estate, Newham, London, 1966. Photographed by Gillian Daniell, then an art student in London, on the morning of the gas explosion in 1968.

Sir Basil Spence, Glover and Ferguson, Queen Elizabeth Square ('Hutchesontown C'), 1960–66.

medium- and low-rise housing, to which system building was better suited. With this knowledge, it is hard to understand the reasons for the sudden popularity of high rise. Several essentially unrelated factors seem to have converged, including an aesthetic ambition on the part of architects, partly for themselves and partly for the future tenants, and a renewed concern about building over too much green-field land, less to protect amenity than to protect agricultural production and its role in the national balance of payments. Added to this were the political motives of having dramatic results to show at election time, and in some cases retaining a Labour-voting population inside an electoral boundary rather than dispersing them to new towns, where their votes would be lost. In a wider sense, the 1960s was a period in which technology was assumed to be benign and all-powerful. This was a worldwide trend, and system building was an international movement. With its powerful labour unions and trade practices in Britain, the construction industry had been resistant to modernization in many respects during the whole century, and here was an opportunity to subdue it.

Only after the peak of high-rise building with 20,000 flats in 1967 did these dark secrets emerge. The decline resulted in part from the government's belated effort to correct its over-liberal subsidy regime, but also from a slow absorption of user feedback. Not all of it was negative, at least initially, but there were so many inherently weak points, such as non-functioning lifts, which multiplied the potential for isolation. In addition, lack of close neighbourliness among residents created opportunities for vandalism and crime. Poor management and maintenance by local authorities magnified small problems into large ones.

It was impolitic to admit to making such large and expensive mistakes, at least until the clamour became an uproar, triggered by a single isolated incident, the accidental gas explosion at Ronan Point, a 23-storey Larsen-Nielsen block in Newham, East London, on 16 May 1968. Causing four fatalities, this collapse of the corner of the block revealed a fault in the system, and also the slipshod way that it had been built by contractors and their labourers. Criticism mounted, but blocks already planned and financed had to make their weary way through to completion regardless.

Coming Down

The instrument used to change direction after 1967 was the 'cost yard-stick', which prescribed an optimum density as a curb to excessive high-rise development. The result was a return to medium-rise schemes, often consisting of linked balcony-access blocks in pale imitation of Park Hill. This was almost a full circle to walk-up balcony-access blocks, after every alternative had been explored and found wanting. The Aylesbury Estate in Southwark (Borough Architect F. O. Hayes, 1967–77) was one of the largest and most notorious of the new-style developments. As Bridget Cherry commented, 'an exploration can be recommended only for those who enjoy being stunned by the impersonal megalomaniac creations of the mid c20'.[10]

In 1959 Leslie Martin and Patrick Hodgkinson published a proposal for medium-rise, high-density housing based on a site in St Pancras. It repeated arguments from the 1930s that the high densities of Georgian terraces proved the viability of contained streets and connected houses, although the building type itself could be refined through a stepped section to offer better quality private outdoor space than the traditional balcony. The St Pancras housing manager appreciated the contrast that their scheme offered with 'the hygienic stillness and television silence of the new housing estates', although he commented that the proposed open planning inside the flats and maisonettes might be too advanced for tenants 'only just about out of the "aspidistra stage" and still only mid-way through the open fire and "nice tiled surround" stage'.[11]

The basic thinking of this proposal, backed by impressive mathematical calculations of the type that Martin introduced to Cambridge in the post-graduate Centre for Land Use and Built Form, fed the opposition to high rise that developed among architects, well ahead of Ronan Point, when their autonomy was taken away by system builders and local government planners.

At Lillington Street, Pimlico (1961–72), Darbourne and Darke also interrogated the cross-section, here rising up to eight storeys without looking either like a slab or a tower. The intention was to remove the institutional quality from public housing, with high-quality landscaping and a brick even redder than Ham Common, with concrete floor plates grinning through in the manner of Maisons Jaoul, partly as a tribute to a fine 'vigorous Gothic' church next to the site by G. E. Street. Colin Amery and Lance Wright wrote in 1977:

> Pre-Darbourne and Darke housing is visibly institutionalised.
> Housing estates were separate and however salubrious and

Darbourne and Darke,
Lillington Gardens,
Pimlico, London.
1961–72.

spacious, visibly apart from the organic spontaneity of ordinary living . . . Under the impulse of collectivisation in the 'fifties the home had become transmogrified and absorbed into something bigger than itself. Homes became clutches of serviced cells. Slowly, in many aspects of this firm's work these are being drawn back into a unity and you have the image of "home" once more.[12]

Low-rise housing was capable of achieving new higher-density forms as well. The Cockaigne Housing Group's development at The Ryde, Hatfield, Hertfordshire, began in 1962 when Michael Baily, the transport correspondent of *The Times*, advertised for supporters to join a co-operative venture 'to work out afresh the real needs of the family of today and the type of structure which would best answer them'.[13] In the years 1963–6 the architects, Phippen Randall and Parkes, built a tightly knit collection of single-storey L-shaped courtyard houses with communal amenities. The Ryde showed a debt to Le Corbusier, but not as the promoter of high rise. Both Lillington Street and St Bernard's, Croydon, by Atelier 5 (1966–70), in common with many other projects of the 1960s, derived their stepped and jumbled forms from Le Corbusier's wartime Rob et Roq housing project in the south of France. Atelier 5, a Swiss practice, was invited to design St Bernard's for the builder-developers, Wates, producing a tidy compact mass of houses with pedestrian access on two levels.

The Dunboyne Road Estate, Hampstead (1966–9), by Neave Brown, was one of many experiments in housing form carried out by Camden's

Phippen Randall and Parkes, Cockaigne Housing Group, The Ryde, Hatfield, Hertfordshire, 1963–6.

in-house architects under Sidney Cook. Dunboyne Road sits as a compact and intricately planned three-dimensional grid of layered uses, from parking at the base, up into flats and maisonettes, and terraces of public and private gardens. Brown went on to design the much larger Alexandra Road estate in 1969 (constructed 1972–8), where the architecture makes its own mountain slopes in a gentle curve aligned to the adjoining railway line. Its sweep of repeating units is undeniably sublime, but construction became notoriously expensive owing to difficulties of inflation in the 1970s, exacerbated by the non-standard nature of the process. The reputation of the most expensive council housing in Britain belonged to Gordon Benson's and Alan Forsyth's Branch Hill, Hampstead (1974–6), the cost of which was partly caused by the value of the secluded and wooded site (on which there was a covenant against building more than

Camden Borough Council (Neave Brown), Dunboyne Road Estate, Fleet Road, Camden, London, 1966–9.

138

Camden Architects' Department (Neave Brown), Alexandra Road Estate, Swiss Cottage, London, 1968–78.

two storeys), and partly by the same difficulties as Alexandra Road. It was perhaps the most idyllic of the Rob et Roq derivatives.

Patrick Hodgkinson's studies in the late 1950s eventually bore fruit at the Brunswick Centre (1968–72), in the heart of Bloomsbury. Like Alexandra Road, it was offered and welcomed as an alternative to a tower block, beginning as a private scheme in which Camden later took a share. The scheme consists of two parallel lines of an extruded stepped cross-section of ocean-liner dimensions, combining flats with a pedestrian shopping street in the middle, a cinema and ample car parking. The stepped 'ziggurat' section, rooted far back in the Modern Movement but increasingly popular in the 1960s, leans backwards in an inverted v. The desirable location lifted the flats from a depressed condition by the end of the 1990s, leading to a substantial refurbishment involving Hodgkinson in the years 2004–6.

At Harlow, Neylan and Ungless's Bishopsfield (1963) created a central civic space raised over parking and ringed by three-storey flats on a minor

Patrick Hodgkinson,
Brunswick Centre,
Bloomsbury, London,
1967–72.

hillock, with Mediterranean lanes leading off in different directions, in complete contrast to the mixed-development neighbourhoods of the 1950s. This was a direct response to the thinking of Team 10 about 'association', based on the assumption that if people lived close to each other, they could halt the alienation of modern consumer society and rediscover some sense of community. The same move towards tighter housing was set as a policy for Cumbernauld, the New Town for Glasgow 'overspill', planned on a hilltop site by Hugh Wilson in 1958–9. This was complemented by a multi-level town centre, designed by Geoffrey Copcutt, which acted as a *Stadtkrone* ('city crown') in the manner of Patrick Geddes's or Bruno Taut's expressionist interpretation thereof. Cumbernauld town centre and the Brunswick Centre were both described as 'megastructures', a word that began to gain currency around 1964, when a number of projects internationally displayed the characteristics of size and multiple and mutable functions inserted into a more or less permanent framework, and the capability of being extended indefinitely, usually in the form of a linear extrusion.[14] Of the two, Cumbernauld was more radical in its open-ended form. A megastructure might include housing as one of its functions, but despite the desirability of combining housing with shops, the compartmentalized and irrational financing arrangements made this difficult.

The whole question of housing in the 1960s remains highly controversial. There were so many genuine problems that for many years the whole body of work was rejected in one piece. Blame was difficult to apportion among designers, contractors, politicians and housing managers, all of whom made mistakes in good or bad faith. The failure of Modernist housing led to a serious loss of self-esteem among architects. The professional magazines reveal an extended period of self-questioning from the late 1960s onwards, challenging not only the ideas of the immediate past, but extending right back to challenge the orthodoxies of the Modern Movement as a whole.

Geoffrey Copcutt, Cumbernauld Town Centre, 1964–8. Copcutt recalled the full proposal, 'like a jeweller fashioning precious metal, I hammered cross-sections and shaped landscape to forge an urban morphology', contrasting it with the built scheme, 'a filleted version of the first phase'.

The historian and journalist Nicholas Taylor made one of the first major attacks on 'production' housing in 1967 in the *Architectural Review*, a magazine that had never abandoned its concern with the gentle philosophy of the picturesque and its respect for places and their past. As he stated at the beginning of his text, '"Housing" is a nineteenth century concept.' This is both historically and philosophically true. The social concept of housing provision from the top down was unchanged from the grudging philanthropy of the Victorians, and the recipients were still expected to like it and be grateful, even in an age of consumerism and choice. When the provision fell so far short of efficiency, and the rise of vandalism began to have an effect, crisis resulted, but the alternatives were not well understood. In terms of action, Taylor and other contributors recommended the rehabilitation of houses of the type that were then being pulled down as slums or 'twilight zones'. Better landscaping and denser settlements were put forward as alternatives, as at Lillington Street, but, as Taylor complained, 'Visual images of community have time and again been used as a substitute for reality.'[15] As old social networks split apart, community was desired more intensely, but no easier to manufacture purely out of building forms.

Office Development and the Private Sector

Under the London Building Acts, street elevations were typically at a uniform height of 80 feet, and any inhabited floors above this level set back in steps. Internal light wells provided a dim outlook for many office

Easton, Robertson, Cusdin, Preston and Smith, Shell Centre, Belvedere Road, Lambeth, London, 1953–63.

Basil Spence and Partners (Andrew Renton), Thorn House, St Martin's Lane, Westminster, London, 1957–9. Described by Sir Nikolaus Pevsner as 'one of the best office buildings of its date in England', Thorn House was remodelled by Renton's successors at RHWL Partnership in 1988–90 as Orion House.

workers. Buildings of this type were heavily criticized by J. M. Richards in the *Architectural Review* as contrary to the urban ideas of Modernism. The height limit of the Building Acts was replaced by the concept of 'plot ratio', first proposed in 1947 by William Holford. This permitted buildings to rise higher, but not to fill a given site with more than the floorspace of an equivalent building under the old regime. The Royal Fine Art Commission was doubtful about breaking upwards, but Richards argued that 'there is nothing wrong with height as such' and that 'a few slim skyscrapers, between which the City panorama could be seen and enjoyed' would be 'less obstructive than large acreages of building of perhaps half their height'.[16] Richards noted the emergence of the fourteen-storey Great Arthur House in the Golden Lane housing estate, and that some tall office buildings were beginning to get planning permission.

It still took some years before taller buildings cut through the skyline. Leslie Martin's plan for the South Bank in 1953 allowed for a 25-storey tower for Shell. Howard Robertson's firm, Easton, Robertson, Cusdin, Preston and Smith, which had a reputation as moderate Modernists before the war, took the commission, and tried unsuccessfully to go higher. The building was stone-clad from top to bottom, and vaguely reminiscent, at least in the lower blocks, of Gio Ponti's much sparkier Montecatini building in Milan of 1936. Ian Nairn grouped it with pre-war skyblockers, as a set of giants, borrowing Blake's opinion of Reynolds, 'hired by Satan to depress art'.[17] As the Macmillan years unfolded, London became the epicentre of the office boom, and tall buildings were one of the devices available to developers and their architects when seeking planning permission from the LCC and interpreting the complex regulations to give the maximum lettable space. As Oliver Marriott wrote in 1967,

> Holford's scheme of plot ratio zoning was designed as a set of theoretical limits on density of workers in given areas. Nobody dreamt that the developers would want to build as much on a site as the plot ratios allowed.[18]

Demonstration by Anti-Ugly Action against the unfinished Kensington Public Library, London, designed by Vincent Harris, 1958.

This is some indication of the LCC's lack of preparation for the office boom. While the guardians of taste in the architectural magazines were generally more pleased if a commercial development was modern than otherwise, it soon became clear that modern could mean many things, not all equally praiseworthy. While the Economist Building used the plot ratio to give space back to the passing pedestrian, Thorn House, St Martin's Lane, by Andrew Renton of Basil Spence and Partners (1957–9), although celebrated as a fulfilment of Richards's intentions in his article of 1954, had less obvious benefits.

In 1957 any architect, especially in London, guilty of persisting with a pre-Modernist elevation, whether overtly historic in character or not, laid themselves open to a visitation from Anti-Ugly Action, a group mainly composed of students from the Royal College of Art stained-glass course, with some Architectural Association students in tow. They devised a novel form of street theatre involving parading a coffin for the death of modern architecture in front of a completed building, such as Bracken House and the Kensington Public Library (by Vincent Harris), and shouting 'It's an outrage'. They caught the public's attention, if only because one of the leaders of the group, Pauline Boty, was not only a talented early exponent of Pop Art, but also glamorously blonde, and probably added vigour to the attempt to unseat the (mostly) elderly academic architects.[19]

One attraction of commercial development for young architects was the possibility of getting things built quickly, and by the beginning of the 1960s developers were not all cautious conservatives. Rodney Gordon was a student at the AA under Peter Smithson and, like many of his contemporaries, joined the LCC Architects' Department. When after a few years one of his colleagues, who had been moonlighting for Owen Luder, one of the youngest 'developer's architects' with his own practice, invited Gordon to meet Luder with a view to designing a competition entry for a shopping centre at Elephant and Castle, 'the bait of designing a major shopping centre was too strong to resist'.[20] The developer for this scheme was Alec Coleman, who explained his philosophy to Gordon: 'A developer is like a prostitute, you've got it . . . you sell it . . . You've still got it.' Gordon and Luder worked on Eros House, Catford (1959–62), an office building in a south London suburb, where Gordon maximized the plot ratio in a

144

Owen Luder Partner-
ship (Rodney Gordon),
Tricorn Centre,
Portsmouth, 1966.

novel way, expressing the structure and services on the outside of the
building envelope in a manner that bridged between Kahn and the
High-Tech manner still in the future. The same team developed shopping centres in Portsmouth and Gateshead, both of which notoriously
introduced a certain brand of New Brutalism into the commercial sector,
with dramatic effect.

Commercial architecture could therefore be more creative than some
of the virtuous architecture of the welfare state, even if Banham declared
that the character was only skin deep. In Birmingham, the Post and Mail
building (1962–5; demolished) by a local practice, John Madin Group,
was a notable example of the Miesian tower-and-podium type. The
Burnet Tait practice continued in the hands of Gordon Tait, who was
initially inspired by Lubetkin's more decorative side, and proved to be a
designer of considerable formal invention and control, even though he
was never 'rated' among the leading architects of the time. His elegant

25-storey tower for the Co-operative Insurance Society offices in Manchester (with G. S. Hay, 1959–62), admittedly a bespoke rather than a spec building, did not suffer from the good taste, administered at the hands of the Royal Fine Art Commission (RFAC), that cut down the Shell Building and Robert Matthew, Johnson-Marshall's New Zealand House in Haymarket to their detriment. Taking its cue from SOM's Inland Steel Building in Chicago, it continued the long-standing sense of a linkage between the northern cities and the United States stronger than the US–London connection.

The developer's architect par excellence in the 1960s was Richard Seifert, a former student of Richardson's at the Bartlett School of Architecture, who might have remained part of an undistinguished majority of practitioners had he not found a distinctive niche on returning from war service in the Royal Engineers, and formed an alliance with the developer Harry Hyams, beginning with the semi-traditional Woolworths Building on Marylebone Road in 1955. With a fresh design input from his partner George Marsh, Seifert designed Centre Point (1963–7), a slender office tower on New Oxford Street, with pre-cast concrete panels and sculptural piloti derived from Marcel Breuer's later works, such as the UNESCO headquarters in Paris. While the un-let building became a symbol of unearned developer's profits, since its capital value accumulated free of rates while it remained empty, it was possibly the first project by a 'commercial' architect to be widely admired as a design by Ernö Goldfinger, among others, who called it 'London's first Pop-art skyscraper'.[21] The opportunity to develop Centre Point came about because of the LCC's desire to effect a road-widening scheme, which it was unable to implement without some form of private-sector partnership, and the council therefore deliberately avoided submitting the scheme to what they anticipated would be a hostile RFAC.

A different form of collusion between the LCC and developers occurred on Euston Road, where the LCC intended to build an underpass, not knowing that the developer Joe Levy had already obtained planning permission for offices on a small but essential pocket of land. Levy milked the situation, first to get LCC help in 'site assembly' for a larger development in a neglected corner of London close enough to the centre to present an attractive office site, and then to exceed the plot ratio for his Euston Centre (1962–72; architects Sidney Kaye, Eric Firmin & Partners), a curtain-walled tower, slab and podium development in green-tinted glass.[22]

In the 1960s British people were still excited by tall buildings. They queued to go up the Post Office Tower in Howland Street in 1967, before an IRA bomb in 1971 caused it to be closed to visitors. As with housing,

G. S. Hay (CWS) and Gordon Tait of Sir John Burnet, Tait and Partners, Co-operative Insurance Tower, Miller Street, Manchester, 1959–62.

a backlash began soon after this date, since towers were increasingly seen as exploiting land values and cluttering the skyline. Seifert gathered further opprobrium (and some grudging admirers) as he went on to add some of the tallest buildings in the City of London in the 1970s, including the 200-metre-high National Westminster Bank (1970–81; now 'Tower 42'). After this, towers went out of fashion until the abolition of plot-ratios in 1993, prompting a proposal by Norman Foster and Partners for the Swiss Re tower on the site of the former Baltic Exchange, damaged by the IRA Bishopsgate bomb on 24 April 1992.

Universities

Compared to housing and offices, universities were a less controversial area of development, but equally typical of the 1960s in their accelerating pace of change and expansion. The children of the baby boom were given primary schools in the early 1950s, and secondary schools in the late 1950s. By the 1960s they would reach university age, and the Robbins Report of 1963 proposed that higher education should be available to all those capable of benefiting from it, supported by tuition and maintenance grants that, while they lasted, made the student experience a state-sponsored release from the realities of economic life. During the decade, the number of universities rose from 22 to 46, with the new ones largely following a pattern of being sited on green-field campuses, usually the park of a defunct country house, a mile or two outside the towns with which they were associated. This model resembled a British boarding school (including playing fields), reflecting a 'new town' faith in the benefits of natural surroundings and a desire to get away from the 'Red Brick' image of the late Victorian and inter-war civic universities. The intention was to house most students on the campus with all their facilities, and it was assumed that sufficient sites in city centres, retrospectively a better solution both for students and cities, would not be obtainable fast enough.

When Keele University was founded in 1949 near Stoke-on-Trent, its faintly neo-Georgian early buildings by Howard Robertson and J. A. Pickavance were seen as a failure architecturally. To prevent any recurrence, later universities were given consultant architects from the start, selected by recommendation rather than competition, and mainly limited to the younger level of established London practices. The Royal Fine Art Commission made a determined and ultimately successful effort to wean the longer-established Nottingham, Exeter and Durham universities off their preference for neo-Georgian and traditional buildings by McMorran, Vincent Harris and Marshall Sisson.[23]

The University of Sussex, designed by Basil Spence and opened in 1962, was slightly ahead of the pack of seven universities that were under simultaneous construction in the first half of the decade. The architecture was typical of Spence: theatrical, warm-hearted and cleverly composed from sources fashionable at the time, chiefly the Maisons Jaoul. Later architects were more cautious about grand gestures, and the opposite end of the spectrum included York, built by Robert Matthew, Johnson-Marshall using the CLASP system developed for schools, and Warwick, by Yorke Rosenberg Mardall, a smooth International Style grid of white-tiled rectangles, carefully zoned and linked by a lower-level road. Architects enjoyed the similarity of campus planning to city planning, and increasingly saw universities as analogies of towns. At Lancaster, Shepheard, Epstein and Hunter created a rectangular agora sheltered from the wind by three-storey buildings and equipped with a long range of steps of the type that Beaux-Arts architects provided

Basil Spence and Partners, Falmer House, University of Sussex, 1960–62.

Yorke Rosenberg Mardall, master-plan model for the University of Warwick, Coventry, 1963.

Architects Co-Partnership, University of Essex, Wivenhoe, 1962–6.

in front of the monumental libraries of American universities, little suspecting that the fashion of the baby boomers was to sit on the ground rather than on chairs or benches. At Essex, the design by Kenneth Capon of Architects Co-Partnership consisted of a series of town squares, in which individual academic departments purposely lost their separate identity. The students were given tall towers of black brick to mark the skyline north of Colchester, and allow them the shortest possible journey from bed to lecture hall. At the University of East Anglia, Denys Lasdun snaked a ziggurat concrete megastructure across the contour overlooking a lake, backed by a 'teaching wall'.

The care taken in designing and building the 1960s universities remains an impressive testimony to a brief period of marital harmony between the British establishment (represented by bodies such as the University Grants Commission) and the architectural profession. Like the students, modern architects were being treated for the first time as responsible adults. By 1968, as with

Denys Lasdun and Partners, the 'ziggurats' in construction, University of East Anglia, Norwich, 1962–7.

housing, there was a turn of opinion against these utopian schemes as a result of experience. Not everything was the fault of the architects. The social changes of which the universities were a manifestation themselves created a more critical climate in relation not only to the physical form of the buildings, but also to the wider ideas and attitudes that they represented. The campus revolutions of the USA, sparked initially in Berkeley in 1964, spread to Britain in the years 1967–9. Few universities were completely unaffected, but events at Essex (where the police were called in as late as 1974) and the LSE became national news stories. Even so, the buildings themselves revealed avoidable shortcomings, ranging from the impossibility of creating a balanced society cut off from ordinary life, especially when so little provision was initially made for agreeable social spaces, to specific problems with stained concrete (East Anglia), falling tile cladding (Warwick), sound-proofing and lifts (Essex). A book of 1972 entitled *Building the New Universities* by Tony Birks was balanced but not uncritical. In 1974 Lord Annan, the Provost of King's College, Cambridge, who had appointed a controversial Vice-Chancellor at Essex, Albert Sloman, reported that 'Numbers of staff and students wrote to me to condemn the architecture of the University and to lay at its door the blame for the unhappy life and hence for the disturbances.'[24] Muthesius comments that no architecture could have been better devised for revolution, 'the more residential and dense the campus, the easier it was for the militants to organise themselves'.[25]

Public Architecture

In the 1930s the design of town halls and similar local government buildings began to reflect Modernism, although never in the latest form. The Victorian and Edwardian traditions of elaborate decoration were modified by the influence of Stockholm City Hall by Ragnar Östberg, completed in 1922, and Hilversum Town Hall by W. M. Dudok (1930). McMorran and Whitby were among a handful of architects who continued to build in a traditional style of load-bearing brick up to the completion in 1968 of Suffolk County Hall in Bury St Edmunds, to which Whitby brought a fresh approach to picturesque grouping absent from the axial formality of pre-war town halls. John Brandon Jones, an enthusiast for the work of Philip Webb and Lethaby, was influenced by one of H. P. Berlage's more conservative followers, A. J. Kropholler, at Hampshire County Hall, Winchester (1959–60). At Brentwood Town Hall (1957, extended 1983) and Staines (1960), his designs appeared old-fashioned and were built against the advice of the RFAC, but they anticipated the return to a regional brick style in the 1970s at Hillingdon Civic Centre and other buildings.

McMorran and Whitby, Suffolk County Buildings, Bury St Edmunds, 1968.

Local government reorganization, the perceived need for more car parking and increasing numbers of local government staff stimulated much new building without the drastic cost constraints applied to housing. Cornwall County Hall, Truro (1962–6), designed by the County Architects' Department in a style with appropriate borrowings from Le Corbusier, was among the most successful, although it was the private firms that tended to attract notice. At Gravesend Civic Centre by H. T. Cadbury-Brown and Partners (1964), a severe style with concrete cladding panels was chosen, although the interior was carefully considered in terms of open space and light. Sunderland Civic Centre (1968–70), by John S. Bonnington (of Sir Basil Spence, Bonnington and Collins), was sited in a park, and described as 'an open town within a town'.[26] Ramps and gentle steps encouraged a feeling of welcome and accessibility.

A much bolder scheme for a new Civic Centre in Liverpool by Colin St John Wilson, working independently of Leslie Martin, was prepared in 1965, after he had been picked from an international shortlist. The site was large and central, and the project contained the first modern atrium conceived as public space. It fell victim to government cuts at the end of the decade. The idea of the atrium had a great future, however, initially in the new public space of the late twentieth century, the covered shopping centre or mall. These initially tended to comprise the bottom end of the market, but architects of repute became involved by the end of the 1960s in schemes such as Lion Yard, Cambridge (Arup Associates, 1968–72), and the Brunel Centre, Swindon (Douglas Stephen and Partners, 1966–75). Both schemes tried to mesh into the existing surroundings, without offering any direct architectural similarity. The Brunel Centre made one of the most successful attempts, at least before Milton Keynes, to transform commerce into civic space, with a grand arched galleria in the manner of Milan.

Working with Martin, Wilson had already begun in 1962 to plan a more celebrated non-event of 1960s architecture, the British Museum Library (as it was then known), originally intended to occupy the whole block of streets south of Great Russell Street. Here, according to the first scheme, there would be an abundance of newly created public space, introducing the kind of thinking then replacing purely functional attitudes towards the city, including 'some of the forgotten symbols of a city: its entry points or gates, its ceremonial ways or public squares and the opportunity that exists of recreating these by the process of building'.[27] The project failed owing to a combination of factors: government cost constraints; a rising tide of conservation opposition to the demolition of a useful and attractive part of London; and a change in the brief to include more library stock and services, resulting in a project that became too big for its site. 'This may conceivably be the way to build a library', wrote the *Architectural Review*, 'emphatically it is not the way to rebuild a central piece of city.'[28] Despite the waste of time and effort, Peter Hall believes that it 'quite suddenly reappeared in a different light as relative planning success', owing in this case to the decision to build on a different site (see chapter Six for the continuation of the project).[29] Alan Bennett welcomed the demise of the British Museum Library in *The Listener*, with the question, 'Have you ever seen a second-hand bookshop in a new building?', and commented: 'London is not to be tidied up.'[30]

In the same year, Leslie Martin's plan for Whitehall was published, which added pedestrianization at the expense of one of London's familiar processional streets. 'Sir Leslie is more concerned with how things could be than with how they are' wrote Terence Bendixson in *The Spectator*. 'Get the facts and measure them is his cry.'[31] But this dogged belief in the calculation of optimal outcomes ignored public attachment to this important symbolic heart of government. Here, again, the desire to revalue previously disregarded buildings such as Sir Gilbert Scott's Foreign Office led to the abandonment of the scheme and the eventual transformation of the existing buildings into highly serviced modern offices, with their ceremonial interiors restored.

Cars, Conservation and Covent Garden

In his special issue of the *Architectural Review*, *Outrage*, in 1955, Ian Nairn recorded a cry of pain about the degradation of the countryside, where the blind and casual spread of ugliness, 'a universal levelling down and greying out', that post-war planning was supposed to prevent was shown to be rampant. It raised the question of sense of place, reinforcing the demand of the Townscape article of 1949 that people should use their eyes rather than refer to abstract theory.[32] The publication of *Townscape* in book form by Gordon Cullen in 1961 signalled the continuing need to stop the rot by more holistic design practices. The American urban theorist Kevin Lynch contributed to developing new concepts for understanding places in *The Image of the City* (1960).

Against this background of pessimism, Jane Jacobs's *The Death and Life of Great American Cities* (1961) was a planning book unlike any written before, dealing directly with issues from the viewpoint of an informed non-specialist who could help professionals to see through the contradictions into which they had been boxed by Modernist ideology, and the degradation they were causing to the public realm through excessive zoning and 'tidying up'.

Many of the problems identified by Lynch and Jacobs stemmed from the erosion of the public realm by motor traffic, especially the growth in private car use. Most modern architects felt obliged to try and accommodate rather than resist the car, but as early as 1957 a new critical attitude was apparent. The book *Mixed Blessing: The Motor in Britain*, by an architect and planner, Colin Buchanan, concluded that cars had produced

> a picture of death, and injury, pain and bereavement, noise and smell, and of vast winding trails of serious damage to urban and country amenities with vulgarity, shoddiness and the plain squalor of mud, dirt and litter . . . In fifty years the motor has turned our transport system inside out without a single contribution to the civic and building record; there is nothing in this country that could conceivably be called the architecture of motor transport . . . Apart from war, it is difficult to think of any previous activity of man that has wrought this kind of dual havoc.[33]

To begin with, British cities developed ring roads on an American model, to ease traffic flow while cutting off the centre from the inner suburbs and accelerating decline. The national motorway network was inaugurated with the Preston bypass in Lancashire in 1958, followed by the first section of the M1 in 1959. As in America, although less blatantly, the rise of the car led directly to the decline of public transport. The railway system, nationalized in 1948 and loss-making after 1960, was pruned after the Beeching Report, 'Reshaping the Railways', of 1963. Although some admirable design work was done within the regional architects' offices of British Rail up to the late 1960s, the system as a whole became increasingly run down.

After something of a false start with Owen Williams's unpopular designs for the M1 bridges, motorway architecture improved. Landscape architects, a profession that was rising in independent significance during the whole post-war period, were employed in the choice of routes and their planting schemes, with Sylvia Crowe's book of 1960, *The Landscape of Roads*, making a timely contribution of good sense. Sir Colin Anderson, a noted design patron from the 1930s (Orient Line ships), chaired the commission in 1962 that selected signage from Jock Kinnear and Margaret Calvert.[34] The system put Britain at the front of the international league in one step, and is still in place more than 40 years later. Thus non-architectural Modernism contributed to removing some of the squalor of the roads noted by Buchanan, in the same way that Alec Issigonis's Mini Minor became a British 'people's car', typifying the lateral thinking of the 1960s.

Most major British towns and cities commissioned plans from consultants in the post-war period, and all of these were concerned with traffic flow.[35] The schemes were on ground level, with roundabouts at intersections. American cities showed a new future with elevated urban motorways and 'stack' crossings where flow need not be interrupted. Buchanan commented that, while appearing exciting, 'they are ruthlessly destructive of ground uses and areas, and it is difficult to view with equanimity the prospect of similar measures applied to our cities'.[36] Despite this warning, urban motorways in cuttings or on piloti began to appear in British cities during the 1960s as an aspect of 'Comprehensive Redevelopment', a phrase that was the key to unlocking central government funding. As Ian Nairn remarked in 1960, the northern industrial cities of Britain, being largely of nineteenth-century growth, were much more like American cities than any others, and similarly suffered from a ring of urban blight between the commercial centre and the suburbs, thus providing the typical location for an inner ring road.[37]

Birmingham and Coventry were cities where cars and their components were made, and for them a suitable display of roadway was a matter of pride. Glasgow was gripped with a road-building fever as part of its designation of 29 Comprehensive Redevelopment Areas in 1960. One of the engineers involved, James McCafferty, has commented:

> a strong element of civic pride was evident: Glasgow was, after all, the nation's largest city and its commercial, industrial hub. And there were also comparisons with the relative inactivity of England in this field.[38]

The *Glasgow Herald* announced that the city had produced 'a blueprint for the first urban motorway in Britain, probably in Europe, and is turning now to consider the proposals for an outer ring route'.[39] By 1974, however, traffic predictions were reduced in line with economic crisis, and the Land Compensation Act of 1973 made councils liable for the inevitable drop in the value of properties next to new roads. Even though the inner ring road was never completed, it established a pattern of car use to the detriment of public transport.

The Newcastle inner ring road and associated developments owed much to the personality of the Leader of the Council from 1959, T. Dan Smith, a Labour politician with a belief in modernization as the pathway to socialism and making Newcastle 'a major cultural city on the western seaboard of Europe'.[40] Visually, the natural contours allowed for a motorway scheme that in parts had its own drama, but opposition was created by Professor Jack Napper at the School of Architecture, especially against the eastern section, which would destroy the Royal Arcade and produce 'a tight necklace to strangle the city'.[41] Smith's collusion with the corrupt architect John Poulson, who also led to the downfall of the Conservative Home Secretary Reginald Maudling, eventually landed both men in gaol, bringing the ring road and similar developments elsewhere into further disrepute.[42]

Following a distinguished performance at the Public Inquiry on plans for Piccadilly Circus, Colin Buchanan was commissioned in 1961 to undertake a study that resulted in the report *Traffic in Towns* (1963), with a talented design and research team. The Steering Group (aptly named, chaired by Geoffrey Crowther of *The Economist* and including William Holford and T. Dan Smith) highlighted the public/private dichotomy exposed by the car, 'a monster of great potential destructiveness' in public terms, and yet one that symbolized personal emancipation. By the 1960s northern cities had abandoned their traditional tramways, as the American cities tore up their streetcar tracks, and, unlike London, they had no powers to take control of suburban rail services. The penultimate paragraph of the Buchanan Report called for a 'sixth sense' of 'motorised responsibility' as 'an almost heroic act of self-discipline from the public'.[43] From a later viewpoint, it is odd that so little attention was given at this time to the improvement of public transport as an alternative to private car use and a means of reclaiming the streets for pedestrians. The operation of 'Parkinson's Law' in terms of new traffic taking to the roads in proportion to roads becoming available was also ignored when making projections of growth. When it came to controversy over the London 'motorway box' proposed by the GLC, it was the economic superiority of the Tubes and buses, better maintained in the capital than elsewhere

Kenneth Browne, illustration from *Traffic in Towns* (Buchanan Report), 1963.

OF COURSE, THE MOTORWAY BOX HAS ENTAILED THE DEMOLITION OF A FEW[1] OBSOLETE HOUSES[2]...

BUT, UNLESS WE PLANNERS HAD ACTED — THE RAPID GROWTH OF CAR OWNERSHIP[3]...

PLUS THE PUBLIC DEMAND FOR INCREASED MOBILITY[4] WOULD HAVE MADE LONDON INTOLERABLE ...

... AS A PLACE TO LIVE IN[5]

out of necessity, that made its abandonment tolerable.

In London, conservation of a very basic kind, based on the desire of largely underprivileged people along the route to defend their homes, was one of the factors that led to the abandonment of 'Ringway One' in 1973. Other factors were rapidly mounting property and construction costs, which skewed the original cost–benefit predictions created to justify the scheme. It became increasingly ludicrous to try and sell the attractions of raised walkways and underpasses once these had been experienced in practice. Whether in the sudden interruptions of the City of London 'pedway' or the fragmented pedestrian links between bus stops and the Town Centre at Cumbernauld, these were clear signals of danger and distress.[44] Stanley Kubrick's choice of underpasses at the GLC's demonstration estate at Thamesmead as a location for the young thugs in *A Clockwork Orange* (1970) confirmed what everyone knew.

During the same period, the GLC was under attack for its plans to redevelop the Covent Garden area in preparation for the closure of the old fruit and vegetable wholesale market in 1973. The Covent Garden story is a microcosm of the whole shift in thinking that occurred in architecture and planning in the course of the 1960s. Despite its central location, Covent Garden was little known or explored by most Londoners, and initially the GLC's intentions were modest. As property values increased, it became necessary to create more development value, and in the process, in order to win the status of 'Comprehensive Redevelopment Area', new road proposals were included around the perimeter, leading to further destruction of original streets. A team of architects at County Hall continued to revise the scheme through the second half

GLC Covent Garden Plan, southern section, 1969.

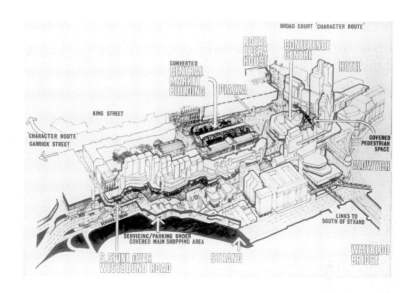

of the 1960s, with an increasing reliance on the contribution to be made by private developers (who had in any case been busy assembling sites) towards its implementation. These planners, a commentator wrote in 1971,

> had learned well from Lewis Mumford, Kevin Lynch and Jane Jacobs to respect the complexities of the city; never would they have committed the solecisms of the pioneers of modern architecture. Nevertheless, they were conditioned to ruthlessness. They thought of Covent Garden as obsolete.[45]

Louis Hellman, cartoon with accompanying notes in *Architects' Journal* (31 January 1973).
(1) 20,000.
(2) All houses built before 1914.
(3) My wife has a car too!
(4) Pressure from small but powerful motoring lobby.
(5) I couldn't have driven direct from Kings Langley to the South Coast at weekends!

Not only urban freeways but also substantial car parking anticipated visitors from outside the area arriving to enjoy the conference centre; and hotels, supported by government funding at £500 per room, left very little of the original streets and the people who lived and worked in them.

Suddenly, one of the planners, a 30-year-old Irish architect, Brian Anson, broke ranks, publicizing his sympathies for the existing residents, who were mostly elderly and lived in poorly serviced, if strongly built, walk-up flats in the area. The GLC could no longer afford to rehouse all those – their constituents – who wished to remain. Besides residents, there was a network of small businesses, profitable in their way as well as picturesque, that benefited from the low rents.[46] Another architect, then a student at the AA, Jim Monahan, helped to found the Covent Garden Community Association. The Vicar of St Martin's in the

Covent Garden
protest, 1972.

Fields, Austen Williams, joined in, and gave convincing evidence at the Public Inquiry held in 1971, which marked the beginning of a rapid climb-down by the GLC (leaving a fragment of its scheme on the ground in Drury Lane, a meagre parody of the Economist Building). Covent Garden remained in temporary limbo, but gradually the developers' properties were refurbished and re-let at higher levels, and the Market reopened in a model restoration as an American-style 'Festival Market' in 1980. After the demise of the GLC in 1986 the market was sold to property investors, with the effect that most of the interesting shops originally courted to move in left as the rents went up.

The Covent Garden story became national news, interwoven with the new trends of student activism, a developing awareness at official levels of the need for public consultation and a resounding identification of modern architecture no longer with compassionate left-wing causes, but as the instrument of property and power. Helped no doubt by its convenient location, it was adopted as a cause by the Architectural Association, which itself had just escaped the cold embrace of amalgamation with Imperial College in South Kensington. What is interesting in retrospect is the gathering together of new ways of thinking, from the physical as well as the social sciences, as a means of giving insight into cities that were not considered in the 1950s.

In Jane Jacobs's book of 1961, the final chapter, 'The Kind of Problem a City Is', drew on complexity theory, the alternative to the 'two-variable solution' dominant in the whole rationalist period of European thought. It was this simplistic mode, Jacobs believed, that underlay the way planners thought, in defiance of the evidence. Their desire for tidiness meant that they failed to see the order present in organized complexity, which was what Jacobs demonstrated with her famous analytical description of life on a street in Greenwich Village in New York. 'To this day', Jacobs wrote,

> city planners and housers believe they hold a precious nugget of truth about the kind of problem to be dealt with when they attempt to shape or reshape big-city neighbourhoods into versions of two-variable systems, with ratios of one thing (as open space) depending directly and simply upon a ratio of something else (as population).

Growing awareness of this fundamental shift in scientific thought began to penetrate general thinking, and around 1970 *Architectural Design* began to include extracts from scientific papers about complexity, citing both the fashionable cybernetics theory of Norbert Wiener and the complexity theories of Bertalanffy and Lancelot Law Whyte, the scientist who had become involved in the *Growth and Form* exhibition in London in 1951.[47]

What was there left for the modern architect to hope for? In a book review of 1971 entitled 'Fifty Years of Phantom Pregnancy', Martin Pawley described him as 'a figure it is beyond the power of reason to save ... We weep to see him groaning in phantom labour over his drawing board.'[48] Reviewing *Parameters and Images* by Lionel Brett, a leading spokesman for modern architecture and a future President of the RIBA, Pawley summarized the message that 'Modern Architecture ... has failed to deliver the goods over the last half century.'[49] When Richard Seifert appeared in a programme on Thames Television called 'Living Architects', Pawley recognized that he had stolen the language of Modernism, literally and metaphorically, and nothing could restore its imagined moral integrity. 'People on chat shows now dare to openly criticize the pack-ice pedestrian plazas of Cumbernauld', he continued, 'high rise living is held to be conducive to madness, and today the phrase "modern architecture has a lot to answer for" is uttered menacingly in public bars throughout the land.'[50]

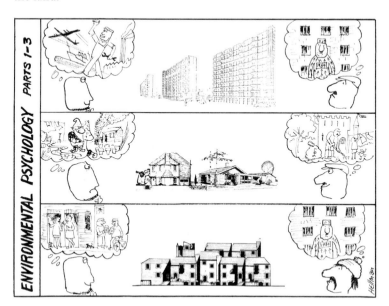

Louis Hellman, cartoon in *Architects' Journal* (20 June 1980).

chapter five

Happiness: The Reintegration of Architecture

The apocalypse of modern architecture at the end of the 1960s was more unexpected, more profound and more deeply destructive of existing ideas than anyone could have predicted. As Udo Kultermann summarized the situation in 1980,

> There was, throughout the world, a loss of confidence in what had been regarded as established architectural values; these were challenged by the social failure of prestigious housing projects, by the energy crisis, by the fact that voices proclaiming that at least some architectural emperors were dressed in new clothes were becoming increasingly audible.[1]

These trends were already in motion, but economic recession following the Yom Kippur War of 1973 between Israel and Egypt, and the subsequent steep rise in world oil prices, triggered a recession and the worst inflation rates ever known in Britain. If the conditions for producing buildings were becoming difficult during the 1960s, they suddenly became infinitely worse. Not only prices, but also strikes in many industries created uncertainty about the future. Building conservation, still a minority concern in the 1960s, made economic sense in the 1970s, since a new construction project would almost inevitably produce a meaner result than any existing building. To this bottom line could be added the attractions of appeal to an increasingly conservation-minded press, planning establishment and public, and new arguments in favour of tourism, energy saving and the avoidance of waste.

The political implications of happiness are being discussed in Britain at the time of writing and have entered the discourse of architecture.[2] It has even been calculated that in 1976 people in Britain were happier than at any time subsequently, showing how, at this time, despite a lack of the material benefits that came later, something unusual was going on.[3] The Modern Movement was meant to make people happy, but it offered a limited set of ways of doing so, and underestimated the complexity of

Fred Lloyd Roche,
Stuart Mosscrop
and Christopher
Woodward, Shopping
centre, Milton Keynes,
1975–9. Perspective
by Helmut Jacoby.

human responses to such compulsion. This chapter links the 1960s to the 1970s by tracing aspects of architecture that recognized a new attitude towards people and their needs, parallel to the turbulent social changes of the period that mainstream Modernism largely ignored. Arguably, it was the non-Modernist architects, equally utopian in their way, who studied the problem of happiness in the Modernist period. With his village development at Portmeirion in Wales, begun in 1925, Clough Williams-Ellis, acting as both entrepreneur and architect, intended to show how a beautiful piece of coastline could be developed without doing damage to its amenities. In its cross between stagy classicism and vernacular, brightly coloured with limewashes, Portmeirion resembled the type of model village often built for international exhibitions, and was supplied with good food and good company. Williams-Ellis, a socialist who knew modern architects as friends but never got far with the style, believed that happiness was a basic human right, and that it was the primary job of architecture to help people towards it. Appropriately, it was in the 1970s, at the end of his long life, that Portmeirion was reappraised and seen as an exemplar for picturesque planning and for the freedom to use architectural styles.

The preaching tone of New Brutalism, with its self-punishing enjoyment of hardship and the jealous watchfulness of the 'elect', seems to bear out the analysis of it as a new architectural Calvinism. The seaside was recognized in British culture as an exception to the prevailing Puritanism, both in codes of behaviour and in architectural freedom, and it is not surprising that the avant-garde Archigram group, apparently the diametrical opposite to Williams-Ellis, made frequent reference to the seaside as a corrective to urban gloom and the Protestant work ethic. There seems to have been a growing awareness that part of the business of modern culture was to shine light into the dark recesses of the British soul. In 1964 *The Listener* commented that a renewed public interest in planning was of a piece with 'the passing of Puritanism and of what has come to be called, with pride or horror, the new morality'. Perhaps, it speculated, a culture more at ease with its physical self would be reflected in an improved public realm, made for enjoyment.[4] The Festival of Britain made its attempt to establish a new architecture of pleasure, and was not unsuccessful, but this was seen as threatening to Modernism's masculinity. Charles and Ray Eames were among those who showed how Modernism and pleasure were not incompatible aims, and in 1966 Peter Smithson gave the view that they made it 'respectable to like pretty things. This seems extraordinary, but in our old world, pretty things are usually associated with social irresponsibility.'[5] The beginning of the 1960s saw the beginning of many forms of liberation, as a new irreverence, wit and permissiveness began to permeate British culture. The rising Pop Art movement, including Pauline Boty of the Anti-Uglies, was anti-establishment but also non-political. A leader in *The Listener* in 1966 commented on a script by the 'design methods' expert Bruce Archer that '"pop art" fashions and designs are ousting our old "functional" principles'. Old-fashioned Germany, still wedded to Bauhaus

Louis Hellman, cartoon in *Architects' Journal* (25 September 1968).

principles, by contrast, 'regards our new fashions in taste as "an aberration which will soon cease"'.[6] The new cycle of taste lasted a long time and left a permanent mark on the ethos of Modernism.

Part of the unavoidable problem was the frequently miserable quality of life in utopian Modernist buildings and environments. James Stirling's residential building for Queen's College, Oxford (1966–71), rapidly became notorious for the discomfort of its rooms. New towns were designed to deal with a quite different set of problems from those of going out for the evening, as a visitor to Cumbernauld reported in 1968:

> It's not Cumbernauld's fault that it happens to be in Scotland, but at 10 p.m. the Golden Eagle, the Kestrel and the Falcon all close, and this is it, as far as Cumbernauld Town Centre is concerned. On the upper terrace the Abatone fish bar keeps going until eleven. After that the centre is deserted, except for a few drunken stragglers weaving their way down the centre of the spine motorway. (After all, it's the best lit route out of the centre, and there's scarcely a car to be seen, except for the odd learner driver practising u-turns round the *piloti*) . . . It's not good enough and it needn't have happened that way.[7]

In October 1964 the MP Tom Driberg, who knew how to find his pleasures in town, declared in the House of Commons:

> Human beings are made and are entitled to enjoy a vast range of activities which may include creative work but which may more often be activities that might be dismissed as mere pleasure or fun. Do not let us dismiss fun as 'mere'.[8]

Petula Clark's rendition of Tony Hatch's 'Downtown', written in response to a first visit to Broadway, Manhattan, celebrated euphoric freedom in the crowd among the city lights and sold three million copies in Britain in 1964, yet in the 1960s few people seemed able to see the point of towns, and the individuality of many of them was declining in the face of low-quality mass leisure, comprehensive redevelopment and ring roads. Independent thinkers began to follow Jane Jacobs in believing that, as Theo Crosby wrote in 1967, 'the city of the newly affluent must be full of old world values'.[9]

Cedric Price, Fun Palace, Lea River site, London, 1961–5.

Fun Palace, interior perspective.

The later pages of the same AA *Journal* that reported Driberg's comments contained images and description of the greatest of the legendary images of happiness through architecture from the decade, Cedric Price's project for a 'Fun Palace'. This was created in 1961 in collaboration with the

166

RIVER SITE

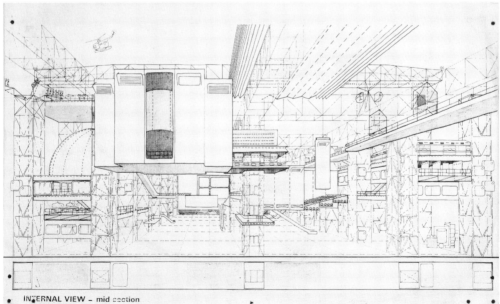

INTERNAL VIEW - mid section

theatre director Joan Littlewood for a site in Stratford, the neglected East End centre where since 1953 she had made the almost derelict variety house, the Theatre Royal, a destination for audiences across the city. The Fun Palace was mentioned by name in Driberg's Commons speech. Price, an architect's son from Stoke-on-Trent who studied at Cambridge and the Architectural Association, became famous for building virtually nothing, and made this fastidious refusal to compromise part of his persona. His approach to architecture was described as 'a philosophy of enabling' (a word that spread in the 1980s to the Community Architecture movement). Royston Landau has commented on Price's affinities to Jeremy Bentham's philosophy of Utilitarianism, at whose core was an unsentimental and entirely secular idea of happiness.[10] For Price, this was to be found in 'the idea of a freedom to be useful'. Joan Littlewood shared his vision of individual capacity and uniqueness. The Fun Palace, in John Ezard's words, was 'a childhood dream of a people's palace, a university of the streets, re-inventing Vauxhall Gardens, the 18th-century Thames-side entertainment promenade, with music, lectures, plays, restaurants, under an all-weather dome'.[11]

Architecturally, the Fun Palace, which would have covered 20 acres on the banks of the River Lea, was defined architecturally in straight lines and right angles,

> a great open framework of steel lattice girders and towers, surmounted by a travelling gantry crane. It is highly flexible in use, can be open to the sky or closed with blinds. Within it, can be slung complete auditoria, studios, workshops or restaurants, with access by mobile radial escalators and tower lifts. Halls and galleries, snack bars and entertainment areas, linked by walkways, can be built and exchanged at will. People of all ages and interests will find space to enjoy their leisure, to relax or be active, at day or night.[12]

Price's next projects, such as the Potteries Thinkbelt and the Pop-Up Parliament, while thought out in complete technical detail, usually involved drastic changes to existing buildings and habits of life that rendered them even more politically improbable. The former, a proposal for an alternative university in his home district of Stoke, combined a highly astute critique of the physical form that higher education was taking in the new universities with a requirement to be site-specific and machinery-intensive that was scarcely necessary to fulfil the purpose. In fact, the Open University, conceived in 1962 and opened in 1969, one of the prime achievements of the Wilson administration, served a much wider constituency without needing any special architecture at all.[13]

Pleasure-zone board game, illustration to 'Montagu Country', Cedric Price's contribution to the Non-Plan special issue of *New Society*, 26 March 1969.

The possibility that planning, as conventionally exercised, might be the problem rather than the solution lay behind 'Non-Plan: An Experiment in Freedom', a proposal made by Price and three other writers, Reyner Banham, the planning academic Peter Hall and the editor of *New Society*, Paul Barker, in 1969. Barker was inspired by a study of American suburbia in its most despised form, *The Levittowners* by Herbert Gans (1967), which showed that life was actually pleasant and fulfilling for the inhabitants. The British were afraid of freedom, he thought. 'Why not, we wondered', recalls Barker, 'suggest an experiment in getting along without planning and seeing what emerged.'[14] Non-Plan was conceived in 1967, and published in *New Society* in March 1969, and its influence will be discussed below.

Price continued to be an inspiration to younger architects (and non-architects) up to his death in 2003. The Fun Palace design happened in the same year as the first issue of *Archigram*, originally a two-sheet magazine by a range of recently qualified students that grew in fame and physical size. Over the course of the first three issues (up to 1963), the group, coming from the AA School and the Regent Street Polytechnic, consolidated as Warren Chalk, Peter Cook, Dennis Crompton, David Greene, Ron Herron and Michael Webb. These core members were working during 1963 in an

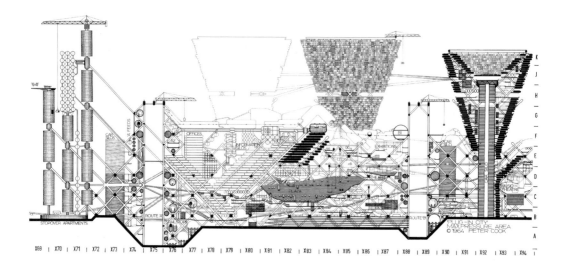

Peter Cook, Plug-In
City: Maximum
Pressure Area,
section, 1964.

office established by Theo Crosby, under the contractors Taylor Woodrow, for the purpose of redesigning Euston Station, until their project was refused planning permission and a more conventional one substituted. Each member brought different talents and products to the magazine and the projects, which were also published in mainstream journals. With Archigram, the Pop movement arrived in architecture, carrying baggage of technological utopianism from Buckminster Fuller, but, unlike him or Price, not caring much whether it would actually work in real life. Peter Cook's 'Plug-In City' offered all the excitement that was missing from Cumbernauld. The concepts of movement defined this architecture, whether the movement of its own separate parts, of the restless fun-seekers within, or, in the case of Ron Herron's Walking City, by the whole structure. Unlike New Brutalism, with its deep crust of specifically architectural knowledge, this encounter between new technology and new social patterns carried no burden of historical memories, other than Lemuel Gulliver's flying kingdom of Laputa.

Archigram and Price both had fleeting contacts with members of the European Situationist International, by comparison with which they appear grounded and pragmatic. What they shared was a belief in the power of the imagination to transform the individual and the environment simultaneously.

Like Price, the members of Archigram were still being fêted by students forty years later as people who had expanded the territory of architectural thinking. Ron Herron built the greatest number of projects, which, while excellent in many respects, did not carry a strong

GLC Architects
(Sir Hubert Bennett),
Special Works Division
(Group Leader Norman
Engleback) with
Warren Chalk, Ron
Herron, Dennis
Crompton and John
Attenborough,
Queen Elizabeth Hall,
South Bank, London,
1960–67.

Archigram stamp. The new LCC (GLC by the time of opening) arts complex on the South Bank, consisting of two concert halls and an art gallery, was a project of long gestation by a team including Chalk, Herron and Crompton under the Group Leader Norman Engleback. While the buildings had atmosphere and presence, they were the antithesis of the Royal Festival Hall's suavity, locked in embrace by the 'Haupstadt'-style walkways, many of which seemed to go nowhere pleasant or useful.[15] The complex was deliberately unresolved in compositional terms, a demonstration of the Brutalist / Team 10 concept of 'crumble' and a fragment of a new city that was never fully 'plugged in'. When the Hayward Gallery finally opened in July 1968, the *Architects' Journal* aptly captioned it 'Love-Hate Complex'.[16]

Instead of building, Archigram members were largely absorbed by teaching and developing their science-fiction comic world with images of immeasurable structures, individual living pods and even a log in the country, lying innocently on the ground, providing all the wiring necessary for long-distance communication. For a time, there was an office and a project for the Monaco Entertainments Centre that might even have been built. As Simon Sadler concludes in his recent study of Archigram, the boring Modernism of the late 1950s and '60s against which the group rebelled was in fact on the point of self-destruction.[17] Their vision of the future stood on a cusp between socialism and consumerism, and, after the failure of revolutions across the world in 1968, it had little choice but to move towards Pop hedonism. Reviewing a collection of pieces from the magazine, published in 1972, in tandem with *Learning from Las Vegas* by Robert Venturi, Denise Scott Brown and Steven Izenour, Martin Pawley showed irritation with Archigram's refusal to confront the 'real' world.[18] Already, however, Peter Cook was contradicting this assumption by recognizing some of the same banal realities of popular culture that Venturi and his colleagues were famous for glorifying, such as John Portman's Regency Hyatt hotels, brash and vulgar developers' architecture with atria and wall-climber lifts that, after some cultural cleansing, were later among the typical features of British High tech.

In 'Notes on "Camp"' (published as an article in 1964 and collected in book form in 1966), the American writer Susan Sontag anatomized the subculture taste that later broke out all over 'Swinging London' at the time of *Sergeant Pepper's Lonely Hearts Club Band* (1967) and Michelangelo Antonioni's film *Blow Up* (1968). 'Camp is a solvent of morality', she wrote, 'It neutralises moral indignation, sponsors playfulness'.[19] Archigram bore some traces of being an 'angry' movement, but its style was really about camp, a quality seldom entirely absent from

Modernism, but deeply subversive of its aspiration to high culture status. In 1971, in a multi-media presentation 'Arcadia', involving music by Delius, Satie, Milhaud, Marlene Dietrich and Emerson, Lake and Palmer, Cook mixed images from English rural pastoralism, Art Nouveau, Disneyland and the Modern Movement. Such promiscuous combinations were typical of the Pop pin-up boards. Cook enjoyed shocking Modernist orthodoxy by enthusing over super-cinemas of the 1930s (of the type that A. J. Price, the father of Cedric Price, designed for Harry Weedon) and the Hoover Factory. Of the latter, Cook said: '[it] not only borrows from the best sources (like Poelzig) but colours it green and orange and allsorts'.[20] 'I'm glad we can begin to relax', Cook said, 'the mood of innovation is interwoven with mystery and the organic: camp reacts to the nature of things.'[21]

Cook was alert to the poetry of everyday life in England, and proposed 'a quietly technologised folk-suburbia'. As he admitted, 'Most of us are, or have been, suburban at some time. It's a nostalgia, a love–hate, a temptation–irritation.'[22] Cook's mood, the same one that the Beatles captured in 'Penny Lane' (1966), reflected the more literal pastoralism into which the London 'scene' had morphed after 1968, often involving a flight to the country, for which a new clothing company, Laura Ashley (founded in rural Wales in 1963), provided the perfect wardrobe in the manner of a costume drama starring Julie Christie. Anticipating British householders' favourite 1980s home improvement, Cook wrote: 'Conservatories . . . represent technologies grappling with the vagaries of the English climate; they were extensions of the basic building structure that provided a totally different environment.'[23]

The 1960s and '70s saw the development of many forms of architectural theory, some of it coming from the same people who were first active in the 1950s in trying to go beyond the simplistic interpretations of Modernism. British journals and architectural schools were still resistant to this kind of critical and cultural theory, and the major British participants, Alan Colquhoun, Kenneth Frampton, Colin Rowe and Anthony Vidler, migrated to teaching jobs in the USA, where Frampton and Vidler were on the editorial board of the influential magazine *Oppositions*, begun in 1975. In Britain, by contrast, theory was often represented by those born and / or educated elsewhere, including Leon Krier, Demetri Porphyrios, Charles Jencks and the proprietor of *Architectural Design* after 1975, Andreas Papadakis, who changed the look and attitude of the magazine by promoting Postmodernism and the revival of classicism. Aldo Rossi's *The Idea of the City*, published in Italy in 1966, but in English only in 1982, was significant in highlighting the historic idea of typology in relation to the history of cities, a theme

Peter Cook, Hedgerow Village, illustrated in 'Towards a Quietly Technologised folk-suburbia', 1972. The original caption reads: 'COEXISTENCE? ROMANTICISM? First thoughts on Q.T.F.S. (Peter Cook, 1971) (*left to right*): (a) Smart, air-conditioned, sophisticated with nice, comfy caravan satellite. (b) "Once you have cross-walls you can do it yourself". The architectural student's dream – painted hardboard etc. (c) As found, log cabin syndrome. (d) Wooden posts as minimum-mega-structure, anything can be slung within. (e) Paper sleeping-bag as domesticity. (f) Travelling-man syndrome'.

explored in Colin Rowe's and Fred Koetter's *Collage City*, written in 1973 and published in article form in 1975. These ideas were inherent in Stirling's change of architectural direction around the same time, leading first to his design for Derby Civic Centre (1970), in which his assistant Leon Krier played a significant role, and, through a series of unexecuted projects in Germany, to his competition victory in Stuttgart for the Neue Staatsgalerie in 1977.

From 1971, the Architectural Association School under the chairmanship of the Canadian Alvin Boyarsky cultivated an international mix of ideas and personalities. In the words of Robin Middleton, Boyarsky 'transformed the AA into the setting for the most vibrant architectural culture to be found anywhere in the world'.[24] Students of the period such as Rem Koolhaas, Zaha Hadid, Daniel Libeskind and Bernard Tschumi became international stars both of theory and design in the late 1980s and early 1990s. Tschumi has commented that 'an economy that was extremely difficult for those who wanted to build was extremely good for research and education'.[25]

While the AA became progressively disengaged from the world of utility, objective methods of architectural research remained current at the Cambridge School of Architecture and at University College, London, under Leslie Martin and Richard Llewelyn-Davies respectively. While their findings were universalized and abstracted through mathematics, they also contributed to the transformation of Modernism, although they needed the input of the human sciences to quantify the cultural aspects of architecture. Geoffrey Broadbent's *Design in Architecture* (1973) tried to fill this gap. Computers were expected to help, less, perhaps, by the complexity of the calculations they could perform than by the alternative logical pathways that they suggested. Broadbent went on to explore the semiotics of architecture, a new application of an academic discipline from the nineteenth century. Charles Jencks, an American history student at the Bartlett, also found in the theory of language one of the ways of reassembling the fragments of Modernism into a morality-free chart of flowing possibilities. The June 1967 issue of *Arena* (the renamed AA *Journal*) on 'Meaning in Architecture', edited by Jencks and George Baird, was the starting point for a long-running exploration of these issues in Britain, later identified by Jencks as the core of a postmodern theory of architecture.[26] In the book derived from his doctoral thesis, Jencks argued for 'a live plurality' as the only possible historiography and approach to the present, and redefined quality in architecture in terms of 'density of meaning'.[27] Old Modernism began to look like a line of dominos. Once the first one fell, it knocked down the next until none was left standing. By the time that Peter Cook was dreaming of a suburban shack city built around a new airport in Essex, he had changed their pattern completely.

A broad range of eclectic options began to open up once the repressive lid of Modernist Puritanism had been lifted. *The Language of Post-Modern Architecture*, Jencks's first work on the theme in 1977, celebrated 'multivalent' communication, regardless of other conventional 'architectural' qualities, matching the mood of image-based fashion from the late 1960s. In 1974 the Smithsons chose the title *Without Rhetoric* for a book of essays, but Jencks suggested that, since some form of statement was unavoidable, architects should consider what they were saying through their buildings: 'We must go back to the point where architects took responsibility for their rhetoric.'[28]

Morality and Architecture, another crucial text of 1977, by the Cambridge architectural historian David Watkin, aimed to discredit the belief that Modernism was the correct and only architecture of progress and the automatic expression of the 'spirit of the age'. With Nikolaus Pevsner as his chief target for criticism, Watkin struck at the inconsistencies and lack of philosophical depth in the British reception of Modernism since the 1930s. His own preferences were for a revived classicism, so he did not consider it necessary to look further into the Modernist canon itself, as other writers were beginning to do, in order to recognize its pluralism.

Milton Keynes

For beleaguered English architects, the new town of Milton Keynes, constructed through the worst years of the 1970s, made a bridge between the
post-war welfare state and the new social, economic and artistic world
of late capitalism that was coming into being. While the earlier New
Towns were prescriptive in what was seen as a benevolent way, Milton
Keynes reflected new ideas about the consumer society and the range of
architecture that it should allow. Even today, mention of Milton Keynes,
designated in 1967, following the rejection by Hampshire County
Council of a GLC overspill project at Hook, is a sure way to raise a
laugh.[29] It has become nonetheless one of the most successful and popular new towns, and currently the subject of massive expansion.

The master-plan competition was won by the practice of Llewelyn-
Davies, Weeks, Forestier-Walker and Bor. Their proposal was influenced
by the writings of the American sociologist Melvin Webber, who com-
mended Los Angeles as the model for future cities on account of the
priority given to cars and roads in a low-density settlement, described
as a 'non-place urban realm'. The objectives of the master plan were
listed as:

1. Opportunity and freedom of choice
2. Easy movement and access, good communications

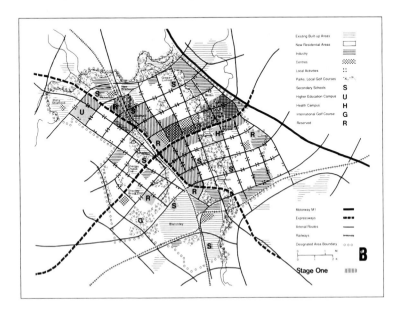

Llewelyn-Davies,
Weeks, Forestier-
Walker and Bor,
master plan for
Milton Keynes, 1969.

3. Balance and variety
4. An attractive city
5. Public awareness and participation
6. Efficient and imaginative use of resources

Up to this point, it had been assumed that working-class people did not own cars, but the Mini and other cheap models changed that. Studies of existing New Towns demonstrated that the post-war ideal of the neighbourhood as a social unit was less important than what Webber defined as the 'community of interest' between individuals who might be geographically scattered across a wide area. Ease of access was therefore more important than actually living side by side. The plan took the form of a grid of roads, loosely laid over the heavy and unproductive clay, at approximately one-kilometre intervals (metrication was a hot issue, applied to buildings, but never to the distances on road signs). At the projected Hook New Town in Hampshire, for which Milton Keynes became a substitute, the idea of putting pedestrians on a raised deck in the central area dominated. Milton Keynes was not only a virtually flat site, but it was also waterlogged, so the roads remained at ground level throughout, with roundabouts for the junctions.

The thinking behind this plan was not solely derived from Webber or exclusive to the problem of planning a New Town. In the partnership, John Weeks had developed since the early 1950s an interest in indeterminacy as a positive attribute of the planning of buildings, allowing for changes in use, rather than locking a plan and structure into a single pattern of use, according to a crude 'form follows function' model. This was behind the practice's design for a large research hospital at Northwick Park, Harrow (1961), where, in a manner similar to early Brutalist principle, the route through the buildings (on foot above or by car below) is the invariable element, and the actual enclosed spaces to either side are expected to grow and change. Flexibility was a popular theme in tune with the 1960s and the general hope and promise of liberation. Weeks wrote in 1971: 'as we know, the shape or appearance of buildings is not very important in the general scheme of things'.[30] At Northwick Park, new medical facilities were added over the course of time, and the original design was able to absorb them without major disruption. To demonstrate a different level of indeterminacy, the elevations had unevenly spaced mullions to prevent the formation of repetitive patterns.

Derek Walker, appointed Chief Architect to Milton Keynes in 1970, described himself as a maverick in public service, and he gathered a

Starting a new life at Milton Keynes, envisaged as a game of snakes and ladders, 1975.

176

team of young designers. Earlier new towns tried to replicate the feel of traditional market-town shopping streets in their pedestrianized cores. At the centre, Milton Keynes was more like a Beaux-Arts scheme in modern dress, employing axial vistas and grand features such as crescents. Two long covered shopping centres, built and initially managed by the Development Corporation, were designed by the Americans Fred Lloyd Roche (an architect and also the General Manager of Milton Keynes) and Stuart Mosscrop, with Christopher Woodward (a veteran of the Smithson office and the Buchanan Plan). The contrast between their stainless-steel glitz and the rough and externally unwelcoming Cumbernauld centre could hardly be greater. Cars were treated in a commonsense manner, with roads and parking provided where they were needed and integrated into the design at ground level, rather than hidden or segregated.

Writing about the stylistic choice made for the covered shopping mall in the centre, Robert Maxwell explained that the open-ended indeterminacy implied by the plan needed 'a low-profile architecture, an architecture that does not claim to provide in itself new laws for the entire city'.[31] To avoid being merely commonplace, a controversial design based on a tight grid in plan and elevation was chosen. The *Architects' Journal* called it 'rigid, boring and inhuman', but by the standards of later shopping architecture it was a model of civic dignity and a sign of Milton Keynes's determination to be different. The shopping building recognized the importance of shopping as the major civic activity by incorporating covered and open spaces for community use and events.

Neo-Vernacular and Critical Regionalism

The housing at Milton Keynes departed from the master plan by retreating to the centre of each square, rather than acting, as originally intended, more like a network of linear cities with shops at the intersections. This is generally considered a weakness, for it reinforced the isolation of each residential area. Housing designs were commissioned from young and work-hungry practices, and Milton Keynes became a catalogue of the varied styles and tendencies of the 1970s, predominantly the 'neo-vernacular' of Martin Richardson, Edward Cullinan and Richard MacCormac, but also encompassing the early High tech of Norman Foster. Neo-Vernacular was one of the great architectural events of the 1970s, although its origins go back to the beginning of the Modern Movement or earlier, with crucial books in Britain by S. O. Addy, C. F. Innocent and Iorwerth C. Peate reflecting the interests and values of the Arts and Crafts period. Bernard Rudofsky's book of 1964, *Architecture*

Peter Aldington,
Turn End houses,
Haddenham,
Buckinghamshire,
1964–8.

Colin A. St John
Wilson, with M. J. Long,
Spring House, Conduit
Head Road,
Cambridge, 1965–7.

Without Architects, made 'non-pedigreed' architecture fashionable again and the term 'vernacular' was extended from traditional rural buildings to include anonymous folk-art of any period, including the industrial. F.W.B. Charles, a pre-war assistant of Walter Gropius, became an expert in the timber-framed buildings of the West Midlands and was instrumental in the foundation of England's first open-air museum of building at Bromsgrove. Increasingly, sophisticated investigation into genuine vernaculars overlapped with the semiological investigation into architectural language.

The relationship between Modernism and the vernacular is a complex subject, with a long history. It was often the result of an architect settling in a particular part of Britain and admiring traditional rural buildings. In the 1950s Tayler and Green (described as 'post-modern' by Nikolaus Pevsner as early as 1962) were pioneers in adapting local style without making it too much of a reproduction of the past. In the 1960s Peter Aldington's tightly clustered group of three houses at Haddenham, Buckinghamshire (1964–8), was a deliberate response to a local tradition of rammed earth walls along the edges of roads and between gardens.[32] The planning idea behind this project had much in common with Team 10's exploration of village form, and similarities to courtyard housing projects by Jørn Utzon in Denmark.

The Cornford House in Cambridge of 1965 by Colin St John Wilson with M. J. Long was a step towards a complex reinterpretation of traditional domestic form, entirely different in spirit from Wilson's own house in Cambridge of 1962, which reflected how Alvar Aalto derived formal and sensual nourishment from pre-industrial building. Wilson was also struck by the theories of the Norwegian Christian Norberg-Schultz, which looked back to vernacular for its essential authenticity. At the University of Surrey, Maguire's pitched-roofed and clustered Stag Hill Court housing (1969–70) was an alternative to the impersonal 'hall of residence', contrasting strongly with the late Bauhaus style of the teaching buildings on the same site by BDP of 1966–9. Maguire claimed that it influenced the design of student housing across the world. The Norwich-based practice of Fielden and Mawson introduced a highly influential adaptation of vernacular with steep roofs at Friar's Quay, Norwich, in 1974, which in retrospect looks like the unwitting source of a flood of inferior imitations.

The project that above all others symbolized the vernacular turn was Byker, the large housing development in Newcastle upon Tyne by Ralph Erskine, instigated by a Conservative council in 1969 in reaction against the previous regime of tower blocks. A refreshing wind blowing from Sweden, where Erskine, English by birth and training, had worked after he was contentedly cut off by the outbreak of war while on holiday in 1939, Byker contained all the antidotes needed to take away the bitterness of system-building failure. Erskine's English work included Clare Hall, Cambridge, a post-graduate college taking the form of a picturesque cluster of residential buildings around communal facilities, fully integrated with its own landscaped courtyards and pathways, using colour and decoration. If this scheme resembled Cullen's *Townscape* drawings, it was no coincidence, since Erskine and Cullen studied together and the book was one of his favourites.[33]

Ralph Erskine Associates, Byker Wall, Newcastle upon Tyne, 1973–80.

Ralph Erskine
Associates, Clare
Hall, Cambridge,
1968–9.

Three further Erskine projects followed Clare Hall in 1969: a housing estate, Studlands Park, for the construction company Bovis near Newmarket, and two in the north, of which Byker overshadowed the uncompleted low-rise housing at Killingworth, an unofficial new town outside Newcastle. In all of these, Team 10 ideas were interpreted in a regional manner closer to Giancarlo de Carlo's work in Italy than to other members of the group. There was no specific 'vernacular' to which Byker referred, but by setting up an office with an English member of the office, Vernon Gracie, on the site of an old undertaker's shop, Erskine engaged with his end users in a way that went well beyond any previous attempts. The wall, backing onto the road and metro rail line, was a given of the brief, but Erskine was able to break down its monotony with surface patterning and colour-stained timber balconies.

Meanwhile, during the period 1973–6, Erskine built the Eaglestone housing area at Milton Keynes, but cost increases during a period of unprecedented inflation compromised the intended quality of the

project, which was only half-finished. More striking as a personal testimony to the transformation of housing architecture between the 1960s and 1970s was the housing at Great Linford (1973 and 1976) by Martin Richardson. After working under Colin Lucas at the LCC, Richardson became, almost by accident, an expert in the Larsen-Nielsen prefabricated system, and built 3,500 dwellings at Hunslet, near Leeds (1964–70), which were later demolished. He already knew that was the wrong direction. By contrast, the Great Linford scheme, in amongst the prettiest of the existing villages on the new town site, was the result of an attempt 'to make a place that is simply quiet and agreeable to live in'.[34]

Pitched roofs were the most potent symbol of the dividing line on the path between Modernism and Vernacular. Mono-pitch roofs, or split dual pitch (letting light in at the apex), were considered modern, but in the 1970s the sheltering familiar roof returned for a combination of symbolic, practical and economic reasons. At Milton Keynes, as well as in housing by Cullinan and MacCormac Jamieson, pitched roofs could be found in housing at Great Linford by Stephen Gardiner (who was also well known as an architectural critic). At Hillingdon Civic Centre (1973–8), Andrew Derbyshire of Robert Matthew, Johnson-Marshall adopted a vernacular style of brick

Martin Richardson, housing, Great Linford 5, Milton Keynes, Buckinghamshire, 1973–7.

Robert Matthew, Johnson-Marshall (Andrew Darbyshire), Hillingdon Civic Centre, Middlesex, 1973–8.

and tile, with an emphasis on roof forms. RMJM had never done anything like this before. Robert Maxwell called it 'a hybrid with all the disturbing aspects of a multi-headed monster'.[35] Equally shocking to the old guard was Ealing Broadway Centre (1979–85), a shopping mall with bold brick towers, more Carcassonne than Corbusier, by the multi-disciplinary practice BDP, hitherto straight Modernists, but on this occasion letting rip with the private dreams of Francis Roberts, a romantic non-believer in Modernism, in response to public demand for an alternative to the standard shopping mall.

Maurice Naunton and George Garrard, Noak Bridge, Basildon, Essex, 1975 onwards.

Such high-profile projects gave encouragement to designers of buildings at all levels. After 1949, the average speculative suburban house showed marked differences from its pre-war neo-Tudor and Georgian equivalents, closer in character if not quality to Tayler and Green's designs. Arthur Edwards has called it 'the Anglo-Scandinavian style' and characterized its use of contrasted textures, such as weatherboarding, tile hanging and pantiles, as 'a dull pattern of architecture, for penny-pinching is almost inevitably dull in its results'.[36]

In 1973 Melville Dunbar and other architects employed by Essex County Council published their *Design Guide for Residential Areas*. It was mainly aimed at creating denser, more urban effects in housing, responding to long-standing criticism of the 'prairie planning' of the new towns, resulting from the old requirement for 70-foot road widths, which was conveniently abolished the same year. More controversially, the *Design Guide* hoped to re-establish local identity, suggesting that 'developments shall generally employ external materials which are sympathetic in colour and texture to the vernacular range of Essex materials' and hoping that 'within the constraints of the Essex discipline the good architect should be able to produce elegant 20th century architecture'. This invitation to vernacular design killed off the post-war 'Anglo-Scandinavian' style all over the country, and developers began to apply a supposed 'regional character' of a very loose description thereafter, finding approval from most local authorities. The results were mostly dreadful, but in Essex itself some exceptions can be found. On the edge of Basildon at

Snape Maltings, Suffolk, original buildings c. 1860, converted to concert hall by Arup Associates, 1967, with later extensions by Penoyre & Prasad, 1999.

Noak Bridge, two architects from the Basildon New Town Development Corporation, Maurice Naunton and George Garrard, decided for a change to design a place they might themselves want to live in. To achieve this, they had to get waivers of regulations for almost every design decision, so regulation-bound had housing become by 1975, although the *Design Guide* gave them backing. Noak Bridge stands as a testimony that 'local character', even on a tight budget, can operate with a hidden ingenuity of planning to keep parked cars off the streets and make a 'walk-able neighbourhood'. In this, it anticipated the targets set by the Prince of Wales for the development of Poundbury at the end of the 1980s.

Conservation drew attention to the aesthetic qualities of brick. One pioneering scheme was the conversion of the principal building at Snape Maltings in Suffolk as a concert hall for the Aldeburgh Festival in 1967, by Derek Sugden of Arup Associates, the engineer who in the 1950s had commissioned a brick house from the Smithsons. Taking the shell of the malting shed 'as found' and cleaning the brick to reveal a rich patina of age, Sugden then introduced detailing that satisfactorily bridged the gap between reproduction and Modernism, and set a new style for building conversion, in line with the way that architects and design-conscious house owners were beginning to strip plaster off brick and sand and stain their pine floorboards.

Neo-vernacular was seen as a danger to good architecture, how-ever: 'dull, hack, with a few tricks attached, quasi-archaeological, highly wrought or semi-Disneyland'.[37] The thinking man's neo-ver-nacular had a different name, 'Critical Regionalism', which was origi-nally derived from the philosopher Paul Ricoeur (1961), and applied to architecture in 1978 by the European theorists Alexander Tzonis and Liane Lefaivre, in relation to a group of young German architects.[38] In 1981 an essay by Tzonis and Lefaivre with Anthony Alofsin estab-lished some lines of discussion, followed in 1983 by Kenneth Frampton's first treatment of the same theme.[39] The 'critical' compo-nent, a reference to Kant and the 'Critical Theory' of the Frankfurt School, was intended to distinguish the movement from purely nostal-gic forms of regionalism, especially those associated with Nazism and Fascism earlier in the century. The phrase, coming from such authorita-tive positions, helped to make these concerns safe for disenchanted Modernists.

Neo-Modernism, Self-Build and Ecology

A third tendency in the housing at Milton Keynes was represented in housing at Netherfield (1972–7) by the 'Grunt Group', the slang term for drafted US infantrymen in the Vietnam War, pinned on them by Peter Cook at the AA.[40] The core of the group comprised Christopher Cross, Jeremy Dixon, Michael Gold and Edward Jones, and the repet-itive plain style of their work was evident as students and in an unbuilt competition scheme for housing at Portsdown Hill, Hampshire. In 1965 they joined the firm of Armstrong MacManus, whose Regent's Park Estate (1957–9) shows the restrained picturesque manner of Armstrong MacManus before the Grunt Group joined them. The Clipstone Street housing for Westminster (1966–71) and two long ter-races of housing in Gospel Oak, Waxham and Ludham (1969–72) represent regression to an earlier form of Modernism, of a piece, per-haps, with the historical and nostalgic mood of the time, and related to Aldo Rossi's well-known Gallaratese housing scheme in Milan of 1967–73. This work was appraised unflatteringly by the German-Swiss émigré Walter Segal in 1972, who accused them of a glib return to the anti-sensual moralism of the early Modern Movement: 'The voice of purism in the 1970s sounds hollow and puritans merely make us uncomfortable.'[41]

Segal himself was for many years a marginal if respected presence in British architecture, but, by a series of unplanned moves, he enjoyed a new fame during the last decade before his death in 1984. Simple houses

were the focus of his attention, but he avoided involvement in the great public housing boom of the 1950s and '60s. In 1962 he needed a temporary house while constructing a new one to accommodate the step-family resulting from his second marriage, and out of economic necessity built it himself, using the simplest means of timber frame and panels. Ten years on, this became the prototype for two housing developments in Lewisham, the brainchild of the journalist-turned-local councillor Nicholas Taylor, scourge of Modernist housing in the *Architectural Review* in the 1960s and author of *The Village in the City* in 1970. The sites were owned by Lewisham Borough Council, but were so steep that it was uneconomical to develop them using conventional building techniques. Segal's method made it possible for the future occupiers to save money by investing their own time in making the buildings. Several were unemployed, and thus learned new skills. All of those involved got to know their future neighbours before moving in, thus creating the kind of bonded community that modern architecture was accused of preventing. Segal was often present on site, and although some freedom was allowed in interpreting his designs, he retained control over the still essentially Modernist character of the buildings.

Segal's initiative was applauded and publicized by members of the gentle anarchist tendency in British architecture, whose ideas of self-help and self-sufficiency gained a wide following in the 1970s as national governments struggled to control their economies in an unstable world. Walter Segal reviewed E. F. Schumacher's classic text *Small is Beautiful* in 1973, commenting:

F. G. McManus
and Partners,
Waxham and Ludham,
Mansfield Road,
Gospel Oak, London,
1969–72.

Walter Segal assist-
ing self-builders at
Lewisham, c. 1977.

it is gratifying to read an author who insists on human freedom, however nebulous and limited; for we are getting tired of being told that there exists no real freedom in the world, an assertion which, undoubtedly, is based on ulterior motives.[42]

Schumacher's book was a timely contribution to the growing litera-ture of alternative economics and social models, which consolidated the revolutionary yearnings of the 1960s into achievable aims. Architects began to accept their own role in improving the quality of life through using resources more carefully, although the origins of ecological or green architecture go back further, to the pioneering heat exchanger fitted in Edward Curtis's Solar House at Rickmansworth in 1956, and the use of passive solar energy using a 'Trombe wall' at Wallasey School in 1961 by the architect Emslie Morgan.[43] The availability of cheap oil and electricity in the 1960s marginalized these issues for a while. The threat of global warming from carbon emission, under investigation from 1958, was still almost unknown, but the oil crisis and the miners' strike of 1973–4 brought these issues to the fore again.[44] In his presidential address to the RIBA in 1972, Alex Gordon discussed 'Long Life, Low Energy, Loose Fit' (abbreviated as LL/LE/LF), which was not only a way of saving energy but also an alternative to the idea that 'form follows function' in terms of fitting a building to a single use, and expecting its demolition if that use changed in the future.[45] This idea could be sold to business clients as a sound investment. Rehabilitation of historic build-ings as open-plan spaces followed as one of the consequences.

For the most part, however, energy saving was the territory of the counter-culture inherited from the 1960s, supported by occasional visionary businessmen such as Gerard Morgan-Grenville, the founder of

Cretan windmill,
erected at the Centre
for Alternative
Technology,
Machynlleth, Wales,
c. 1976.

Alex Pike, Autarkic
House, Cambridge,
1974.

Edward V. Curtis, Solar House at 14 Beacon Way, Rickmansworth, Hertfordshire, 1956.

the Centre for Alternative Technology in an abandoned quarry at Machynlleth in North Wales in 1974, which had a strong architectural basis, adopting Walter Segal's self-build methods and trying different means of power generation. Buckminster Fuller re-emerged as an elderly but irrepressible witness to the future, appearing at Westminster Central Hall in 1970, where he spoke for two-and-a-quarter hours non-stop, and again, supported by Cedric Price, at a 'Think-in' organized for the World Design Science Decade in 1977. Fuller's geodesic domes became a symbol of 'alternative' living, especially in the USA. Stewart Brand's *Whole Earth Catalogue* (1968–72), published by Penguin in Britain, helped to spread the word. At Cambridge University, Alex Pike began to develop the 'Autarkic' house at the Martin Centre, and built a test model in 1974.[46] Experiments in solar water heating were made at Central London (formerly Regent Street) Polytechnic by Steven Szokolay, and applied in Milton Keynes, where the first of two batches of demonstration low-energy houses was built in 1981 in Bradwell Common, including two 'Autarkic' houses, by Donald Forrest.

The counterculture also encompassed the urban squatting movement that gained pace in London, combining a criticism of local authorities for allowing houses in their ownership to remain empty and unused, with a desire, usually on the part of young educated middle-class people, to make common cause with local working-class populations by stimulating

Farrell/Grimshaw Partnership, Service Tower, International Students' Club, Paddington, London, 1967. This innovative pod structure by Nicholas Grimshaw (right, standing next to Buckminster Fuller) rivals Reliance Controls as the first High-Tech building in Britain.

a sense of community. The story of Tolmers 'Village', an area around Drummond Street, near Euston, demonstrated the potential for social and architectural transformation of the urban development process. Students from the nearby Bartlett School of Architecture at University College, London, began researching a community that had already united in opposition to a covert development plan by Joe Levy, intended to match his Euston Centre on a nearby site. They drew public attention to collusion between Levy and the Labour council (leader Frank Dobson) to remove most of the existing population. As at Covent Garden, campaigners stressed the inherent virtues of having residential populations of mixed income and housing tenure integrated in the inner city, contrary to the assumption that nobody wanted to live there. In a bold move in 1973, the journalists Benny Gray and Christopher Booker (author of a recent book, *The Neophiliacs*, which moralistically discredited the 1960s belief in progress) set up their own property company to challenge the Levy proposals with a real alternative. This suspended the Levy scheme until new legislation in the form of the Community Land Act under the newly elected Wilson government in 1974 allowed Camden to exercise a compulsory purchase of the crucial property, at which point lengthy negotiations began about redevelopment. During this period, some of the original group of students, plus many others, moved into empty houses and created gardens, festivals, organic food shops and similar activities typical of the hippy movement. Eventually, with Camden as developers, a low-rise architectural scheme by Levitt Bernstein Architects replaced the primary architectural set piece, Tolmers Square, with typical brown-brick housing of the period, and a mirror-glass office block facing the main roads, signalling a pyrrhic victory, since many businesses were driven out by higher rents. Nick Wates, one of the student squatters, wrote *The Battle for Tolmers Square* (1976), a valuable analytical account of the different stages, and began a career in enabling local communities to take more control of their own future through 'Action Planning'.

In 1969, responding to public concern about architecture and planning, a government report on Participation was published, known as the Skeffington Report. This set the tone for the rise of local involvement and later 'community architecture', as an attempt to overcome the anonymous and often misdirected efforts of local authorities. Where the Westway, the major completed section of the 'Motorway Box', passed an existing community in decaying housing known as the Swinbrook estate, the tenants persuaded the GLC to rebuild their accommodation between 1971 and 1984. Ninety-three per cent of the tenants participated in a consultation, and as a result the existing street pattern was largely retained. In other respects, the community was disrupted and no comparable level of tenant involvement followed. Working in Basildon, Ahrends, Burton and Koralek employed a social psychologist, Peter Ellis, on the later phases of the Chalvedon housing area, building in brick with timber facings and pitched roofs. After his early success in house design, Peter Aldington formed a partnership in 1970 with John Craig, an artist then working in advertising with no training as an architect but a genius for liaising with the client and abstracting the dynamics of the project as a catalyst for design. A book of 1980, *Architecture for People*, featuring Aldington and Craig, Erskine, Darbourne and Darke and Walter Segal, represents some of the achievements of the 1970s in correcting the mistakes of the past and finding a related set of architectural forms in which to do so.

High Tech

The Californian Case Study Houses, mostly built of steel and glass, were relatively little known in Britain before the early 1960s, except to architects such as John Winter who had worked in the States. Lighter, both physically and intellectually, than the classics by Mies van der Rohe such as the Farnsworth House, they were one strand of inspiration that eventually led to High Tech, the movement that was in formation during the 1960s and broke through during the 1970s as a living and continuing stream of pure Modernism.

Richard Rogers and Norman Foster returned from studying at Yale in 1962, and had such problems with builders using conventional materials and methods in their first joint projects that both chose thereafter to work as far as possible with 'light and dry' materials that clicked together on site. Typical clients came from industry, such as Reliance Controls, whose factory at Swindon was designed by Team 4, the practice including Rogers, Foster, Georgie Wolton and Wendy Cheesman (1965–6). Here, in Bryan Appleyard's words, Foster and Rogers 'were to discover most of the elements that would compose the originality of their mature styles'.[47] Unlike the controlling aesthetic of Hunstanton School, Reliance suggested a more flexible ethos appropriate to the time, including an egalitarian attitude to working practices. Plan and structure had the simplicity of a diagram; technical innovations were made with lightweight steel cladding; and the result was proclaimed to be quick and cheap. The practice divided, and Richard and Su Rogers, working independently with the technical support of John Young, developed a theoretical 'zip-up' house, published in 1968, in the Buckminster Fuller tradition of factory making and rapid site assembly. It proposed the use of Neoprene gaskets to seal the windows,

Team 4, Reliance
Controls, Swindon
(demolished), 1965–6.

not for the first time in architecture, but in a deliberate way that set the tone for future 'technology transfer'. Foster picked up a number of industrial clients, combining a rather blank architectural look with 1960s colour schemes. A single-storey office building at Cosham, Hampshire, for IBM (1970–71) was entirely clad in tinted glass on the outside, virtually disappearing with reflections, with full air conditioning to maintain the mainframe computers in a steady state. Foster's housing at Bean Hill, Milton Keynes (1971–3), differed from the other schemes there in attempting a form of system building, with a timber frame and aluminium cladding. It was cheaply built, and suffered for it, even losing its landscape budget and the potential softening of the gaunt repetitive rows. Still, even with pitched roofs added in the early 1980s, Bean Hill completes Milton Keynes's catalogue of 1970s architectural trends.

The breakthrough building for Foster was the offices for Willis Faber Dumas in Ipswich, completed in 1975, with its sheer but undulating three-storey glass wall, without visible support. For Banham, Foster's building turned the tables on all the spoilers of modern

Frank Dickens, cartoons showing the advantages for employees of relocating to the Willis Faber Dumas Headquarters.

Foster & Partners,
Willis Faber Dumas
Headquarters (now
Willis Limited), Friar
Street, Ipswich,
Suffolk, 1971–5.

architecture – contextualists, energy conservationists, craft-lovers and concrete-haters – since it answered their objections, apparently without deviating from the forward path of Modernism. In designs such as Lloyds at Chatham and the Central Electricity Generating Board at Bristol, both of 1973–8, Arup Associates made an important contribution to the development of office typology, with their grid plans of repeating pre-cast concete elements, but Foster's space-frame roof and deep service floors were more apt for cutting to shape on the irregular Ipswich site and made better photographs. Willis Faber gave a new look to the wide spans and deep column-free floor plates of open-plan office interiors that followed German and American working practices.

At Ipswich, open-plan office typology was merged with the escalators of a department store, the atrium of a John Portman hotel and the visibility of a transport interchange, all images of escape from the clammy grip of what Philip Larkin called 'the toad *work*'. To show the Willis Faber workforce, who were being moved out of London, the benefits of their new building, Foster commissioned cartoons from Frank Dickens, whose suited, moustached and hatted businessman 'Bristow', familiar from the *Evening Standard*, skipped in the street outside the glass sheath,

Foster & Partners,
The Sainsbury Centre
for Visual Arts,
University of East
Anglia, Norwich,
1974–8.

sat down coolly in the air-conditioned spaces and avoided long journeys down corridors.

Foster was selected by Sir Robert Sainsbury to build a museum for the Sainsbury Collection at the University of East Anglia, combined with a faculty of Art History, and a staff club and public restaurant. Foster's building stood well apart from Denys Lasdun's concrete megastructure and its gathering damp stains. Clad in aluminium, it presented a form of aircraft hanger with one large internal space, a solution that some commentators felt was poorly adapted to the functional brief, but which still had undeniable panache and a quality of euphoria long absent from such buildings. Where Lasdun's building, and most new university buildings since the 1960s, had signalled that academic work was a solemn duty, and that even relaxation could not admit the frivolity of the everyday, Foster's project included a pleasant airy restaurant, open to the public and also serving students and staff together. Even the quality of the food was superior to the normally abysmal catering of the mid-1970s, although this may not have been solely the architect's responsibility. It is hard to imagine anyone penetrating the campus of Essex or Warwick in search of a recreational lunchtime gallery visit with friends, but the Sainsbury Centre projected invitation.

Richard Rogers made a spectacular transition from commerce to culture when, in 1968, in partnership with Renzo Piano, he won the competition for a new art museum and cultural centre in Paris on the Plateau Beaubourg. The competition scheme was closer to Price's Fun Palace than the built design, with a less prominent external structure and more intermediate floor levels. The external load-bearing structure of steel tubes was thickened during the design process to create column-free changeable internal spaces, which proved to be unnecessary for the operational needs of the building. The Centre Pompidou found its imagery not in the flashing billboards proposed in the competition scheme, but in brightly painted coloured service pipes and the snaking plastic tube of its escalator. On close analysis, this new hedonistic, almost childish, version of Modernism used function largely as a form of decoration, but it changed the sense of what a cultural building could become.

High Tech never established a theoretical basis or felt the need for one. In this, it was typically British, appealing to a combination of pragmatism and unreasoned emotions that had no logical connection, but worked if not examined too closely. It borrowed or was lent pieces of theory about urbanism, the social uses of space, energy saving and mass production that seemed relevant, although they could equally well be used to support other architectural outcomes. Its self-image as the authentic line of Modern Movement development after Postmodernism depended on a rather narrow reading of Modernism itself, of the type proposed by Reyner Banham at the end of *Theory and Design in the First Machine Age*, in which he identified technology as the sole validating factor. As the diversity of architecture and planning ideas in the 1970s demonstrated, modernity was alive but no longer universally accepted as an unmixed blessing, while Modernism fragmented into a new kind of eclecticism. The benefit, and the justification for this chapter's title, was that spaces opened up in the previously rather tight culture of Modernism through which a better view was obtained of the world beyond, and the architectural means through which it might still be ameliorated.

DOGLANDS

Hellman

THE LONDON DOGLANDS DEVELOPMENT CORPORATION AGM IS IN SESSION

FRIENDS, I AM HAPPY TO REPORT ON YET ANOTHER SUCCESSFUL YEAR FOR THE COUNTRY'S LARGEST UNPLANNED *ENTERPRISE ZOO*...

WE HAVE REASSURED THE INDIGENOUS MONGREL POPULATION OVER ANY DOG-IN-THE-MANGER RESERVATIONS THEY MAY HAVE HAD...

MONGREL RELOCATION PLC

WE HAVE ATTRACTED THOUSANDS OF YOUNG ENTERPRISING PUPPIES* INTO THE AREA BY PROMOTING POST MODERN DOGHOUSE DEVELOPMENTS...

FOR SALE
WOOF WHARF
PRESTIGIOUS DEVELOPMENTS FROM £ 300,000

* PEDIGREED UPWARDLY MOBILE PROFESSIONAL POODLES

...AND OUR GREATEST ACHIEVEMENT...THE SALE OF *CANINE WHARF* ON THE *ISLE* OF *HUMANS* TO OUR TRANSATLANTIC COYOTE COUSINS... A DYNAMIC DEVELOPMENT...A NEW BUSINESS CENTRE WHICH RESPECTS THE CHARACTER OF THE OLD CITY...

chapter six

Conscience: The Architecture of Fruitful Anxiety

From the perspective of the future, the period after 1980 will offer as much scope as any other in this book. It already feels like a defined era in world history, irrevocably changed from what went before. From the perspective of Britain, there have certainly been storms in the teacups of the rarefied world of architecture that have spilled over into the public mind and left their mark. To all appearance, the architectural story is one of near-disaster followed by triumphant recovery for Modernism. There is evidence that the recovery resulted from a hard process of learning and experience. Modern architecture is less unpopular now, and there is no widely accepted alternative to it, but it still has a marginal place in the national consciousness. Britain occupies a far more prominent place in the international architectural scene than in 1980, but this is partly because many of the best British architects have achieved their best work overseas.

In May 1979 Margaret Thatcher became Prime Minister, leading Conservatives who presented themselves as the party of hard-headed efficiency in the form of monetarism, run by experienced business-men. In retrospect, it appears that they were opportunistically making up their policy week by week in response to events, often without great consistency, but their victory, reinforced in the elections of 1984, 1987 and 1992, showed the inability of Labour to present voters with a credible alternative. The 100-year-old problem of failing British manufacturing was solved by removing subsidies from uncompetitive nationalized industries, including coal, steel and car manufacture, and subsidizing the social cost with the revenues from North Sea oil. Films such as *The Last of England* by Derek Jarman (1987) turned protest into aesthetics, evoking fascist violence and homoeroticism as the mood of the time.

Privatization of former state-owned utilities from telephones to railways purported to offer choice to customers, pushing up standards of service. It was in tune with the spirit of the age that the RIBA changed its Code of Professional Conduct in January 1981, in response to the shrink-

Louis Hellman, cartoon in *Architectural Review* (April 1989).

ing of public-sector employment, and the view that the existing codes preventing architects from advertising or engaging in property development and the construction business were no longer valid.

Eric Lyons, whose work with SPAN exemplified the potential of architect and developer collaboration, wrote:

> The tacit acceptance by RIBA/ARCUK that architects and architecture ought properly to be part of public daily life means that there now remains but a small rational step to take. That is to liberate architects from the promotional constraints that are manifestly impractical, inconsistent and against the spirit of our time.[1]

Lyons was the founder chairman of the Association of Consultant Architects in 1973, the successor to the Association of Private Architects. The ethos of the organization was one of professional responsibility and accountability, combined with outreach to potential clients. Although they were now permitted to do so, architects seldom took to paying for advertising space for their practices, but their attitude had to become more proactive if they were to prosper in the changing business climate. They began to find and develop their own opportunities for work, nurturing clients and acting as 'enablers', in place of the old way of waiting for a client to arrive with a brief in hand. Roger Zogolovitch (a founder partner with Piers Gough of CZWG) was one of a small number of architects who became developers, finding himself able to 'control the process of architecture with integrity, enjoyment and imagination at the opposite end of the scale to that former shadow of a professional – the development architect of yesteryear'.[2]

Another way to get work by merit rather than recommendation was through architectural competitions, which were encouraged by Michael Heseltine, who as Minister of Environment from 1979 to 1983 brought a strong interest in architecture to the job, saying in 1980:

> I know that people are often sceptical about architectural competitions because of the risks associated with them – expense, delays, wild designs. But if the competition is properly run, the cost should be insignificant set beside the cost of the building. There need be no unacceptable delay.[3]

It also became possible for architectural practices not only to become limited companies, but also to 'go public' on the stock exchange, in order to raise additional capital for a type of business that had historically always been undercapitalized.

The change in the professional code was timely, since public employment dropped drastically with the government's moratorium on funding new public housing. The Labour government in the 1970s had already begun to see subsidized housing as a default mechanism limited to places where the market could not provide. Even before Thatcher's campaign to centralize government, the Urban Fund was set up as a mechanism to pay for housing and urban regeneration directly from central government rather than through local councils, which were increasingly seen as inefficient, corrupt and mired in the problems of public housing.

The Conservatives went further, and in 1980 offered tenants in public housing the 'right to buy', which they took up enthusiastically, with generous discounts of 33 per cent on the value of the houses. In addition, the tax rebates on mortgage payments made home ownership of all kinds an obvious option for anyone with the means. Token though it was, the choice of the style of your own front door, permitted to freeholders but not to tenants, became a mark of freedom.

Architects in public offices were the victims, and many of the generation who had started their careers in the 1960s never developed independent careers after losing their salaried jobs. The GLC housing department was almost empty by the time that the council was abolished in 1986. Housing specialists with higher profiles, such as Neave Brown and Martin Richardson, found work in the Netherlands in the 1990s, while others who had made a start in housing, such as Benson & Forsyth, diversified into other building types. The one local authority architectural department that managed to evolve under the new conditions and create and commission high-quality work was Hampshire County Council, where rising population supported by the growth of defence industries and other technology required new schools. According to standard practice, these would have been built with the CLASP system, but owing to the Conservative council Leader (1976–93 and 97–9), Freddie Emery-Wallis, and his support for an outstanding County Architect (1973–92), Colin Stansfield Smith, it turned out differently. Each school was individually designed, either by members of staff, such as Nev Churcher, or by practices ranging from the High Tech of Michael Hopkins to the 'Romantic Pragmatism' of Edward Cullinan and Peter Aldington.[4] Stansfield Smith was keen to match architects to the sites and the divergent views of the head teachers involved. Hampshire demonstrated that public-sector architecture could be fully compatible with the individualistic spirit of the times, but caring and socially responsible with it, and Stansfield Smith was awarded the RIBA Gold Medal in 1991, elected President of the RIBA and knighted for the achievement of the department.

The 1980s was known as 'the Me decade', and a new attention was paid
to tenants' preferences in housing, which tended towards the small scale,
vernacular and intimate. As Alison Ravetz reported on research of the time,

> There is a strong dislike of drabness, monotony, a non-homely
> scale and any distinction of size or material, any oddity of
> design, that make an estate look like a 'camp' or 'barracks'.[5]

If council housing was built at all, it now tried to fit in with existing urban
patterns and to look as little like council housing as possible. Jeremy
Dixon's Lanark Road scheme in Maida Vale (1981–3), containing small
starter flats, was built on a Westminster City Council site in partnership
with the developer Michael Taylor as a way of circumventing the housing
moratorium, and exemplifies the new direction, since it was designed for
sale to the tenants. A neat pastiche of early Victorian paired villas, the flats
contrast with the three eighteen-storey LCC towers of 1959–64 that stand
in front of them. Equally striking is the development in Dixon's work itself
since his participation as a member of the 'Grunt Group' in the design of
the ultra-anonymous Netherfield Housing at Milton Keynes (1971–3).

Hampshire County
Council (Nev
Churcher), Woodlea
School, Bordon,
Hampshire, 1992.

In Liverpool, where during the 1980s depopulation had made land cheap, the extreme left-wing City Council built two-storey brick houses in culs-de-sac on the sites of the 'heroic' inter-war brick flats by Lancelot Keay and later tower blocks, replicating as far as possible the product of the free market. In London, where property prices rose steeply through the 1980s, the effects of the national rise in homeless households from 5,000 in 1977 to more than 45,000 in 1990 was visible in the number of street sleepers.[6] Deprived of the capital to build new dwellings, local authorities tried to fulfil their housing obligations by paying high prices for substandard bed-and-breakfast accommodation for families.

Edward Heath's Conservative government (1970–74) had hoped to replace public authorities with housing associations as the major providers of rented housing, through the provisions of the 1974 Housing Act, which channelled public money to them rather than to councils. Their share of rentals rose from 470,000 in 1981 to 1,588,000 in 2001 at a time when private rentals remained static. They were in the business of commissioning new housing, but in contrast to the ponderous bureaucracy of old-style public housing, they aimed to introduce a new broom of efficient management after the tenants moved in. The practice of Pollard Thomas Edwards, formed in 1974, was one that grew up on this new patronage. The founder partners all wanted to work in housing, but not in the old way. Instead of creating large-scale redevelopments, they realized the potential of smaller sites, often weaving in their new work with retained and converted historic buildings, losing the stigma attached to council housing largely through its architectural form. They built in the forms that people would buy if they were buyers, something the old 'social' architects would have seen as a betrayal. Later, Pollard Thomas and Edwards enabled developments that mixed finance and ownership by councils, housing associations and private developers, the last being a role that they themselves took at times.

There remained large housing estates all over the country whose deterioration from the late 1960s contributed to the whole crisis of confidence in public-sector housing. Small changes brought genuine results. Electronic entryphones and other security measures made amends for the absence from all public housing of permanent on-site *concièrges*, not included as part of housing management in the 1960s. Some local authorities changed the image of their housing with decorative facings in brick and Postmodern skyline details to disguise the identity of the hated flats and provide an external layer of insulation.

Pollard, Thomas and Edwards, Field Court, 77 Fitzjohn's Avenue, London, 1977–8.

Public Building in the Age of Privatization

In an often-quoted interview for *Women's Own* magazine in 1987, Margaret
Thatcher said: 'there is no such thing as society'.[7] In the eyes of architects,
her enthusiasm for self-reliance resulted in a counter-productive meanness of attitude towards state expenditure on building; this had not been
seen, even in the worst times of financial stringency, since the infamous
Liberal First Commissioner of Works in the 1870s, A. S. Ayrton, had per-
secuted George Edmund Street over the construction of the Royal Courts
of Justice. This was a parallel made by Colin St John Wilson in telling the
story of the British Library after 1975, a project that demonstrated national attitudes towards architecture during the final quarter of the twentieth
century.[8]

The rise and fall of the scheme to place the Library next to the British
Museum in Bloomsbury was outlined in chapter Four. In 1976 the site of
the St Pancras goods yard was purchased from British Rail and a new
chapter of the saga began. Wilson's new design was ready in 1977, and it
was announced that construction would begin in 1979. In response to
the disastrous strikes that had delayed the Barbican in the City of
London, the World's End housing in Chelsea and the GLC's last big redevelopment, Thamesmead, the Library was broken down into three
separate construction phases, becoming supposedly less vulnerable to
union activity, although not exempt from other contractual problems at
a higher level. The incoming Conservative government, prompted by its
fear of the unions and relative unconcern about cultural issues, was
determined to break it down even further. Construction began in 1982,
under a 'stop-go' funding system described by Wilson as 'like pulling a
plant up by its roots to see if it was still alive and then cutting a bit off
before shoving it back in the ground'.[9]

The consequent delays lasted, symbolically perhaps, beyond the seemingly endless period of Conservative rule, until the Library opened in the
autumn of 1997 under New Labour. In 1988 the government announced
its intention to sell off the remaining five acres of the site, so that the full
scheme can never be realized, although a modest addition of a conservation building was begun in 2005. In terms of architectural semiotics, the
Library is teasingly complex, a building with a cloaked personality from
outside, but which opens up within, undeniably romantic, but avoiding
monumentality and sentiment. The quality of materials and finish, so
much at risk during these years, was sustained, and it has become a solid
and well-used addition to national life. Wilson's commitment to generous public space set a standard for lottery-funded arts building projects
at the end of the 1990s.

Colin St John Wilson,
The British Library,
Euston Road, London,
1973–97.

The commissioning of works of art for the building from Eduardo Paolozzi, Ron Kitaj and others denotes the movement of the rebels of the 1950s into the establishment of the 1990s. During the 1980s public art was widely seen as a way of making buildings and public spaces more expressive and popular. Art galleries became one of the defining building types of the 1980s and '90s in Britain, combining technical requirements with a call for sensitivity to public perception, existing architectural context and works of art themselves. In Frankfurt, a clutch of new museums by international architects during these years gave the city a much higher profile, and other European and American centres took note. The National Gallery was keen to build an extension on a government-owned bombsite adjoining the existing building in Trafalgar Square, an easy-enough operation in earlier years, but since, as *The Times* commented, 'the era of public patronage, so strong since the last war, was over', it was deemed necessary for the development to pay for itself.[10] A competition called for developers to fund the galleries on the upper level in return for gaining the use of the ground floor, on a lease of 125 years. Seven designs were short-listed, and members of the public were invited to vote on their preferences, selecting Ahrends Burton and Koralek (ABK), Arup Associates and Richard Rogers. The pattern of voting was confusing, however. The Rogers design was among the most popular and the most unpopular at the same time, and the Gallery itself preferred a design by Skidmore, Owings and Merrill that was disliked by the architectural advisers. ABK, in some respects a compromise choice, were instructed to prepare a new scheme, and it acquired a prominent tower, capped with masts and banners. After a public inquiry, this was allowed to proceed, but immediately afterwards, on 30 May 1984, the Prince of Wales made the scheme a subject of particular criticism in a speech at the RIBA Gold Medal ceremony, which was one of the decisive moments of the decade. It was already in the doldrums, but the royal reference to 'a monstrous carbuncle on the face of a much loved and elegant friend' killed it.

The situation was retrieved by the offer of funding from the three Sainsbury brothers, who were beginning to assert themselves as architectural patrons in their own supermarket grocery business. This removed the government and the developers from the equation, and put the Gallery trustees in a position of greater control, anxious not to repeat the mistakes of the first round of designs. 'Where else but in late twentieth century Britain could the fiasco of the National Gallery extension have taken place?' asked the *Architects' Journal*, although it went on to comment that the Burrell Collection in Pollock Park, Glasgow, which was won in

Barry Gasson Architects, Burrell Collection, Pollock Park, Glasgow, 1972–83.

competition in 1978 by Barry Gasson and John Meunier, and completed in 1984, was 'arguably the most successful museum to be built in Britain for a century'.[11] This building, a hangover from an earlier age of public order, represented the anti-monumental, vernacular-inspired style of the 1970s, and has retained a lasting respect.

For a second National Gallery competition, an invited short list from Britain and America included James Stirling and Piers Gough. All the schemes typified a high tide of cultured Postmodernism very different from the brassy Rogers offering. The selected design was by Venturi, Scott Brown and Rauch of Philadelphia, the practice of Robert Venturi, whose book of 1966, *Complexity and Contradiction*, has as good a claim as any to being the foundation of Postmodern architecture. Venturi declared his interest in Sir Edwin Lutyens, whose attraction to Italian Mannerism had gained him several illustrations in *Complexity and*

Venturi, Scott Brown, The Sainsbury Wing, National Gallery, Trafalgar Square, London, 1986–91.

Contradiction at a time when his classical work was deeply unfashionable in Britain.[12] For anti-Modernists, the rehabilitation of Lutyens became a symbolic campaign, and in 1981 an exhibition of his work, designed by Piers Gough, was held at the Hayward Gallery. Despite misgivings on the part of the Arts Council that sponsored it, it proved to be immensely popular. The Sainsbury Wing was mannered and clad in Portland stone. Beyond this, it had little in common with Lutyens, and by the time it opened in July 1991 enthusiasm for Postmodernism was fast fading.

The Prince of Wales

Prince Charles's speech at the RIBA's 150th anniversary award ceremony in 1984 articulated a deep public mistrust of modern architecture that had not been placated by the changes of the 1970s. In the words of his biographer, Jonathan Dimbleby, the prince's instinctive traditionalism 'had long been offended by what he saw as the ugly and impersonal environment that post-war architecture had imposed on the urban landscape, and especially on the inner cities'.[13] From the support he gained, it was clearly a widespread view.

Rod Hackney (*right*) at Black Road, Macclesfield, 1984.

Apart from the National Gallery, the prince singled out another project still at a sensitive planning stage, condemning the 'glass stump more suitable for Chicago than the City of London' that the developer Peter Palumbo was seeking to build at No. 1 Poultry, to a design made some years earlier by Mies van der Rohe.[14] While this project had been welcomed when first presented to the press in 1969, it had taken the whole of the 1970s to assemble the site, which included several listed buildings. A long and high-profile public inquiry, in progress during May 1984, divided the architectural world and created a climate of controversy about Modernism, contextualism and the preservation of the 'urban grain' of small dense streets as something inherently desirable. The Mies project was rejected, although Palumbo was offered the opportunity to come back with a different design. A decade after the inquiry, James Stirling's and Michael Wilford's more contextual project for the site was unveiled, but deemed an anti-climax.

In the 1980s the onset of each spring brought news of riots from communities far removed from the aesthetic niceties of the capital. St Paul's, Bristol, was first, in April 1980, followed by Brixton, London, in 1981 and Toxteth, Liverpool, in July the same year, the month of the Prince of Wales's wedding. In this situation, the Community Architecture move-

Louis Hellman, cartoon in *Architects' Journal* (27 February 1985).

ment, dating from the 1970s, offered an appropriate vehicle for the prince's desire to become involved in architecture at a grass-roots level. Rod Hackney, a little-known architect in Cheshire before the date of the famous speech, was singled out with Edward Cullinan as representatives of the new people-friendly trend, and acquired instant fame. The prince undertook some visits with Hackney, describing how 'it is only when you visit these areas . . . that you begin to wonder how it is possible that people are able to live in such inhuman conditions'. The problems were caused in part by the rapid collapse of the British manufacturing indus-try in the 1980s, and the prince stressed the value of the skills that resi-dents had acquired when restoring their homes in Macclesfield. Was this, as Lionel Esher asked, 'a change as profound as the one we associ-ate with the Renaissance, but almost its mirror image . . . the retreat from heroic plans, from mass solutions and from self-indulgent architecture, like other British retreats, not a defeat but a victory'?[15] For architects, there was a major lesson to learn about communication with users and, as Nick Wates put it, 'a change of attitude away from the elitist vision of the architect as team leader to that of mediator and active participant in a team'.[16]

The most lasting contribution by the Prince of Wales was Poundbury, a model project for an urban extension at Dorchester, Dorset, on land owned by the Duchy of Cornwall, where he was able to influence the way that development would take place. From an idea first launched in the late 1980s, the first phase started on site in 1993, attracting inevitable crit-icism from the architectural world for its use of historic regional styles. The fact that these were designed and executed to a higher standard than

Leon Krier (master planner), Poundbury, Dorchester, Dorset, 1989, phase one, 1993 onwards.

normal made them more threatening to the Modernist cause. Leon Krier, a former assistant to James Stirling who declared his alienation from modern architecture and much of the modern world in brilliant lectures and cartoons, was and remains the master planner. The radicalism of Poundbury lay in its planning concept rather than in its architecture, which successfully reversed most of the space requirements for cars imposed by planners on behalf of road safety since the war, thus achieving higher densities, more considered public spaces and a feeling of a European rather than an English or American settlement. Separate zoning of residential and commercial areas (including light industry) was abolished, so that residents could find employment in walking distance of home, while also having access to fine countryside on foot within a few minutes.

As Dennis Hardy explains,

> Krier's notion of modernity is everything that modernism is not. Whereas the latter is collectivist and alienating, the former is essentially democratic; while modernism builds in concrete, glass and steel, a more traditional approach will use materials gathered locally; the one fragments the city into functional zones, the other seeks to bring the various parts together; modernism builds high, traditionalism uses height only for buildings of civic importance or as landmarks.[17]

These generalizations could be challenged, but Poundbury raises questions of definition usually left unanswered. A large number of its proposals, or their equivalents, are now widely adopted in urban design. Poundbury, however, is not democratic by process of choice, since the Duchy imposes its preferences on developers working there. There is no difficulty about this, except among Modernist critics, since the houses have always sold well. The use of representational styles from the pre-Modernist period sticks in the throat of most architects, but the reasons for this cannot objectively be found. If Poundbury gives you the creeps, you are probably a Modernist.

The New Right and Style Wars

The anti-Modernist mood that was so pervasive in the 1980s almost inevitably favoured a wider return to more literal renderings of classicism, thought by many to be a dying art. There were a few younger 'conviction classicists' like Quinlan Terry, the successor to Raymond Erith following the latter's death in 1973. Richmond Riverside for Haslemere

Erith & Terry,
Richmond Riverside,
1985–8.

Terry Farrell, Comyn
Ching Triangle, Seven
Dials, Westminster,
London, 1978–85.
The corner building
is new, the remainder
refurbished.

Estates (1985–8) enabled Terry to step out of the country-house world
in which classicism had largely been confined since the 1950s, and offer
the picturesque quality of Portmeirion to an appreciative public. This
looked for a time as if it might herald a run of similar projects, but
while the classical counter-proposal by John Simpson for rebuilding
Paternoster Square was successful in halting a selected scheme by Arup
Associates in 1988, its successive reworkings by Terry Farrell and William
Whitfield, and the long delay in construction, launched it finally in 2002
as something substantially different from the first Simpson scheme. As
public space, it seems as successful as it could be in a non-residential
area, and the lack of distinction in the individual buildings by
MacCormac, Eric Parry and others does not diminish its effectiveness as
a neutral background to St Paul's Cathedral.

Terry Farrell's reconstruction of the 'Comyn Ching' triangle of
Georgian houses near Covent Garden (1978–85) was a model of the urban
thinking that combined restoration of old buildings with new work, and
restored the original street lines and heights. Farrell argued that the housing crisis could be solved better by property management of what existed than by new construction, which was usually too rigid in plan to
allow for adaptation. He foresaw the architect's future role chiefly as
'resource management of old buildings' and welcomed this as 'a labour

intensive activity, challenging to the imagination and involving the architect in strategic areas he has all but abandoned to other professions'.[18] Farrell flirted with classicism in the popular temporary garden centre for Clifton Nurseries in Covent Garden (1980–81), but it was a playful engagement, like his masterpiece of billboard architecture, the TV-am headquarters in Camden Town, where the finials were made in the form of breakfast eggcups. Piers Gough did something similar in a witty but urbane reinterpretation of the Georgian terrace type for the developer Kentish Homes.

In 1980 the first Venice Architecture Biennale, *The Presence of the Past*, indicated the internationalism of the anti-Modernist movement, although nowhere outside Britain did it make such inroads into public consciousness or the architectural establishment. The prince's conviction that the past offered superior models for most things was widely shared in the 1980s, pervading television, advertising, branding and even pop music. Modernists were a beleaguered minority, but the view of Jürgen Habermas, that modernity was 'an incomplete project', began to gain credence as Postmodernism revealed its limitations, and the work of the Modernist masters began to be explored in greater depth.[19]

By 1986 the architectural establishment was on the rebound, and the symbolic vehicle for the counter-attack was the exhibition *Foster Rogers Stirling* curated by Deyan Sudjic at the Royal Academy in London, where the emphasis was less on style or technology than on the issues of public

Foster Associates, model of Hong Kong and Shanghai Bank, Hong Kong, 1979–86, at the exhibition *New Architecture: Foster Rogers Stirling*, Royal Academy of Arts, London, 1986.

Louis Hellman, cartoon in *Architects' Journal* (27 June 1984).

space and urban development. Foster's project for a new BBC building in Langham Place with a public way through it introduced concepts of permeability missing from his earlier designs. Stirling's extension to the Staatsgalerie in Stuttgart, designed in referential quasi-classical language belonging to the world of Rossi or Colin Rowe's book, *Collage City* (1978), had recently opened to great acclaim and formed the centrepiece of his display, somewhat at odds with his High Tech stable mates. The Lloyds Building in Leadenhall Street by Rogers, completed in the course of 1986, brought the innovations of the Pompidou Centre to London, no longer as a people's palace of culture but as a temple of capitalism, the symbolic monument for the revival of Modernism in the high period of Thatcherism. Foster's Hong Kong and Shanghai Bank in Hong Kong did something similar on the far side of the world. Was this actually modern architecture? Not according to the elderly troublemaker Berthold Lubetkin, who described Lloyds as 'an assembly of nuts and bolts, scrap iron, celebrating a confusion of fancy props, the glorification of ironmongery and triumph of mega-technology for its own sake'.[20] For the time being, it was essential to banish concrete from view, and with projects like

the Inmos Microprocessor Factory (1982) at Newport in Wales by Rogers, the Renault Distribution Centre (1983) at Swindon by Foster, and Michael Hopkins's Schlumberger Research Laboratories at Cambridge (1984), High Tech consolidated its position as the smart face of knowledge-based manufacture in post-industrial Britain.

High Tech's suitability as transport architecture led to Foster's glamorous Stansted Airport (1986–91), whose lift to the spirits provided the perfect setting for the ultimate democratization of air travel in the 1990s. Nicholas Grimshaw's train shed at Waterloo Station for the Eurostar (1994), set on a curve with an elaborate carapace of overlapping glass designed to shift and shake with the train movements, was an obvious application of the style to recreate the glories of Brunel and Victorian engineering, and symbolize a new proximity to Europe.

The completion of two Hopkins projects in 1991–2 showed a change of direction in his work in response to significant symbolic sites

Richard Rogers and Architects, Lloyds of London, Leadenhall Street, City of London, 1978–86.

in London. The Mound Stand at Lord's Cricket Ground (1984–91) achieved a stylish match of contextual brickwork in the base, facing the street, with a jaunty stretched canopy on top, a reproach to fake traditionalism with real load-bearing brick. In these matters, conservatives and radicals might join hands, as they had done in the first generation of Modernism in Britain. Hopkins followed this opening innings in the new game with the partial rebuilding of Bracken House by Sir Albert Richardson, after it had been saved from demolition by becoming the first post-war listed building in 1988, when its original owners, the *Financial Times*, followed the exodus of the newspapers to Docklands.

Two ends of the architectural spectrum came together at Bracken House, at a time when the rhetoric of resurgent Modernism remained strongly anti-conservationist. Hopkins managed the reconciliation with aplomb, and nearly all his subsequent work has shown the value of reintegrating solid construction with the High Tech stream, both in visual and operational terms, since its thermal properties have come to be increasingly significant. Hopkins completed his journey to the heart of the British architectural establishment with the new Glyndebourne

Opera House (1989–94), reaffirming equilibrium between high culture in a general sense and the high culture of architecture, which, since the completion of Denys Lasdun's National Theatre in 1976, had temporarily lost its voice and identity. In many ways, the path was set in these projects for a new respectability for Modernism, achieved through use of traditional materials and forms, while stopping short of actually using historical detail or decoration. For this trend, European architects such as Rafael Moneo and Alvaro Siza provided exemplars. With this near classicism, a truce was declared in the style wars, but there was also an underlying feeling that individuals from a variety of positions could unite in a shared ethical position and a joint opposition to the crudity of the common run of commercial architecture.

Postmodernism was a different type of truce, but many doubted whether its theoretical basis could be transferred into the new ethical climate of the 1990s, since it was so widely considered as a superficial eye-catching veneer applied to buildings lacking inherent interest. Because of this condemnation, no architect now wishes to be called Postmodern, even in retrospect. Arguably, Postmodernism finished too soon and deserves a more discriminating appraisal, with the best examples celebrated for their intelligence and sensitivity. If any architect could carry Postmodernism with conviction, it was James Stirling, apparently so uncaring about any kind of ethics, public communication or explanation, but devoted to the building as a work of art on a 'take it or leave it' basis, as he had been at the beginning of his career against the background of the welfare state. Pleasing neither the historical purists nor

CWZG, China Wharf, Bermondsey, London, 1982–8.

the puritanical anti-historicists, he scrambled the history of architecture into previously unimaginable conjunctions.

Piers Gough, fulfilling the promise of his student years, was a more dashing version of Stirling (he called his work 'B movie architecture') with bold gestures of form and colour and over-scaled architectural jokes, as in China Wharf, Bermondsey (1982–8), and The Circle (1987–9) nearby in the regenerated Shad Thames area, and the more ambitious Cascades on the Isle of Dogs (1986–8). He avoided preciousness in the use of materials, which some architects began to cultivate in the 1990s, but usually hit all the 'urban' buttons. Terry Farrell brought a broad imaginative sweep to several large projects whose weakness lay in a lack of fine detailing and lumpy massing. Alban Gate, his development on London Wall on the former 'Route 11', destroyed the unity of its 1960s Miesian office slabs, while Embankment Place (1987–90) realized the value of airspace over Charing Cross Station, stitching together some of the pedestrian routes in the area at the same time.

John Outram created his own learned synthesis of historical references in brightly coloured patterned detail, with a pumping station in Docklands (1985–8), which became another architectural emblem of the period, while his New House at Wadhurst Park, East Sussex (1976–86), classical in some respects, showed how decorative effects could just about remain on the Modernist side of the divide. Even more than Stirling, Outram was the joker in the pack of six British architects (all London-based) presented in 1992 at the Venice Biennale. In the following years, he converted a Victorian hospital in Cambridge into the Judge Institute of Management in a sympathetic improvisation on the rather weak original buildings, with a product fantastically out of sympathy with the tight-buttoned aesthetics of Cambridge, left or right.

A lesser-known example of English Postmodernism was the Civic Offices at Epping, Essex, by Richard Reid (1984–90), which combined aspects of Lutyens and Venturi in a loose 'Townscape' arrangement that made a positive contribution to the town. This was the Italian Rationalist

John Outram,
Judge Institute of
Management,
Cambridge, 1991–6.

Richard Reid
Architects, Epping
District Council
Offices, Epping,
Essex, 1984–90.

aspect of Postmodernism (Reid was a former Rome Scholar in Architecture), with a basis in theory. It used exaggerated and simplified forms to which Stirling had shown the way, as did the sheltered housing in Essex Road, Islington (1987–92) by John Melvin, for the Mercers' Company, in which the demonstrative architectural statement responded to several London traditions, while taking nothing away from its skill in planning or quality of construction. A non-architect, Ian Pollard of Flaxyard, was even able to make bad architecture amusing, with the Marco Polo building at Battersea and a notorious store for Homebase, a subsidiary of Sainsbury's, in Warwick Road, Kensington (1988–90), which parodied Stirling's Stuttgart gallery with Egyptian trimmings.

Postmodernism was damaged by its imitators in the same way as Modernism had been before; it had access to a wide range of theory, yet often resulted in superficial application of ideas. In retrospect, its overt mannerism belongs in what, in a wider sense, could be called the long B-movie tradition, beginning with Elizabethan classicism and continuing into late seventeenth-century English Baroque, with all the improper but often engaging 'applied' styles based on communication that have been opposed to the Platonic versions of classicism and Modernism.

The opposition to Postmodernism was part of the resurgence of architectural ethics in the late 1980s and early 1990s, constructing a platform from which architecture could be re-launched. This was achieved partly by moving the architectural discourse outside the walls of its own institutions and into the general press (for which the Prince of Wales's publicity was a boost), broadcasting and other institutions, such as the Arts Council, where Peter Palumbo, as Chairman from 1988 to 1994, set up an 'Architecture Unit'.

Figures such as Edward Cullinan, Richard MacCormac and David Lea, seen as modern successors to the Arts and Crafts Movement, were more important for the recovery of credibility during the 1990s than the big names of High Tech, Postmodernism or Classicism. Of these three, Lea has been the least prolific but probably the most high principled, admired for his rigorous use of sustainable materials with the kind of sophistication of space and detailing that were usually missing from the emergent Green Movement in architecture. Cullinan was a figure noted in the 1960s who really made his name in the 1990s with projects such as the Visitor Centre for the National Trust at Fountains Abbey (1988–92), which offered the kind of decorative use of materials still desired in the 1980s, although falling out of fashion in the 1990s. It became increasingly important in the new climate of scrutiny and participation to be able to talk a lot more often, and to explain projects to non-architects using references they could understand. Where there was a way to situate the

Edward Cullinan
Architects, Visitor
Centre for the
National Trust,
Fountains Abbey,
North Yorkshire,
1988–92.

project historically, so much the better, and where the older generation of architects might have looked for explanations based on economics or performance, Cullinan was one of the many who developed a new language of architectural exegesis. His office was the seedbed for another generation of practices such as Penoyre & Prasad and Short & Ford, spreading the same values in the way that Norman Shaw's pupils in the 1880s created a similar leavening in the architectural culture.

Richard MacCormac and his practice, MJP, became known for his use of shallow pitched roofs, overhanging eaves and regional materials, often developed into quite complex forms. He and Cullinan developed ways of fitting new buildings into historic contexts with enough references to keep the planners happy. As President of the RIBA (1991–3), MacCormac was one of the first for several years who had a high reputation as a designer. He organized a major exhibition, *The Art of the Process*, arguing that

MacCormac,
Jamieson, Pritchard,
Cable and Wireless
Group Telecom-
munications College,
Coventry, 1992–4.

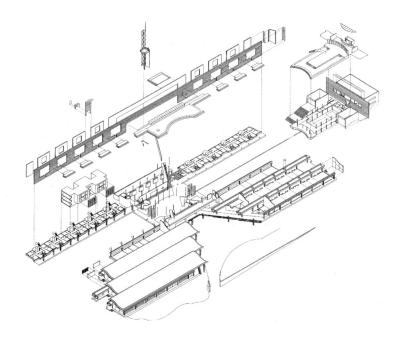

architecture is the least understood intellectual skill in the building
industry today, and that architects must respond to the changing
perception of the profession in society by demystifying and opening up to scrutiny what it is they actually do when they design.[21]

The nature of the gap between newly sensitized architects and their
more simple-minded clients comes across in Andrew Saint's description
in the catalogue of MacCormac's own offering, the Cable and Wireless
Group Telecommunications College:

> Cable and Wireless has long been teaching telecommunications
> to students, many from the old colonies, on a bitty site in
> Cornwall. It wanted something smarter and less hierarchical,
> somewhere in middle England. It knew its technical needs and
> had secured 10 business-park acres outside Coventry for its
> college . . . MJP's response was not to lead off with a simple
> generative diagram. Instead, it dished up for discussion a menu
> of mixed-use-places-in-isolation, ancient and modern: castles,
> colleges, Palladian villa-farms and so on. But Cable and Wireless
> was more at ease with decision-taking than with prolonged
> debate. It wanted to get on with the job. Soon enough, MJP had
> to hold its nose and jump.

Evans & Shalev,
Courts of Justice,
Truro, Cornwall, 1988.

As Saint went on to explain, a number of decisions were justifiable on purely rational grounds, apart from the green ceramic coating on the roofs, inspired by a Han dynasty figure that MacCormac had seen in Singapore.

Some architects who had begun as New Brutalists happily found an outlet for a more representational approach in a climate less insistent on abstraction. Eldred Evans was considered one of the major talents of her generation, but her partnership with David Shalev had produced relatively few buildings before the Law Courts at Truro, Cornwall, completed in 1989, a building that retained essentially Modernist concepts of light and movement through space, although it was almost axially symmetrical and entered beneath a vestigial pediment. This led on to the commission for a new outstation of the Tate Gallery at St Ives, also in Cornwall, which anticipated the lottery projects of the 1990s in its requirement to act as a symbolic focus for regional regeneration.

Something in the City

Commercial architecture was widely derided in the 1960s, but as the welfare state declined, it attracted more enterprising designers and patrons. The 1970s recession was part of the key, since Stuart Lipton, then a young developer, took time off in the USA and studied construction methods that shortened the time on site by using steel frame rather than concrete for the structure as part of a 'fast-track' system, in which the building might begin on site before all the drawings were complete. In

contrast to the drawn-out, strike-prone accidents of a British site, this became a revolutionary transformation that also changed the look of buildings.

Lipton, in partnership with Godfrey Bradman, is chiefly associated with the Broadgate development, using the site of the demolished Broad Street Station in the City and the adjoining new ground created by claiming 'air rights' (an American practice) over the tracks of Liverpool Street Station. The first phase, 1 Finsbury Avenue, by Peter Foggo of Arup Associates (1982–4), marked a transition in the firm's work from external concrete framing to steel, with a frame fully erected in thirteen weeks. After many years of crass 'commercial architecture', this building brought a new sophistication, not only on the exteriors, but in the atrium at the centre (a calm contrast to the busyness of the Lloyds' spectacular) and, unseen yet crucial, the wide floors of the open-plan offices, each with a deep service void to allow rapid and constant updating of electronic equipment.

The acknowledgment of the temporal dimension in office building, both in construction time and operational use, was a major conceptual shift, aided by the continuing researches of Francis Duffy, similarly inspired by American practice. 'Never before, not even in Chicago in the 1880s, has the office building been so central to society nor loaded with such significance', Duffy wrote in 1981.[22] The opinion was not exaggerated, although in 1988 he contrasted the British obsession with 'the extent to which façades are decked out in classical motifs' with a more practical attitude in Europe, where, as he noted, people buy office buildings and rent homes, the opposite of Britain. Arups were stretched to complete the early phases of Broadgate, and the American firm SOM, no longer under the spell of Mies, designed the later parts, where postmodern gestures began to creep in.

Even so, Broadgate represented a breakthrough on many fronts. Godfrey Bradman raised money abroad to avoid the stifling restrictions imposed by British institutional investors. Not only the public art, but also the public spaces in which it stood, were completely new elements in the scheme, configured in a comfortable and restrainedly picturesque sequence to avoid the agoraphobic dotting of buildings in a void as at La Défense in Paris, a development of similar period with a strong urban form. The ideal of efficiency, expressed as American know-how with European polish, had come round full circle again. As Duffy explained, the architect's visible role was reduced, in most places, to a 10-centimetre thickness at the face of the building, where character could be achieved by hanging slices of granite, not unlike Albert Richardson's early borrowing before the First World War of the architectural vocabulary of Karl Friedrich Schinkel to clad steel frames quickly and efficiently.[23]

The deregulation of financial services in 1986, known as 'the Big Bang', was an event of worldwide importance, bringing additional business to the City of London, owing partly to the accident of its ideal position between the time zones of the two other major financial centres of the world. Half the volume of offices in the City of London was rebuilt between 1985 and 1993. This stimulated expectations for a secondary financial centre in the former dock area of the Isle of Dogs, part of the vast areas of the London Docks that presented a spectacle of political and financial stasis throughout the 1970s. Then the London Docklands Development Corporation was established in 1981 as one of a series of Urban Development Corporations with wide discretion in terms of planning, inspired by *New Society*'s Non-Plan issue of 1969, as well as by the liberal economics of Thatcherism. Canary Wharf, the largest development, was the work of the American architect César Pelli for the original developer, G. Ware Travelstead, forming part of a plan for a high-density business centre laid out on a grid with a raised street deck, also involving SOM. A Canadian developer, Olympia and York, took over the scheme in 1987, and completed the tower and adjacent buildings in 1991, when recession stalled the scheme for several years. In 1995, after complaints

Ian Ritchie Architects,
The Watergarden
(Roy Square), Narrow
Street, Limehouse,
London, 1986–8.

about the dominance of American firms, Troughton McAslan contributed a building. Some modest, Erskine-like offices were built at Heron Quays by Nicholas Lacey, showing modest ambitions at the beginning of the development, but Docklands was brash and American, while Broadgate was European in spirit and urban context, and perhaps each was appropriate to its place. By the end of the 1990s it was clear that international finance could be conducted without as much marble, granite or other kinds of stone facing as previously supposed.

Docklands also generated a quantity of private-sector housing, by architects who included Jeremy Dixon and CWZG. At Roy Square, Limehouse (1989), for the developer Roy Sandu, a leading member of the London Hindu community, Ian Ritchie, normally a High Tech designer, produced a notable paraphrase of Georgian classicism that avoided being pastiche or Postmodern.

London's docks have not been the only area of waterfront regeneration, although the Merseyside Development Corporation, founded in the early 1980s, has delivered nothing so spectacular in Liverpool apart from the temporary Garden Festival in 1984, although Stirling converted part of the Albert Dock, a building he had admired as a student, into Tate Liverpool (1984–6). Cardiff Bay offered a similar opportunity, where the chance to build an opera house by Zaha Hadid was thrown away following her competition victory in 1994. This has been described as 'the greatest loss to British architecture over the last generation'.[24] A temporary Visitor Centre in the form of a gleaming tube by Will Alsop

(1990) was for a long time the main representative of metropolitan Modernism in the new quarter. In the late 1990s the two towns facing each other across the River Tyne, Newcastle and Gateshead, enjoyed their riverfront revival, culminating in two adjacent arts projects on the Gateshead side, the Baltic, a flour mill converted as an art gallery (2003), and the Sage, a new building by Foster and Partners for music (opened 2005), with an elegant and attention-grabbing pedestrian bridge, by Wilkinson Eyre (1997–2001), connecting them to the conserved and regenerated north bank.

The alternative to the office in a redeveloped 'brown-field' area of existing city was the business park, situated on a virgin piece of 'green-field' land, an idea borrowed from France and the USA. Out of sight and mind, most buildings of this type were unremarkable. In the 1970s Cambridge University began to develop its Business Park on the western side of the city, close to the new M11 motorway, where Hopkins's Schlumberger breaks the skyline. Firms such as CWZG began to publish smart and memorable decorated sheds, for Aztec West, near Bristol, the second of the type. Close to London, Stuart Lipton commissioned a master plan from Arup Associates in 1985 for Stockley Park, Chiswick, a non-traditional location influenced by its proximity to Heathrow. Landscaping with trees and water, works of art and taut, tasteful buildings were the hallmark, creating an anthology of current architecture by Arup, Foster, Ian Ritchie, Troughton McAslan, Eric Parry and Richard Rogers, up to 1990.

The shift represented at Broadgate towards a greater focus on efficient delivery was part of a significant overhaul during the period 1980–2000 of the way that architectural practices operated. Architecture at the end of the 1970s was notorious for overspending, whether or not this was avoidable. Following American practice, more intermediaries came into the process to prevent this, such as project managers and client representatives, displacing the architect from his former direct triangular relationship to the client and the contractor. 'Design and Build' packages were favoured by developers and public bodies for the assurances of tight control that they offered, but the architect's control was substantially reduced, with a loss of quality. To counteract doubts about their performance, architects became less blasé about their services, listening to such American analysts as Donald Schon, inventor of the phrase 'reflective practitioner', which became widespread in defining one aspect of an architect's offering, and Robert Gutman, a major influence on Duffy's thinking, who took a cool outsider's look at what architects actually did and separated their skills into separate strengths of ideas, service and delivery, which were not necessarily found combined in one individual or even one practice.[25]

Recession and Recovery

The Recovery of the Modern was the title of an anthology of writing from the *Architectural Review* of the period 1980–95, published for the magazine's centenary in 1996. As Michael Spens wrote in his introduction, it was

> one saga in the set of wider circumstances over the past twenty years that led to the survival and recovery of Modernism, as a continuity of culture whereby the 'new' is considered to be more of a preoccupation creatively than what has been.[26]

Postmodernism, he argues, fell short of the equivalent cultural achievements going under the same name in other disciplines, and the alternative was found in a more international outlook and a renewed sense of morality. Architects turned away from the demands of the public and looked for approval from their peers. New Modernism was a more gentle if still insistent strain, 'existing again in recurring pluralities . . . and enriched as never before'.[27]

The task was to use hard thinking and moral integrity to recover the good bits of Modernism and leave out the bad, or somehow redeem them through historical and theoretical interpretation. In 1986 E. M. Farrelly described the 'New Spirit' as 'tough, iconoclastic, streetwise; acerbic, often aggressive and very highly strung'.[28] This was represented by the projects of Nigel Coates and his NATO (Narrative Architecture Today) group, which were generally not buildings in the conventional sense, but schemes to stimulate activity in public spaces, trailing with them some of the radical chic of the Punk rock revolution of the mid-1970s. Projects by Hadid and Alsop had similar intentions, seeking bizarre forms without human scale. Some work qualified for the title 'Deconstructivist', another term taken from literature, and adopted in architecture in 1988. The international trend had an avid following as an alternative to Postmodernism, with which it shared a desire to make Modernism more visually interesting, regardless of issues of tectonics or structural rationalism, and to pursue analogies between architectural form and linguistic structure. Deconstruction looked back to previously unexplored areas in the history of Modernism, especially the Russian Revolutionary avant-garde. Rem Koolhaas, a tutor at the Architectural Association in the late 1970s with Hadid among his students, went to Russia to research architects such as Ivan Leonidov, whose work was almost entirely in the form of unbuilt projects. This encouraged Hadid to focus on presenting her competition schemes as exquisite near-abstract paintings. Deconstruction aligned itself with fine art on a formal and conceptual level, while retaining lofty notions of its social significance, which were emphasized in the first major European project in this manner, the extension to the Jewish Museum in Berlin by Daniel Libeskind (1989), a design that also reflected the cult of the Russian avant-garde at the AA, where Libeskind was a tutor.

German commissions for English-based practices were a feature of the decades following Stirling's Staatsgalerie, including several of his own significant later works. Other architects have included Grimshaw, Rogers and Foster, who won the symbolically important job of rebuilding the Reichstag in Berlin as the seat of government for the reunified Germany. In the former East Germany, Ian Ritchie designed a new entrance for the Leipziger Messe, the major trade exhibition venue. Zaha Hadid's commissions have now included major buildings in Wolfsburg and Leipzig. Ian Ritchie observes that 'maybe there is between one and three percent more cultural awareness of architecture as an art in the general populace than here and that can make a vast difference in terms of the approach the public take towards new ideas'.[29]

The worldwide expansion of theory in schools of architecture during the 1970s and '80s meant that a return to Modernism at this point was not a simple recapitulation, but involved a new awareness of the potential depth within the subject, with an intention to avoid the formulaic. In Britain 'The Other Tradition' was formulated as an antidote to monotony and loss of the sense of place. Peter Blundell-Jones contributed to the rediscovery of its German heroes, Hans Scharoun, and Hugo Häring, while there was a resurgence of interest in Alvar Aalto, a popular figure among British architects since the 1930s, but latterly upheld as a hero of modern 'resistance' architecture and a strong influence on Wilson's British Library. Peter Davey, the editor of the *Architectural Review* from 1982 to 2005, was sympathetic to this trend and acknowledged the continuity from the Arts and Crafts Movement to Regionalism, which he described as 'a philosopher's stone that will transmute the mundane to a built poetry that can unite us all, of whatever background, in homecoming'.[30] The Arts and Crafts belief in the haptic (an element largely ignored in Deconstruction) was supported by the growing influence of phenomenology in schools of architecture, especially in the teaching of Dalibor Veseley from the 1980s onwards at the AA and Cambridge. This was part of a global discussion in Finland, Japan, Germany and the USA, which influenced architects such as Eric Parry, a long-time enthusiast for Philip Webb, in reworking Modernist precedents and gave British architects a way into international thinking without losing their cultural roots. Phenomenology as a philosophical movement involving thinkers such as Edmund Husserl, Martin Heidegger and Maurice Merleau-Ponty aimed to undermine and supplant the positivism of the nineteenth century that fed the efficiency doctrines of modern architecture and thus, for those who cared, served as a way of addressing the mounting sense of global ecological crisis, less by mechanical than by spiritual means. The school of English Minimalism owed much to this perception, although it was paradoxical that some of its first products were fashionable restaurants or shops for luxury goods, designed in the 1980s by David Chipperfield, Stanton Williams and John Pawson and Claudio Silvestrin. During the 1990s Minimalism, which was inherent in most of 'first-generation' Modernism up to 1930, became a media phenomenon, appropriate for the shallow contrition of economic recession, since it was far from cheap to produce. While international in its reach, Minimalism was given a local habitation in Herbert Ypma's book *London Minimal* (1996), where Georgian fanlights and red pillar boxes provide a visual counterpoint to empty white rooms.

Minimalism required high-quality finishes, which in an age of deskilled building crafts added to its exclusivity, while providing a reassuring material weight to theoretical ideas. To pick a single figure acting as guru, not just to Minimalism but to a younger generation in search of the line of the future, rather as Philip Webb did for the Arts and Crafts Movement, one might select Tony Fretton, whose work became widely known with the Lisson Gallery (1985–93). Fretton worked as a fine artist for a while, bringing to architecture the formal discipline, intellectual reach and 'the power to be affecting and communicative' that he found in Donald Judd, Barnett Newman and Louis Kahn. 'Plainness and a sense of naturalness' were qualities he sought.[31] While apparently concerned with pure aesthetics, Fretton still spoke of a desire to communicate to society at large. The Lisson Gallery, set in an 'everyday' streetscape rather than the rarefied art dealers' quarter, was excessively plain and spartan for its time, but also slightly quirky. It set what for England was a new model for Modernism, 'an architecture this country has never known', as Kenneth Frampton called it in 1992, remixing familiar elements from Adolf Loos, Alvaro Siza and Brutalism with exquisite understatement.[32]

Tony Fretton, Lisson Gallery, Bell Street, Marylebone, London, 1985–93.

228

David Chipperfield,
Museum of the
River and Rowing,
Henley-on-Thames,
Oxfordshire, 1998.

Florian Beigel, Jon Broome, Suresh A'Raj, of Architecture Bureau, Half Moon Theatre, Mile End Road, London, 1985.

Loos's devotion to the standard products of British equipment of 1900, men's suits and chairs, was reassuring in a regionalist way, while more than any other Modernist master, he explored space, the aspect of Modernism that Postmodernists were deemed to have neglected. The Loos revival is seen most strongly in the Walsall Art Gallery by Caruso St John (1995–2000), a practice marked by

Caruso St John, Walsall New Art Gallery, 1995–2000.

> a concern for authenticity: the search for a strategy for avoiding or subverting / resisting the apparently inevitable commodification of architecture under global capitalism and for tactics for resisting the neoliberal markets' imperative for novelty.[33]

This description could cover a subsection of the London architectural world during the past ten years. In their lineage, they acknowledge Florian Beigel, in whose office they came together. Beigel's Half Moon Theatre in Mile End Road was a crucial work of the early 1980s that stood for the continuity of Modernist values in a spirit of community engagement. The risk that these works run is to be too precious and introverted. Even so, they can be contrasted with the more pretentious if popular modernisms emanating from London or passing through it, which are more concerned with formal invention on a global stage.

The 'high-style' revival of Modernism was matched by its spread as a normal style for restaurants and bars in the slow climb out of recession in the early 1990s, affecting even the traditional British pub, where in fashionable locations curtains, carpets and upholstery were removed to expose hard surfaces. Enthusiasm for vintage modern furniture among collectors acted as a spearhead for architecture, and the word 'retro', referring to this revival, confusingly became a synonym for modern.

Political Change in the 1990s

During the 1980s Britons looked enviously at François Mitterrand's series of 'Grands Projets' in Paris and at the secondary level of high-quality urban renewal there and in other French cities. British firms occasionally contributed, as with Norman Foster's Carré d'Art at Nîmes of 1984–93, his first seriously contextual urban building. The Lottery brought a similar *largesse* and freedom, and was the beginning of an extraordinary boom in public architecture in Britain, which was timed to pick up the 'New Spirit' and give it physical form all over the country. Projects were selected by competition, open to architects in Europe as well as in Britain, and contributed to an accelerated move into the European mainstream, with the Swiss practice Herzog & de Meuron making a strong impact with their conversion of Bankside Power Station into Tate Modern (1995–2000) and following it with the Laban Dance Centre in Deptford.

While it was relatively easy to commission individual arts projects with lottery funding available from 1995 onwards, the inherited complications of Britain's post-war housing have taken longer to sort out. After the Conservative government's dismantling of the welfare state housing system in the early 1980s, initiatives were launched to rebuild inner cities, although the task was massive and the expertise still undeveloped. By the early 1990s new mechanisms of change were taking shape, as can be seen in the story of the Hulme Estate in the southern part of central Manchester, planned by Hugh Wilson and J. L. Womersley and built between 1968 and 1972. A few years on, the original streets of terraced

houses might have been saved by 'Community Architecture', but instead they were replaced by the biggest deck-access scheme in the country by the once-praised masterminds of Park Hill and Cumbernauld, which was immediately beset by technical and social problems directly attributable to lack of forethought and realism in the design ('Europe's worst housing stock' as the *Architects' Journal* later described it), and culminating in the promise in 1992 to use £37.5 million of government 'City Challenge' money to destroy the whole project and replace it with something closer to what had been there before. Intensive involvement of local residents, using techniques of 'Action Planning', produced a master plan allowing for accretive growth in place of a single style or method, although controlled by the newly popular design codes originating from the New Urbanist movement in the USA. The resulting architecture avoided the historicism associated with the New Urbanists, but was inspired by Ralph Erskine in permitting visual variety to stem from the wishes of individuals. The project included a housing co-operative, 'Homes for Change', in the form of a four-sided block, funded by the Guinness Trust, as well as private-sector housing. A new generation of architects based in Manchester, such as Roger Stephenson and Stephen Hodder, used the greater freedom in planning constraint in the mid-

1990s (compared to central London) to create new models for inserting modern design within historic buildings.

In Birmingham, urban regeneration in the 1990s, led by Les Sparks as Director of Planning and Architecture, concerned itself with mitigating the adverse effects of the 1960s ring road, and creating a network of rehabilitated and new buildings along the canals in the city centre. Thus an alternative city centre was created, including Brindleyplace, a canal-side development based on the primacy of public space, around which a deliberately eclectic collection of new buildings marched in visually coordinated step to show the possibility of pluralism. In Birmingham, Manchester and Belfast, new concert halls, with acoustics superior to the older halls of London, affirmed the excellence of provincial culture. These were the Symphony Hall, Birmingham (1987–91), and Bridgewater Hall, Manchester (1993–6), both by RWHL Partnership, and the Waterfront Hall, Belfast, by Robinson McIlwaine, a project originated in 1978 and completed in the years 1993–7, the most visually distinguished of the three.

London lacked a central coordinating authority following the abolition of the GLC in 1986, and the inability of local councils to fill the role was seen in the poor quality of public infrastructure and the generally cosmetic level of improvements, which failed to solve underlying problems and created a mood of decline, 'a downward spiral of infrastructural and human problems that will prove hard to halt' as the historian Roy Porter wrote in 1994. The grim ironies of a city with low self-esteem were captured in the film *London* (1994), a fictionalized portrait of the year 1992 in the capital, which is portrayed by the director, Patrick Keiller, a former architect, as a limbo of lost souls in a shabby prison camp. In the director's synopsis of the film, Robinson, the unseen protagonist, speculates that the 'nineteenth century, England's reaction to the French Revolution and the failure of the English Revolution itself may all be to blame for London's decline and its imminent isolation and disappearance'.[34] In the film, Robinson and his companion pause outside William Morris's house in Hammersmith and remember

> what we used to think of as the future: sophisticated engineering; low consumption; renewable energy; public transport; but just now, London is all waste, without a future, its public spaces either void or stage sets for the public spectacles of nineteenth century reaction, endlessly re-enacted for television.[35]

Although *London* reflected the gloom following the re-election of John Major in 1992, his Minister for Environment from 1993 to 1997, John Gummer, commissioned a discussion paper on 'Quality in Town and Country', as well as starting the process of recreating a unified government for London which was continued in the Labour manifesto of 1997, promising a new elected Greater London Assembly. The example of Barcelona was ever present, where, between the death of Franco in 1975 and the Olympic Games in 1992, the city had been revived both economically and physically through a renaissance of locally generated architecture. Barcelona inspired Glasgow and Dublin to use architecture as a catalyst for regeneration. As Richard Rogers pointed out in his Reith Lectures of 1995, cities were becoming more effective at working towards long-term targets for limiting their ecological impact than national governments.[36]

When Tony Blair became leader of the Labour Party, his campaigning emphasized youth, innovation and connection with the culture of Europe; in a word, 'modernizing'. Socially excluded sections of society were to receive new help, although the fatalism of old-fashioned 'welfare' was to be avoided. This was a message in tune with a revival of a socially conscious Modernism, and Rogers collaborated with the Shadow Arts Minister, Mark Fisher, in a party publication, *A New London* (1992). Following his election victory in 1997, Blair began to implement these policies, not without controversy and some falling short of the original intentions, but with an overall result that, combined with steady economic growth, gave a boost to architecture through funding and enabling new buildings of many kinds, especially hospitals and schools. The London Borough of Southwark showed the capacity of architecture to create economic and social benefits, from the international scale of the Tate Modern to the local effect of Will Alsop's Peckham Library (1999), a colourful and sculptural equivalent to the boisterous public libraries of the 1900s. Most architects regret, however, that by continuing the Conservative Private Finance Initiative

Cross-section through a residential district showing a tree-lined street enclosed by buildings with ground-floor retail and commercial facilities and upper-level apartments enjoying views of private and communal gardens. Design by Andrew Wright Associates, illustrated in *Towards an Urban Renaissance* (1999).

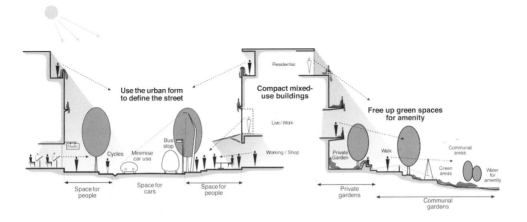

scheme to offset the capital cost of many of these projects, architects have been involved in large amounts of needless paperwork and administration with no tangible benefits at the end for the public.

A new Cabinet role was devised for the Deputy Prime Minister, John Prescott, as head of a newly configured Department of Environment, Transport and the Regions, with a national overview of planning policy. The Urban Task Force appointed by him in 1997 and chaired by Richard Rogers recommended denser settlement patterns, better public transport infrastructure and the use of brown-field land for new housing among a range of issues that had been brewing for ten years or more prior to its report of 1999.[37] The strong rural preservationist faction was placated, and demands for sustainability partially satisfied. Implementation was patchy, and the government proved unwilling to come into conflict with some of the vested interests of commercial house builders, so that the long-term problems of new housing have been addressed only in a piece-meal way. There were no tough measures for reducing car use, out-of-town retailing and other agents of impending ecological crisis, or for gen-erating better public services in suburban areas of low density that com-prise a large amount of the inherited housing stock, although city centres did show signs of improvement. A follow-up report, *Towards a Strong Urban Renaissance*, in 2005 noted that

> England's cities are very different places from the post-industrial centres of unemployment and failing public services of twenty years ago . . . They stand more confidently on the international stage.

Manchester, which took advantage of an IRA bomb in the city centre in 1996 to remove previous unpopular developments, was the prime show-case for design-led change.

The period since 1980 saw the invasion of formerly subjective areas of life by attempts to quantify and account for everything. New Labour redoubled efforts in this direction, and special interest groups had to respond in kind. The RIBA's report *The Value of Architecture* (2000) was upbeat about the general situation, while noting the loss of qualified architects and planners in the public sector since 1985, dropping by 50 per cent and 95 per cent respectively. Their lack was felt when complex urban regeneration projects had to be steered to acceptance without being stripped of design quality in the name of economy. The 'flagship effect' of art museums and other prominent public buildings generated tourism and growth, but the value of good design was not universally accepted. The report quoted the *New Statesman*:

Alsop and Störmer,
Peckham Library
and Media Centre,
London, 1999.

The idea that an identity – for a city, or region, or country – can be physically constructed troubles many people in Britain. Manchester is now learning, but in England generally the invention of a tradition through architecture is not a conscious process.[38]

The report's author, Ken Worpole, stressed how urban design could affect quality of life through 'greater feelings of safety and security, greater legibility and assurance, and in a greater sense of locality, identity, civic pride and belonging'.[39] The theories of Kevin Lynch and others going back to the 1950s were finally being applied. Pedestrianization of town centres had a bad reputation, but urban designers began to acquire more subtle ways of handling motor traffic and balancing it against other users, despite resistance to change of any kind. The partial pedestrianization of Trafalgar Square in 2002, based on the research of the

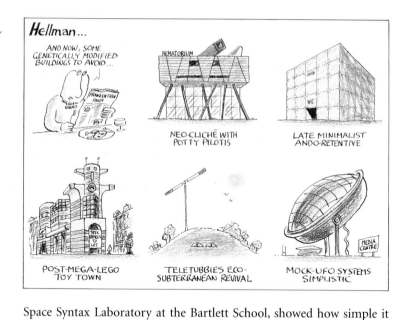

Hellman...

AND NOW, SOME
GENETICALLY MODIFIED
BUILDINGS TO AVOID...

NEO-CLICHÉ WITH
POTTY PILOTIS

LATE MINIMALIST
ANDO-RETENTIVE

POST-MEGA-LEGO
TOY TOWN

TELETUBBIES ECO-
SUBTERRANEAN REVIVAL

MOCK-UFO SYSTEMS
SIMPLISTIC

Space Syntax Laboratory at the Bartlett School, showed how simple it could be. The office-building sector has often led in sustainability of construction and operation. The Canon Headquarters at Reigate, Surrey (2000), by David Richmond, showed a temperate use of simple passive methods of thermal-mass, sun-shading and stack-effect ventilation, with a roof made of the company's own photovoltaic panels. These were good building blocks for a simple version of Modernism. The Norwegian architect Nils Thorp's headquarters for British Airways at Heathrow was praised for similar achievements, with a working environment that looked pleasant to be in. Architects who insisted on cladding their entire building with glass had more difficulty in being

David Richmond
& Partners, Canon
UK Headquarters,
Reigate, Surrey,
cross-section through
offices, 1995–9.

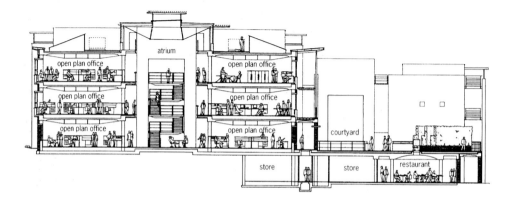

convincingly green, although Rogers, Foster and others consistently claimed this for their buildings, including the controversial but unmissable 30 St Mary Axe (first called the Swiss Re tower but popularly known as 'the Gherkin') in the City of London, completed in 2004.

An old debate about the comparative worth of 'icon' buildings (memorable and newsworthy designs by 'signature' architects) and high-quality background buildings surfaced in 2005, with some renewed attention to the latter category. A practice such as Bennetts Associates shows a strong ethical impulse combining ideals of collaborative design, energy saving and community involvement, represented in a number of office buildings and in the Central Library and Jubilee Development, Brighton, a PFI project praised for retaining high quality, creating not only a public building, but a new square and realigning the street pattern to an original grid. The architects commented: 'environmental engineering is the Trojan horse for structural and spatial expression'.[40]

The weakest point in the bright horizon of British architecture at the turn of the Millennium remained private-house building. In a heated sellers' market, there was little incentive for developers to improve the aesthetics, planning or sustainability of their product, and they continued to rely on 'kerb appeal', the first impression created by the front of the house. Initiatives by CABE, the government's own architectural advisory body, failed to make any major breakthrough. Individuals had small successes, including Wayne Hemingway, a successful fashion designer who criticized the design of Wimpey Homes in the press, and

Louis Hellman, cartoon in *Architects' Journal* (27 February 2003).

was invited to collaborate with them in a project at Gateshead. The houses were commercially successful, but the company reverted to its former designs. John Prescott was persuaded by the New Urbanist arguments for design codes, including the usually rather historical designs that went with them, as promoted in the USA by the Congress for New Urbanism and in Britain by the Prince's Foundation for the Built Environment. This was a recognition that most modern architects who had offered sample schemes for new house types failed to understand the emotional needs of the market, which would tolerate modern architecture in places of work and entertainment, but not necessarily in homes. Various television programmes have attempted to show Modernism in the Netherlands as an alternative, so far without much effect.[41] *Towards a Strong Urban Renaissance* cited the Millennium Village on the Greenwich Peninsula (still a slightly forlorn and isolated group of dwellings, partly by Ralph Erskine, who resigned in protest at alterations to his scheme), and partly by a young practice, Proctor Matthews, who developed a distinctive style to match Erskine's, using bright coloured panels like medieval heraldry. In Manchester, the development company Urban Splash, set up in 1993, pioneered inner-city loft living in converted historic buildings, a phenomenon previously restricted to London, and by 2000 was spreading its influence to other cities. Also mentioned were 'many visionary Peabody housing projects in London'. These were largely the initiative of Dickon Robinson as Director of Development, who commissioned the partially prefabricated housing at Murray Grove, Islington (1999), by Cartwright Pickard, in an attempt to overcome the construction-time over-runs of conventional building methods. It was completed in 27 weeks, although the cost overran by 15 per cent. The result was elegant enough, in the new metropolitan manner, and others followed, such as Raines Court by Allford, Hall, Monaghan Morris. These changes were in line with the recommendations of the Construction Task Force (the Egan Report) of 1999, which returned to the issues of 1900 about inefficiency throughout the industry as a factor in rising construction costs. Architects were alarmed at the possibility of being left out of the building process, but also looked forward to a phase of 'mass customization' akin to the direction taken by the car industry, in which design ingenuity and individual difference could exist within an overall streamlining of production.

Peabody's most radical scheme was BedzED – Beddington Zero (Fossil) Energy Development (2002) – at Beddington, Surrey, by the architect Bill Dunster, who had left Michael Hopkins after contributing to the pioneering energy-saving Nottingham Trent University Campus and Portcullis House. At BedzED, Dunster worked with the consultancy

Cartwright Pickard, Murray Grove Housing, Islington, London, 1998–9.

240

Bioregional to create a model of sustainable development not only in the sourcing and use of materials, but also with the minimum of energy in use. The greatest novelty was to design in ways by which residents could live more rewarding and simultaneously less wasteful lives than they could expect in the conventional three-storey flats built alongside the Bedzᴇᴅ site. The result attracted much interest and some controversy. Not without teething problems, it remains the major demonstration site of its kind, when its example could well have been developed elsewhere. In a text reviewing British architecture from the 1950s to 2004, Peter Buchanan commented:

Bedzᴇᴅ is both high-density housing and a business park. For those who use all the facilities it offers, it achieves the feat of allowing a western European lifestyle within the ecological footprint the earth can support (which is less than a quarter of the average Londoner's footprint) ... [W]e need a new vision of creativity,

Bill Dunster Architects, Bedzᴇᴅ, Hackbridge, Surrey, 1999–2001.

FAT (Fashion Architecture Taste), Islington Square new housing, New Islington, Manchester, 2006.

not as competitive ego-expression, but (recapturing some of the humility of the fifties) as collaborating in the flowering of all forms of evolution – natural, historical and personal.[42]

This is a different way of stating the ethical theme to that of Caruso St John and their fellow 'new materialists', yet similarly reminiscent of Arts and Crafts ideals of the everyday and anonymous. It is a condition that many architects currently practising in Britain may suppose they have attained, arriving at a degree of consensus without conformity that would have been unimaginable fifteen years ago. In 2006, however, the press welcomed a return to Postmodernism in the form of the Woodward Place housing in Manchester by FAT (Fashion Architecture Taste), a scheme quite unlike the solemn approach of most housing architecture. These were the architects preferred by the local population,

Proctor and Matthews, consultation meeting with local residents, Dale Mill, Rochdale, Lancashire, 2005.

who were going to be re-housed by the Manchester Methodist Housing Group within the New Islington development by Urban Splash. The houses followed traditional plan models, but with a more flexible set of potential future uses. Externally, they had cut-out shapes on their gables, little balconies, all ironic enough not to be mistaken for the Poundbury of the north, but in reality not far removed in intention.

While demand for housing in the South-East drove prices beyond the means of most first-time buyers on a single income, declining population and employment opportunities in many northern cities presented the government with problems in its attempt to equalize opportunities in British society. Ethnic and religious tensions in many northern cities led to outbreaks of violence, and in 2002 the ODPM launched its Housing Market Renewal Pathfinder Initiative to focus investment on demolishing houses deemed to be incapable of occupation, and replacing them with modern housing. This scheme was criticized for appearing to return to the bad practices of the 1960s, in which lives were disrupted by planning blight as habitable houses were condemned. The inequality between the cost of rehabilitation work, which attracts 17.5 per cent VAT, and new construction, which is zero-rated, was again pointed out as a wasteful and illogical discrepancy, but no serious action was taken to amend it.

Pathfinder may falter with Prescott's exit from power in 2006, but a scheme by Proctor Matthews for a small site, Dale Mill, in Rochdale indicates the approach taken to

> provide a robust and high-quality urban design framework that balances key issues such as housing density with increased internal space provision and the creation of attractive external spaces providing clear definitions between public, private and communal space.

Gordon Cullen's Townscape theories were cited in the competition-winning report, indicating that a picturesque approach has enduring persuasiveness.

There are other circularities and persistent themes apparent here. Comparing this situation with 1900, the problem of providing adequate housing in cities, supported by a physical environment and public realm attractive and affordable enough to stabilize populations and draw investment, remains as far beyond the scope of immediate solution by architecture and planning professionals as it was then. There are new energy-based arguments in favour of more concentrated populations, although the decline of agriculture has created social problems in rural areas since the late 1990s.

There is a concerted attempt, almost for the first time in 100 years, to persuade people in Britain that urban living is preferable, despite the conviction revealed in a survey in 2002 that 80 per cent of people would sooner choose to live in a bungalow.

chapter seven

Difference: Local Action and Global Thought

'Since the 1970s there has been a sense of crisis about what it has meant to be British', wrote the historian Paul Ward.[1] It is now widely understood that Britain is not a natural 'nation', but an agglomeration of individual nations, of which England is the largest and economically most powerful. The rise of Britain in its final form has been linked to the imperatives of imperial expansion, and the decline of Britain's status as a world economic and military power since 1945 has in turn been reflected in the pressure to restore greater autonomy to the parts that Ward calls 'Outer Britain': Scotland, Wales and Northern Ireland. Each of these has an individual history in relation to England and the construction of the 'United Kingdom of Great Britain and Ireland', dating in its most complete form from the Act of Union with Ireland of 1801 and in its present form from 1922. This story has become an especially important aspect of the late twentieth and early twenty-first centuries, with the European Union diminishing the economic and legislative hold of the London government. In spite of globalization and the rise of a multi-cultural society in England, or perhaps because of it, the definition of English identity has become a matter of widespread discussion, based on anxiety that it might not exist, or that, once found, would prove unattractive and unfitted for the modern world. While national identity has become a positive attribute for architecture in 'Outer Britain', for England it remains largely unarticulated, despite a widespread feeling that it has played a part in the Modern Movement.

Modern architecture is an inherently paradoxical medium through which to study national identity, since modernity implies a levelling of cultural differences through technology and the flow of information and populations. On the other hand, the historian Robin Okey claims that 'industrialisation and the emancipation of suppressed ethnic groups are the twin shaping themes of modern European history, and far from being antagonistic they have proved largely complementary'.[2] Not only in architecture, but also in the whole tendency of culture, the rediscovery of local difference has been a form of resistance to modernization, and also a way of rescuing Modernism from periodic crises of

O'Donnell and Tuomey,
Blackwood Golf Club,
Clandeboye, Co. Down,
1992–4.

credibility. The dangers for the creative artist should not be underestimated, yet the poet and painter David Jones was a passionate enquirer
for the spirit of Welshness, while fearing that any attempt to differenti-
ate Welsh culture would be

> either a dubious difference, a mere propagandist difference, or
> something imposed by purely utilitarian motives, unintegrated
> and thin, and, of course, peculiarly loveless, though no doubt of
> the highest efficiency and the product of considerable combined
> intelligence and most careful experimentation.[3]

The paradox of regional Modernism is that regional authenticity must
be sought in the study of the past. Iorwerth Peate's book *The Welsh
House* (1940) was a major contribution to understanding Welsh vernacular, where, in the words of Greg Stevenson, he proposed, as Finns, Poles
and Hungarians had done for their countries in the 1890s, that 'Welsh
architecture was in fact the vernacular architecture of Wales, rather than
the architect-designed polite architecture that was largely influenced
from outside'.[4] 'We have suffered from a perverted creed of progress and
utilitarianism' wrote George Scott-Moncrieff in 1952 of development in
Scotland.[5]

Is regionalism always and necessarily a conservative tendency, or does
it offer a different and better modernity from which to derive a critical
regionalist architecture? Is regionalism simply another way of saying
'provincialism', with its implication of lagging behind the centre and
receiving each phase of Modernism too late? Sometimes this seems to
be the case, but 'high-end' architecture has a long history of mobility.
Buildings in Dublin and Edinburgh at the end of the eighteenth century
were perhaps 'in advance' of London, but maybe the decline of autocratic
patronage created a greater effect of time lag in the twentieth century,
despite improved communications. At the beginning of this book, we
saw how the geographical margins were the earliest places in Britain to
manifest major technological change in building construction around
1900. Aesthetically, a few trend-breakers have occurred in the interven-
ing years, but only Dublin has a consistent record of getting 'ahead' with
buildings such as Busáras, the central bus station by Michael Scott
(1956), and later works by his practice. Conversely, there have been times,
such as the late 1930s and the 1970s, when loss of confidence in the high
Modernism of the centre gave the periphery the opportunity to become
the avant-garde by offering the return of lost architectural meaning.
Beyond the particularity of a single region, moreover, lies a generic and
transferable sense of identity that has enabled modern architecture to

respond to place in a non-literal way and thus resolve the paradox of 'backwards' and 'forwards'.

Broadly speaking, therefore, the study of regional Modernism includes the universal and the particular, and neither can be assumed to dominate. It has been generally agreed that literature and, to a lesser extent, music have provided the dominant artistic media through which 'Outer Britain' has debated and celebrated its identity, while the contribution of architecture has been less clear-cut. Scotland is the exception, for Scottish architects have achieved international significance for centuries while retaining aspects of their national identity, but even well-informed English people might have difficulty in naming a single Welsh or Northern Irish architect.

The economic realities of the nations within Great Britain during the twentieth century have contributed to the inequalities. Architectural development normally arises where the money is, and Scotland, Wales and Northern Ireland all suffered from having grown in the nineteenth century on a relatively narrow base of heavy industry. Their rural areas remained much less developed than in England during this time. The sharp decline of their 'traditional' industries after the First World War led to crises of unemployment and emigration in the 1930s. Architecturally, Scotland, the largest of the three countries, suffered least. Its architectural culture was institutionally strong, with two schools of architecture in both Glasgow and Edinburgh, and further schools in Dundee and Aberdeen, all founded before 1914. The Welsh School of Architecture in Cardiff was founded in 1923, and the Department of Architecture at Queen's University, Belfast, only in 1965, prior to which many Ulster architects trained at Liverpool.

In political history, each country has had a different relationship to England. Wales has the longest history of political union, dating from 1536, and entered the modern world (in its widest sense) without separate laws or institutions. On the other hand, the Welsh language survived as a spoken vernacular far more widely than Gaelic in Scotland, becoming the chief symbol of separate identity, together with sporting and musical activities; and Nonconformist worship, evidenced by the number of large chapels in Welsh towns and villages, may have influenced the priority given in the culture to music and the word. Separate legal and educational systems in Scotland have provided a basis for difference from England since the formal Union of 1707, and language mostly in respect of dialect. Nationalism in both Scotland and Wales had strong historic links with religious independence, which in turn gave common cause with the labour movement, all associated with the perception that religious, political and capitalist oppression had their origin in the London parliament, where Liberal and later Labour governments depended on the support of Scottish and Welsh MPs. The landed and governing classes in each country, both indigenous and immigrant, were anglicized in speech, religion and career opportunities, but were in some cases stronger advocates for their countries of origin than the local population.

Ireland was placed under the English crown in 1542, but the north resisted English rule until a programme of devastation was followed by colonial 'plantation' in 1607, resulting in the establishment of a Protestant loyalist population locally that held economic and political advantage and was anxious not to be cast adrift from London. Following decades of agitation for Irish Home Rule, culminating in the Easter Rising in Dublin of 1916 and the military conflicts of the immediate post-war years, the southern and greater part of Ireland achieved independence by a series of steps, leaving the 'six counties' of Ulster with their dominant Protestant population hardened by conflict and resistance, as part of the reduced United Kingdom in 1920, possessed, unlike Wales or Scotland, of its own parliament. Northern Ireland not surprisingly looked more to England for its culture, architecture included, than to Dublin, where the vigour of the Georgian and Victorian local school was in abeyance. The principal building of Belfast at the start of the new century, the City Hall, was won in competition by Alfred Brumwell Thomas, a London architect, in 1896, and completed ten years later. The commission to create buildings for a new parliament at Stormont went to a Liverpool architect, Arnold Thornley, in the competition of 1923, in what was seen at the time as the international style of Franco-American classicism, in white Portland stone. In this it resembled the local government and national cultural buildings in Cathays Park, Cardiff, from 1897 onwards, the first of which to be the work of Welsh-based architects was the Cardiff Technical College in 1912 by Ivor Jones and Percy Thomas. This was the beginning of Thomas's career as the principal architect in Wales, whose influence extended to London and the RIBA presidency. The practice continued after his death in 1969, making a shift into Modernism after the Second World War.

Neither of these commissions stimulated any debate about appropriateness of style, as did the design of Imperial Delhi by Sir Edwin Lutyens in 1910. Although Charles Rennie Mackintosh showed how Scottish building styles could be abstracted to make antecedents for Modernism, and although a self-conscious adoption of regional styles formed a basis for Scottish architecture for more than 100 years prior to 1900, they would have seemed a retrograde step for any major institutional building. In the early years of the twentieth century, Sir Robert Lorimer, a more conservative adapter of national tradition, was the dominant influence rather than Mackintosh, but his influence waned with the onset of Modernism. The competition for St Andrew's House, Edinburgh, the northern headquarters of the London-based Scottish Office, was a marker in replacing any outmoded call for a literal Scottish style with the idea, after three years of lobbying against a proposal by the London-based government architect, that, regardless of style, the competition in 1933 should be open only to Scottish architects, who were presumed to be able to capture the essence of Scottishness as nobody else could. In the House of Commons, the popular writer John Buchan warned: 'we are in danger very soon of reaching the point where Scotland will have nothing distinctive to show the world'.[6] The competition winner was Thomas Tait of Burnet, Tait and Lorne, with impeccably Scottish credentials and an Edinburgh office, although the firm worked internationally and in a range of styles. While Tait's design has much to commend it, nothing about it is especially Scottish, and instead it belongs in the Art Deco style, as widely used after 1930 for entertainment and leisure buildings. Even the National Library of Scotland (1934–55), by the Arts and Crafts church architect Reginald Fairlie, was reticently stripped classical rather than attempting regional references.

By the 1930s Mackintosh was invoked as an alternative starting point, and in 1934 the architect Robert Hurd described a 'modern Scottish idiom', which he identified in Mackintosh, believing that 'freedom of design is a natural aptitude of a Scottish architect properly founded in his country's past architectural achievement'.[7] The Saltire Society, founded to encourage and recognize Scottish culture, gave building awards from 1937 onwards that recognized 'a quality of straightforwardness' rather than either Modernism or 'a proliferation of crowstep gables and wrought iron thistles', and it influenced the revival of non-literal regionalism after the war.[8] The Empire Exhibition at Glasgow in 1938 represented a transition between the stripped classicism of Wembley in 1924 and the levity of the Festival of Britain in 1951. Tait was appointed as architect-in-chief, and many younger designers were given opportunities, even if under the names of senior figures. The white buildings were broadly Art Deco, some tending to regional styles, some more modern, within the same range seen at the international exhibition in Paris in 1937. Spence contributed a model house for the Scottish Council for Art in a vernacular style, and there was a 'clachan' or traditional village, reproduced from plaster casts of authentic buildings. Apart from a few other self-consciously Scottish buildings, the issue of national identity was secondary to the desire to perform to an international standard. For J. M. Richards, the exhibition represented 'a whole-hearted acceptance of the spectacular as well as of the functional possibilities of the modern idiom'.[9]

Art Deco was as far as Modernism went in most provincial parts of the British Isles before 1945. The conviction with which it was handled was unlike the dilution in the name of good taste that often occurred in England, and showed how, since the late Victorian period, the greater the distance from London, the stronger the likelihood of American influence. Art Deco came via America from Paris, but one of its French masters, Rob Mallet-Stevens, apparently said: 'If I were God, I should design like Mackintosh', so that in one sense it was coming home.[10] It was the style of cinemas, where even the unemployed might enjoy warmth and comfort for a few hours. In Northern Ireland, three local cinema specialists emerged, John McBride Meill, Thomas McLean and Robert Sharpe Hill, who matched the sophistication of London designers. Their work has virtually disappeared.[11] The north coast of Wales, with its summer tourist economy, developed some spectacular holiday camps, such as Pontin's, Prestatyn. The local architect S. Colwyn Foulkes built restrained cinemas in Rhyl, as well as excellent housing. From time to time architects were able to abandon ornament and symmetry, and work in a fully developed Modern Movement style. The Rothesay Pavilion on the Isle of Bute by J. and J. A. Carrick (1936), a northern equivalent of the De La Warr Pavilion in its function and form, with a projecting bow at one end, is the most notable example. The Strangford Lough Yacht Club (see p. 59) is a smaller version of the same compositional theme. In Edinburgh, the St Cuthbert's Co-operative Association in Bread Street (1935), by T. P.

J. & J. A. Carrick,
Rothesay Pavilion,
Isle of Bute, Argyll
and Bute, 1936–8.

R. S. Wilshere,
Botanic Primary
School, Agincourt
Avenue, Belfast,
1939.

Marwick & Sons (see p. 46), was exceptional in the whole of Britain as a glass curtain wall standing forward from a concrete frame (now converted in an appropriately neo-Modernist style into the Point Hotel). At the Infectious Diseases Hospital, Paisley (1932–4), Burnet, Tait and Lorne built their most straightforwardly modern building anywhere to date. Schools in Scotland responded slowly to changing ideals of education, spreading in plan and reducing in height, with larger windows.[12] In Northern Ireland, R. S. Wilshere, education architect to the Belfast Corporation, progressed from neo-Georgian to the large metal-framed windows in brick walls seen at Botanic Primary School (1939). After the war, Wilshere was extensively involved in low-rise housing, and built schools using the 'Bristol system' with prefabricated aluminium section, produced locally by Shorts Aircraft.

Mackintosh's lead in converting the harled (rough plastered) surfaces of Scottish houses into abstract forms was followed by William Kininmonth and Basil Spence in the 1930s, with some inflexion from Continental Modernist models of the 1920s. In Wales, the few 'white Modernist' works were mainly by English practices, such as a flamboyant holiday house in Llandudno by Harry Weedon, the Birmingham cinema architect, for a Manchester baker. In Penarth, 5 Cliff Parade by Gordon Griffiths (1939) was a local product, like some of the English Modernist houses that looked to the Regency. In Northern Ireland, Bendhu, on the edge of the sea in Co. Antrim, a flat-roofed concrete house by Ben Cowser for the artist Newton Penprase (1936), was something of a one-off in its eccentricity.[13] In location and 'pioneering', it could be paralleled by the first white modern house south of the border, in a similar seaside location, Geragh, Sandycove, Co. Dublin (1936–7), by Ireland's leading Modernist, Michael Scott, for himself.

More than for England, the end of the Second World War marked the effective beginning of Modernism in 'Outer Britain'. Even this was a slow start, and Robert McKinstry recalled that 'in the comparatively cosy and certain little Ulster of the early fifties there were, as yet, very few buildings that could be called modern'.[14] This situation began to change with houses and other buildings by younger practitioners such as Henry Lynch-Robinson and Noel Campbell, whose Dhu Varren at Portrush (1958–9) and a house at Brocklamont Park, Ballymena, were outstanding, the former on the edge of the sea, the latter a cool Miesian pavilion enlivened with sculpture and murals out of doors.[15] Campbell never disdained the decorative aspects of 1950s Modernism, and the same can be said of Max Clendinning, a Belfast-born and trained architect with a speciality in all-white interiors in the 1960s, who was involved in the curved timber roof of Oxford Road Station, Manchester (1956–60). The most exceptional new churches in Northern Ireland, almost all Catholic on both sides of the border, were the work of Liam McCormick, who left Ireland to study in Liverpool in the 1930s. Between 1947 and his death in 1996, McCormick built churches of great variety and power. Some show the influence of Le Corbusier's Ronchamp rather strongly, but the principles of concealed

Noel Campbell, house at Brocklamont Park, Ballymena, Co. Antrim, 1959–60.

Liam McCormick,
Our Lady of Lourdes
Church, Steelstown
Road, Londonderry,
Co. Londonderry,
1976.

lighting and sculptural form were generalized, and local materials used to excellent effect.[16]

In Scotland, Basil Spence was the only pre-war Edinburgh practitioner to make a British national reputation, consolidated by his success in the Coventry Cathedral competition. His small project for Fishermen's Housing at Dunbar (1949–52) was a reversion to his pre-war vernacular, at which he was very adept. His Edinburgh office remained as Basil Spence, Glover and Ferguson, and was involved in buildings for Edinburgh University, Glasgow Airport and the notorious 'Queenies' or Hutcheson-town c housing in the Gorbals (see pp. 133–5). His Mortonhall Crematorium, Edinburgh (1967), was one of the few in the British Isles to aspire to the architectural dignity of similar buildings in Scandinavia through a generic white-walled vertical Scottishness. As a church architect, Spence was rivalled in Scotland by the spectacular run of buildings by

Sir Basil Spence,
Glover and Ferguson,
Mortonhall Crema-
torium, Edinburgh,
1967.

Isi Metzstein and Andy MacMillan from Gillespie, Kidd and Coia, although they shared Spence's talent for theatrical effects.

Robert Matthew, a contemporary of Spence's, returned home to Edinburgh from the LCC in 1953 and established a large practice, adding an English dimension through his partnership in 1956 with another ex-public-sector architect, Stirrat Johnson Marshall, although they operated virtually as separate entities. Matthew continued to build the kind of housing he had admired in Sweden, and encouraged at Alton East – individual towers set in a romantic landscape. Spence's ability to operate equally on both sides of the border was matched by Robert Matthew, whose firm grew to international dimensions. In Edinburgh, the Royal Commonwealth Pool (1970; project architect John Richards) was a serious building, and Richard Murphy later commented: 'In these days of exotic plastic leisure centres, the dignified restraint of this design is a lasting relief'.[17] Spence's former

Peter Womersley,
Group Practice
Consulting Rooms,
Kelso, Roxburghshire,
1967.

associate, William Kininmonth, remained an Edinburgh figure, taking over
the supremely establishment practice of Rowand Anderson and Paul, and
showing a proto-Postmodernist ability to swing in and out of Modernism
at will, including a tough but well-integrated urban infill, the Scottish
Provident Institution Head Office in Edinburgh (1968).

An English-born architect, Peter Womersley (1923–1993), made a
significant contribution to architecture in Scotland following his first
and widely publicized house at Farnley Hey in Yorkshire (1954). Without
being connected to any of the networks of the time, Womersley found
his own way to developing architectural forms. Working mostly on his
own, he designed further memorable private houses, but also health
buildings, such as the admired doctors' group surgery at Kelso (1967),
one of the few to show any direct Scottish character. In other respects,

his work helps to build up an image of Scotland in the 1960s as a country with good opportunities for patronage and a planning system that did not get in the way.

In Wales, the Percy Thomas Partnership became the dominant single office in the more populated and prosperous south, with Thomas's son becoming involved with and welcoming the up-to-date contribution of the Welsh-born Dale Owen on his return from the USA, where he had worked for Walter Gropius and The Architects Collaborative, in the late 1950s. Owen designed the BBC headquarters in Llandaff (1967), which has nothing distinctly Welsh about it, but is a bold and clean statement in the language of strong horizontal banding then in use by the two Basil Spence offices in Edinburgh and London. He went on to design the Great Hall and Bell Tower for University College, Aberystwyth (1970), a more romantic concept, comparable in grandeur to work by Jørn Utzon. Northern Ireland depended more on London-based designers to create some its most modern buildings, such as the Belfast Synagogue of 1961–4 by Yorke Rosenberg Mardall and their Altnagelvin Hospital (1949–60), a twelve-storey slab sited on a hill top, distinguished by works of art by William Scott and F. E. McMillan, both Ulster artists in origin. The extension to the Ulster Museum by Francis Pym (1963–71) was the sole major work by this London-based architect, who resigned from the job in 1966, but a very remarkable one, responding to an unfinished inter-war classical building by clasping it in a composition of concrete planes in relief, planned internally as an upward spiral journey, more

Percy Thomas Partnership (Dale Owen), Great Hall and Bell Tower, University of Wales College, Aberystwyth, Ceredigion, 1970.

Francis Pym,
extension to the
Ulster Museum,
Belfast, 1963–71.

like recent projects by Zaha Hadid than the Guggenheim Museum in
New York with its similar circulation system. There is nothing intrinsi-
cally Northern Irish about this, apart from the apparent freedom to
'keep in keeping' in a non-literal way, which might not have been possible in London, even at this high period of experimental freedom.[18] The
construction period ran into the time of 'The Troubles' in Northern
Ireland, when the Catholic minority community began to protest
against their situation, initially in the wake of the Civil Rights movement
in the USA. This interrupted a wave of modernization that was beginning to produce new buildings for new institutions. Since the mid-1960s
the architecture of the province has been irrevocably marked by the
fluctuating but never fully resolved conflict. The new University of
Ulster at Coleraine, founded in 1963 and constructed between 1968 and
1977 to designs by Robert Matthew, Johnson-Marshall, joined the same
firm's universities at Stirling, the only completely new campus in
Scotland, and York, a severe design composed mainly of three- and four-

storey blocks with regular window mullions. The new town of Craigavon, designated in 1965, was built to link existing towns on the southern edge of the large inland Lough Neagh, but the onset of the 'Troubles' reduced population growth and left housing uninhabited, until after 2000, when some parts were redeveloped.

Given the confidence in Modernism's international claims, it is not surprising to find that the 1960s was the decade in which national differences were least considered. Writing in 1962, Patrick Nuttgens suggested that, in contrast to the 1930s, 'the problem of being Scottish, which tangled up a lot of good architects of an earlier generation, has probably given way to the greater need of being wholly alive and a part of the world', citing the pithead colliery buildings in Fife by the former Bauhaus student Egon Riss in the 1950s, the new work of Gillespie, Kidd

Egon Riss, Rothes Colliery, Kirkcaldy, Fife, 1957.

Graham Brooks,
The Capel House,
Llandaff, Cardiff,
1966.

and Coia, and the effect of Robert Matthew on changing official taste, becoming 'the almost automatic choices for universities and hospitals'.[19] In 1977 Peter Willis praised the recently completed Bridgegate House and shopping centre in Irvine new town by the Development Corporation's architects (1976), which crossed the river previously dividing two parts of the town. While associating this with American inspiration, Willis felt that it exemplified the 'imaginative, not to say spatial aspect of recent Scottish architecture'.[20]

Private houses were a medium for mildly regionalist experiments, in the prolific work of firms such as Law & Dunbar-Naismith and Morris and Steedman. In Wales, Capel House, Llandaff (1966), by Graham Brooks, is an example of the simple but sensitive work of the period. Ian Campbell's house overlooking Belfast Lough consists of two linked wings at right angles to each other, each with monopitch roofs, similar in this respect to Dewi-Prys Thomas's Entwood at Birkenhead (1959), a study in extrapolating from the Welsh vernacular, accidentally situated across the border in the Wirral.[21] In the 1960s and '70s there was a generic regional Modernism that could be found in any of the areas of 'Outer Britain' and in England as well, thus complicating any claims for its unique relationship to any single nation or landscape. The similarities are owed to the generic qualities of 'upland' vernacular in the whole northern and western areas of the islands, where materials were historically scarce and often limited to hard and intractable stones that benefited from a whitewashed render coat. As abstract forms, these lent themselves well to construction with concrete block, and matched modern needs and sensibilities, with the insertion of larger windows and split-roof pitches, letting light into the centre of the plan, a device popularized by a group of houses at Klampenborg, Denmark, by Arne Jacobsen of 1947–55.[22] Their influence on architects looking for non-literal ways of interpreting vernacular can be seen in the Fair-a-Far housing at Cramond, West Lothian, by Philip Cocker and Partners (1973).

In Northern Ireland, high-rise housing was much used as a solution to slum clearance, and much of it has since been demolished.[23] In Wales, Swansea Council commissioned thirteen tower blocks in 1961, in contrast to the cottages and low flats that characterized Welsh public housing, but vandalism and letting difficulties followed soon after, and no more were built.[24] Scotland had four new towns, at East Kilbride, Glenrothes, Irvine and Cumbernauld, all designed for Glasgow 'overspill', the last being the only one to achieve widespread architectural fame. In Wales, Cwmbran, between Newport and Pontypool, was designated in 1947 and begun in 1952, on a hilly site, with terraces and closes of housing.

As well as welcoming Modernism, Nuttgens believed that 'the Scots . . . have not let it arrive without a protest. Or let it in unscathed.'[25] He attributed this to the extreme weather, which in turn limited the range of effective building materials. With Art Deco and classicism *démodé*, vernacular provided an alternative that was popular and practical. Chessel's Court (1958–67), by Robert Hurd and Ian Begg, was an infill development on the south side of Edinburgh's historic Canongate, not unlike the rebuilding of many bombed historic German city centres. Ian Nairn recognized the success of Wheeler and Sprowson's more abstracted urban renewal schemes in Kirkcaldy, in which 'the old rhythms have been caught and effortlessly translated'.[26] The Small Houses Scheme launched in the historic seaside towns of Fife by the National Trust for Scotland shared the same approach, preserving historic buildings as cultural yeast for sustaining a community in relatively remote places and finding modern equivalents to fill the gaps between them. The idea began before the war, and was carried forward with imagination, becoming a 'revolving fund' that covered its own costs.[27]

Arguably, regional consciousness in architecture rose and fell in much the same cycle during the course of the century in the Cotswolds or Cornwall as it did in Ceredigion or Caithness, but the dissolution of the

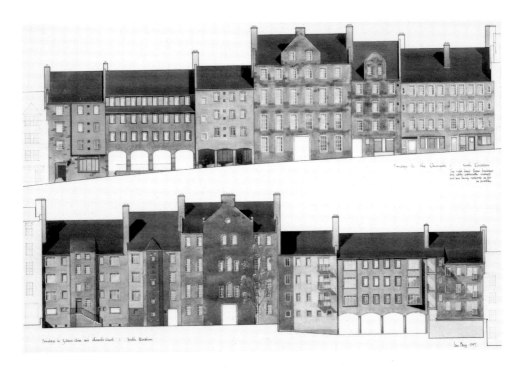

Robert Hurd and
Partners, Chessel's
Court redevelopment,
Canongate,
Edinburgh, 1957.

Modern Movement at the end of the 1960s coincided with an unprecedented rise in political awareness among the Scots and Welsh. Nationalist
parties came and went before 1970, but the Westminster parliament was
unperturbed by them. By March 1979, however, the situation had changed
to the point where devolution for Scotland and Wales with separate elected assemblies was put to a referendum, although it failed to pass according to the demanding criteria imposed. In both countries, artists of all
kinds felt that they had a role in raising national self-consciousness. In
Cardiff in the 1960s, Dewi-Prys Thomas would show students a slide of
the Acropolis, followed by one of a simple stone barn on a Welsh hillside,
and simply say: 'look at the stone'. As Peter Lord wrote, 'Dewi-Prys's gift to
his students was to enable many of them to understand this and to sense
the implications for their lives as architects', going on to qualify that 'sensing the genius loci is about sensing people not about the kitsch manifestation of the new idolatry of the nature'.[28] Pencadlys Gwynedd, the county
offices in Caernarfon (1980–85), was an attempt to create a building that
'historically might have been there for the previous two or three centuries',
where in the opinion of many Dewi-Prys failed to avoid the risk of kitsch
in architectural style, although the urban form of the building, in the
historic centre of the town rather than on a green-field site, was exemplary

Merfyn H. Roberts and Dewi-Prys Thomas, Pencadlys Gwynedd, Caernarfon, 1983.

in matching the progressive spirit of the time. As Richard Weston has commented, '"national" expressions are not passed on in the genes or consciously designed, but rationalised post facto out of a mass of conflicting evidence'.[29] In Scotland, Hurd's partner Ian Begg continued the picturesque style of Chessel's Court with more rather than less historical conviction, even though his Cathedral Visitor Centre in Glasgow (1990) was known derisively as 'Fort Weetabix'. Modernism balanced regionalism in the scales to produce the Plas Menai outdoor sports centre by Bowen Dann Davies (1977–82), not far away from Pencadlys, which has been considered a greater success, lying low in the mountain-backed vista across the Menai Straits, beneath slate roofs, with chunky stone and timber inside and out, 'the most persuasive built manifesto of the search for a Welsh architecture'.[30] The Ben Lawers Mountain Visitor Centre, Perthshire (1973), by Moira and Moira, is an equivalent Scottish building in use and style. In Cardiff, the new buildings for the Museum of Welsh Life at St Fagans (1968–81), by Dale Owen, were more Modernist than vernacular. The Northern Irish equivalent, Ferguson and Mcilveen's Ulster Folk and Transport Museum (1980), tips the balance the other way.

These examples might give a false impression that Modernism was always on the back foot after 1970. Some significant buildings continued themes from the 1960s, such as the Department of Music at University College, Cardiff (1970), by Alex Gordon and Partners; the Welsh Industrial and Maritime Museum, Cardiff (1977), by Burgess and Partners; the Portadown Technical College, Co. Armagh (1976), by Shanks, Leighton, Kennedy and FitzGerald; the Dundee Repertory Theatre (1982) by Nicoll Russell: and the headquarters for Distillers Company, Edinburgh (1984), by RMJM. These were at the end of their line, however, for when Modernism returned, the starting point was more self-consciously contextual and referential. The difference is highlighted by Malcolm Fraser, a leading Edinburgh architect, recalling the bankruptcy of the discipline 'under the burden of its hubris', exemplified in a speech by Robert Matthew in 1977 in which he claimed: 'there is not a single social or industrial problem of

Richard Rogers and Partners, Inmos Microprocessor Factory, Newport, Gwent, 1982.

importance that can be solved without new buildings, often on a vast scale'.[31]

The election of the Conservative government in May 1979 led to terminal collapse of the surviving heavy industries, coal, steel and shipbuilding. By the end of the 1980s, there were more Welshmen working in banks than in coal mines, and such new jobs as existed were found in new, cleaner technology, often in Japanese companies. One of these was Inmos Microprocessor, whose factory at Newport was the first to make silicon chips in Britain. It was designed by Richard Rogers in 1982 and boasted a highly serviced dust-free environment, as well as an eye-catching exterior. In Scotland, North Sea oil arrived in time to provide new economic resources, while Glasgow, described in a book title as 'the city that refused to die', began to direct its regeneration towards conservation rather than blindly destructive redevelopment.[32] The marketing campaign 'Glasgow's Miles Better' in the early 1980s branded the city and marketed it for tourism. Mackintosh, whose buildings the city council had been happy to demolish for years, became an integral part of the brand. The Cardiff Bay Development Corporation, established in 1987, presided over a mixture of conversions and relatively undistinguished new building, until the Welsh capacity for architectural patronage was tested and found wanting with the Welsh Opera House competition in 1994, in which Zaha Hadid's design was selected and then discarded in favour of spending money on a new rugby stadium. 'Instead of living with the world's great cities, we had opted for provincialism', as Stephen Evans wrote.[33] Cardiff therefore missed its opportunity for a 'Bilbao effect' through a single landmark building. In Edinburgh, the Royal Scottish Museum extension (1991–8), by Benson and Forsyth, fulfilled multiple symbolic purposes, as a building to represent the history of Scotland while explaining it through objects, and as a demonstration that Modernism was alive despite lack of support from the Prince of Wales, which temporarily threatened the project. While the language was Modernist, the meaning was Postmodernist in its layering of reference and significance, responding to the sense among architects that the public would be pacified provided that every gesture carried an explanation.

Zaha Hadid, competition design for the Welsh Opera House, Cardiff, 1994.

In an opinion poll of 1992, 50 per cent of Scots favoured independence for Scotland. Devolution was part of New Labour's promise of local autonomy and the reduction of central power in Tony Blair's election campaign of 1997, and a new referendum on devolution in September produced a vote of 74 per cent in favour of a Scottish parliament. A simultaneous referendum in Wales produced a small but sufficient majority in favour of a Welsh assembly. In both cases, existing historic buildings were adapted to enable the assemblies to meet, but there was a strong desire for new buildings to symbolize these historic changes. In both cases, the process of completing the buildings was far from smooth. Each went far above its original budget and timescale, attracting predictable criticism. Neither was designed by an architect with local connections. The Scottish Parliament, on a site near Holyroodhouse, the historic royal palace in Edinburgh, was strongly supported by the First Minister, Donald Dewar, who, like the Catalan architect Enric Miralles, did not live to see it completed. The choice was appropriate for Scotland's historic links with mainland Europe and its aspiration to emulate Barcelona in bringing economic success in the wake of independence, manifested in and generated by popular modern architecture.

Benson & Forsyth, extension to the Scottish National Museum, Chambers Street, Edinburgh, 1991–8.

Like the Royal Scottish Museum, this design was heavily metaphorical, although never too literal. As Miralles wrote,

EMBT (Enrico Miralles
and Benedetta
Tagliabue) with RMJM,
Scottish Parliament,
Edinburgh,
1999–2004.

The parliament should be able to reflect the land which it
represents. The land itself will be a material, a physical
building material. From the outset we have worked with
the intuition that individual identification with land carries
collective consciousness and sentiments.[34]

'We had lost the intuitive, the letting go, that change of consciousness
that is necessary to rediscover the poetic', wrote Neil Gillespie of the
finished building, 'Miralles, acting as our shaman, recovers a sense of
place.'[35] This attention to place was as major a theme for the late
twentieth century as it had been for the late nineteenth, neatly brack-
eting the international Modern Movement. What had once been the
preoccupation of the sensitive few at the fringes became a mainstream issue not only in architecture but also in the fine arts, film and
literature.

268

Frank Gehry, Maggie's Centre, Dundee, 2003.

The counter-puritan jollity of the Parliament and its international star quality are shared by a contemporary project, Maggie's Centres, a series of cancer-care buildings devised before her death by Maggie Keswick Jencks, the wife of the critic Charles Jencks, whose roots were in the lowlands of Scotland, as a result of which the first examples have been built in Scotland. Architects have included Frank Gehry (Dundee, 2003, his first project in the British Isles) and Zaha Hadid (Kirkcaldy, opened 2006), as well as leading Scottish architects such as Richard Murphy (Edinburgh) and Page & Park (Glasgow). At a time when healthcare buildings have been sucked backwards into utilitarianism as a result of the constraints of the Private Finance Initiative (PFI), these buildings have shown what can be achieved with a little more cost and imagination. During the second half of the 1990s, the bounty of the national lottery was deliberately directed away from south-east England, and fell on Scotland, Wales and Northern Ireland alike, giving the opportunity for major arts and heritage projects, with special European funding available in the more remote and underprivileged areas. The Festival of Architecture in Glasgow in 1999 was a skilfully managed event, recalling the same city's year as European City of Culture in 1990. The Scottish Executive issued *A Policy on Architecture in Scotland*, which recommended a campaign of public education (similar to CABE's in England), attempting to get beyond the gap dividing a handful of 'star' buildings and the mass of undistinguished ones.

The relative lack of confidence in the transformative capacity of architecture in Wales in the past has not been entirely lost, although the past ten years have given a stronger indication than any previous decade that it might be changing. As well as the loss of the Opera House, a scheme by David Chipperfield for the Mid Wales Arts Centre at Powys Castle fell apart in 1996 when the local council failed to commit to its share of funding. The architect commented; 'The people of Welshpool are losing out on £8 million of investment into one of the poorest areas of Europe for the sake of local politics. It is completely irresponsible behaviour.'[36] Despite such cold-footedness, the Welsh-based architect David Lea believed that Wales's position might augur well for the future, through focus not only on local materials as a form of symbolic decoration, but also as part of a sustainable way of living:

our small and energetic population inhabits a magnificent green landscape capable of providing almost everything required for a wonderful quality of life: clothing, food, shelter, tools, and energy. Agenda 21 frameworks arising from the Rio Summit offer the opportunity to being these resources into a creative relationship.[37]

Wales is also the home of Christopher Day, an architect known for his books about building in harmony with nature and human feeling, partly based on the architectural traditions of Rudolf Steiner. Day's Steiner kindergarten at Nant-y-Cwm, near Llancefyn, Dyfed (*c.* 1990), made the material aspects of a building inseparable from its intention to create feeling, and much of the work was done by hand by volunteers.

Day's buildings, or Lea's usually more conventionally architectural ones, might seem a paradigm for an architecture in touch with the Welsh landscape, but their search was far from unique in Europe, and by the mid-1990s there were examples that combined this impulse with a recognizable line of modern architecture. In *Touchstone*, a magazine whose foundation coincided with the new wave of devolutionary enthusiasm, Adam Voelcker wrote of Peter Zumthor's Thermal Baths at Vals in Switzerland, with its abundant use of local slate, that in future Welsh buildings might match its level of sophisticated contact with the elements, 'with maybe some better architects and an improved competition

Christopher Day,
Nant-y-Cwm school,
near Llancefyn,
Dyfed, c. 1990.

Richard Rogers
Partnership, The
Welsh Assembly,
Cardiff Bay, 2006.

track record'. Yet, as he went on, it would take more to level the national differences, including a less subservient attitude to safety and 'the whole formulaic mentality into which we seem to have become locked'.[38]

The Welsh Assembly building was the subject of a selection process in 1998 for the same site as the Opera House, facing onto Cardiff Bay. Compared to Edinburgh, there was a less intense sense of context. It was won by Richard Rogers Partnership with a scheme similar in some respects to their Law Courts at Bordeaux and the European Court of Human Rights at Strasbourg. Some changes came into the design as security concerns heightened after the attack of 11 September 2001 on the World Trade Center in New York, so that the idea of transparency, which is represented in the glass box enclosing the chamber, beneath its overhanging roof, is not transmitted through the actual way that the people are allowed to enter the building. The Assembly opened early in 2006. Welshness was sought through the use of a slate plinth for the building, while the oak underside of the canopy, rising in the centre to

cover the debating chamber in a dome with an air-extract cowl, is the most visible surface material. While the cost increases, the time delays and the transfer to a Design and Build contract in 2002 all contributed to controversy, the general reception of the building was positive.

This cannot be said for the Wales Millennium Centre on the adjoining site, which was a substitute for the cancelled Opera House, offering a space not only for opera but also musicals and a circus. The designer was Jonathan Adams of the Percy Thomas Partnership, who was Welsh by parentage if not upbringing. Here he introduced a symbolic quality that he felt was lacking from the Assembly. From most angles, bands of slate forming flanking walls are highly visible. From these emerges the large shell of the auditorium, clad in stainless steel, with a giant inscription cut away to create window openings in the shape of letters. It may seem like a parody of an 'icon building', although the foyers inside are less insistently representational and their undulating balconies are reminiscent of Aalto. Comparing the two buildings, one may feel that nationalism in architecture has failed to win its case, and may fall out of favour as fast as it did following the National Romantic phase in European architecture a century before.

In Northern Ireland, nothing so dramatic has been attempted, wisely perhaps, given the emotive connotations of nationhood. Instead, there have been a number of projects that have shared in the growing architectural sophistication of the Republic of Ireland, especially following the economic boom of the 'Celtic Tiger' period in the 1990s. In addition to the Waterfront Hall (see p. 234), Belfast enjoyed its own Modernist revival, with buildings such as the Central Fire Station, Bankmore Street (1991), and the Glenveagh School, Harberton Park (1993), by Kennedy Fitzgerald and Associates, who were also the designers of the new St Brigid's Roman Catholic Church (1996–7). Taken together, these designs cover a similar expressive range to those of Michael Hopkins. The regeneration of the riverside area where the Waterfront Hall provided the focus has included the high-tech Hamilton Building (1995–6) by Christopher Campbell Architects, and the more traditional Clarendon House (1998), by Knox and Maxwell. The Dublin architects Sheila O'Donnell and John Tuomy designed the Blackwood Golf Club at Clandeboye, Co. Down (1992–4), which, in its deliberate breaking down into parts, reminded Shane O'Toole of 'the ancient and sacred acropolis of Cashel', the seat of kings and bishops for 900 years. In Armagh, often the site of modern conflict, the architects Glen Howells, based in Birmingham and London, contributed a new theatre and arts centre, completed in 2000, which was acclaimed for respecting the civic context and avoiding 'spurious notions of a regional vernacular', continuing the austere and colourless classicism of some of its historic neighbours.[39] It offered an escape into cosmopolitan sophistication, in this context one of Modernism's positive assets.

With such generally optimistic reports coming from Outer Britain, how does England consider itself in relation to possessing a national

Christopher Campbell Architects, Hamilton Building, Belfast, 1995–6.

style of modern architecture? On the one hand, it is usually convenient for architects to assert their interest in locality, since it has now become an approved concept in planning regulation. How it is to be achieved is a less certain matter, beyond the literal replication of materials and building forms often demanded by planning committees with results that seldom justify the effort. Since Pevsner's *The Englishness of English Art* in 1956, no attempt at a general theory of Englishness has been attempted, and the simplicity of his visually based criteria would probably be deemed superficial if reworked. Pevsner noted the ways in which English medieval cathedrals differed in plan form and aesthetic intention from French ones, even in a period when architecture and religion were more international than they have ever been since. He noted a divorce between structure and ornament and a tendency to achieve expression through excessive length or height. These characteristics could be clues to the English problem with Modernism, at least in its guise as an architecture of structural reason, subordinated and rationalized ornament, and essentially classical aesthetics of balance, not that modern architecture in Europe or America has necessarily conformed to these criteria at all times.

Another long-term trend that is relevant is the way that England has been a net importer of architectural ideas at almost all times. Admittedly, its forms of pre-modern timber framing are completely distinctive, suggesting the possibility of a national style, but in the realm of polite architecture the traffic across the Channel has been one way.[40] This argument has often been used in defence or extenuation of Modernism's apparent alien invasion in the twentieth century. Thus John Summerson wrote in 1946:

> from time to time, in all the arts, the English have developed an enormous appetite for foreign influence; its immediate effect has sometimes been slightly irrelevant, but it has invariably stimulated new vitality and creation.[41]

On the other hand, if one were to accept that the abstract and plain qualities of Modernism were alien to the national character of design in England, one would have to exclude the powerful and enduring consequences of the religious Reformation from the Tudor period onwards. This also was a European movement, originating with Luther in Germany and Zwingli and Calvin in Switzerland, but it transformed the look of English and Scottish places of worship. By the time of Oliver Cromwell in the mid-seventeenth century, almost all signs of sacred representation had been effaced, and plain white walls were considered the proper and least distracting context in which to fix one's attention on the abstractions of divinity through the ministry of the word. What David Brett has called 'The Plain Style', founded on prejudice against the decorative excesses of the Counter-Reformation in Catholic Europe, have been the symbols of good citizenship, masculine virtue and moral integrity ever since, a code shared equally with North America. The history of styles in England partly consists of an ebb and flow between the plain and the fancy, frequently combined with moral and religious justifications for each position. When King Edward VII, one of the least overtly moral monarchs in English history, finally succeeded his mother, Queen Victoria, in 1901, one of his first actions was nonetheless to paint the polychrome interiors of Buckingham Palace in white. Thus Modernism arrived in England at a time when plainness was in the ascendancy, although its revolutionary intentions prevented its rapid or complete adoption by cautious and conventional people.

These qualities could be linked to the satisfaction felt by English people in denying their intellectualism. Perry Anderson attributes the lack of systematic thought in the cultural field to the fact that while mainland Europe followed Roman law after the 'Dark Ages', with its basis in principle, English law has been based on precedent. Consequently, European education was based on abstract reasoning, while English was empirical and pragmatic, and all our major twentieth-century thinkers have been *émigrés*.[42] By extension, it is not uncommon to claim, as Summerson did, that in architecture we need a periodic boost of foreign logic along with the strong coffee to set the sluggish and muddled English mind in motion. Stefan Collini has recently questioned the truth of anti-intellectualism in England, arguing that our conception of Frenchmen endlessly discussing philosophy in cafés before declaiming truth from the barricades is a caricature, as is the comforting sense of isolation adopted by those in England who identify themselves as a lost tribe of thinkers.[43] Despite the apparent ascendancy of London as a world centre for architecture, the paradigm of English stupidity is certainly alive in architectural discussion in 2006. Thus David Chipperfield, who has largely built overseas, complains that

> the big difference between working in Britain and Europe is that here, you are not really expected to debate ideas. Money and marketing are what matters most . . . Original thinking and debate have been overwhelmed. So we get a lot of slick and often thoughtless architecture put up at speed. It doesn't matter much how it works, but how it looks, and whether or not it fits the latest fashion profile.[44]

Like Chipperfield, and other typical intellectuals in internal exile, Tony Fretton is homesick for another country, and says that being based in London

> only works if you get on an aeroplane and get out of England with its nonsensical planning system and lack of architectural leadership and courage, and the declining intelligence of the institutions that surround architecture.[45]

The metaphorical notion that Modernism is a definite destination as simple to reach as Zurich or Berlin can be comforting, for the complaints about England are not unjustified. Yet its reification in aesthetic or technical terms has been the cause of previous overreaching and breakdown. Deborah Saunt, on the other hand, suggests that the oyster of English Modernism needs the irritant of an adverse culture to produce its pearls, praising Fretton's ability 'to assimilate contradiction without compromise, and to see that as a creative starting point rather than as a negative thing'.[46]

Certainly, the route of media promotion by which modern architecture has been restored to public favour, including the Stirling Prize, lends itself to such shallowness both of input and output, a paradox that seems to justify the restriction of Modernism's discourse once more to a smaller circle of initiates, as it has been for most of the twentieth century. Deyan Sudjic, reviewing the first ten years of the award (1996–2005), asked whether it was time to bring back the concept of memory, embodied in Stirling's own work:

> it would be encouraging to think that an award could be used to convey a more complex message than the triumph of spectacle, and that an architectural prize can still be about more than the egotistical object or a reward for corporate good manners.[47]

At the same time, Rem Koolhaas, an outsider who has chosen London as one of his several bases, believes that England has accidentally got the right qualities for the time, enjoying a belated flowering of Modernism, and that 'through this Anglo-Saxon fluidity and the fact that the market has always been a determinant of values here, has been able to manipulate forces in a much more sophisticated manner'.[48]

Saunt's view supports the reading of plurality as a constant condition in English architecture and not necessarily a disadvantage. Plurality can be a deliberate goal, or an accidental result of failing to reach some other, more defined position. If, as Koolhaas claims, fluidity is an Anglo-

Saxon quality, then it may have found its moment in an age defined by another immigrant thinker, Zygmunt Bauman, as Liquid Modernity.[49] This concept, arising from observation of social and technological trends in the 'second modernity', conforms to the broadening sense of the architect's field of action extending beyond the construction of new buildings to a more general sense of intervention. There is nothing about current conditions to suggest that stability, literal or metaphorical, can be attempted or achieved in the near future.

References

chapter one: Efficiency: From Modernity to Modernism

1 Martin Wiener, *Between Two Worlds: The Political Thought of Graham Wallas* (Oxford, 1971), p. 129.
2 See Tricia Cusack, 'Mouchel, Louis Gustave', *Oxford Dictionary of National Biography* (Oxford, 2004) (with bibliography).
3 As reported in Patricia Cusack, 'The Reinforced Concrete Specialist in Britain, 1905–08', *Architectural History*, xxix (1986), p. 185.
4 See Alan Powers, 'Architectural Education in Britain, 1880–1914', PhD thesis (University of Cambridge, 1982).
5 See *The First Fifty Years: History of the Brixton School of Building, 1904–1954*, London County Council (1954), and Alan Powers, 'Professor Pite', in *The Golden City: Essays on the Architecture and Imagination of Beresford Pite*, ed. Brian Hanson (London, 1993), pp. 95–103.
6 See Alan Powers, 'Liverpool and Architectural Education in the Early Twentieth Century', in *Charles Reilly and the Liverpool School of Architecture, 1904–1933* (Liverpool, 1996), pp. 1–23, and 'C. H. Reilly: Regency, Englishness and Modernism', *Journal of Architecture*, v/1 (Spring 2000), pp. 47–64. See also Christopher Crouch, *Design Culture in Liverpool, 1880–1914: The Origins of the Liverpool School of Architecture* (Liverpool, 2002), and Peter Richmond, *Marketing Modernisms: The Architecture and Influence of Charles Reilly* (Liverpool, 2001).
7 Ian Nairn, *Nairn's London* (Harmondsworth, 1968), p. 150.
8 *Drapery Times* (20 November 1909), quoted in Dan Cruickshank, 'Reinforcing Classicism', *Architects' Journal* (12 February 1992), pp. 22–34.
9 *Ibid.*, p. 28.
10 John Brodie, 'Concrete Dwellings, Eldon Street: Report of the City Engineer, 22 April 1905', *Proceedings of Liverpool City Council, 1904–05*, quoted in Richard Moore, 'An Early System of Large-Panel Building', *RIBA Journal* (September 1969), pp. 383–6.
11 Reyner Banham, *The Architecture of the Well-Tempered Environment* (London, 1969), p. 76. For better illustrations, see Annette Becker, John Olley and Wilfred Wang, eds, *Ireland* (Munich and New York, 1997), pp. 90–91.
12 Wyndham Lewis, *Blast*, 1 (1913), p. 23; Desmond Mountjoy [Desmond Chapman-Huston], *A Creel of Peat: Stray Stories* (London, 1910), p. 5.
13 H. Muthesius, *The English House*, ed. Dennis Sharp (London, 1979), p. 4.
14 See J. H. Archer, *Partnership in Style: Edgar Wood and J. Henry Sellars*, exh. cat., Manchester City Art Gallery (Manchester, 1975).
15 Lawrence Weaver, *Smaller Country Houses of Today* (London, 1910), pp. 202–7.
16 Wagner's address is printed in the volume of *Transactions* published by the RIBA in 1908, pp. 109–11.
17 For a comprehensive account of Burnet's career, see http://www.codexgeo.co.uk/dsa/architect_full.php?id=M001684.
18 See Alan Powers, 'Angleterre', in *Encyclopédie Perret*, ed. Jean-Louis Cohen, Joseph Abram and Guy Lambert (Paris, 2002), pp. 370–72.

19 Beresford Pite, C.F.A. Voysey and Reginald Blomfield, 'L'Art Nouveau: What It Is and What Is Thought of It', *Magazine of Art* (1903), p. 169.

20 Nikolaus Pevsner and Enid Radcliffe, 'Randall Wells', *Architectural Review*, CXXXVI (November 1964), pp. 367–70.

21 'Engineering and Architecture', *Builder*, CXI (1931), p. 54.

22 Roger Fry, *Architectural Heresies of a Painter* (London, 1921), p. 9.

23 A. Trystan Edwards, *Good and Bad Manners in Architecture* (London, 1924); Howard Robertson, *The Principles of Architectural Composition* (London, 1924); Clough Williams-Ellis and Amabel Williams-Ellis, *The Pleasures of Architecture* (London, 1924).

24 This account relies heavily on Mark Swenarton, *Homes for Heroes* (London, 1981).

25 Wyndham Lewis, *The Caliph's Design* (London, 1914), subtitle to book.

26 Colin Davies, *The Prefabricated Home: A Non-Architectural History* (London, 2005), p. 60.

27 Thomas Jones, *Whitehall Diary*, ed. Keith Middlemas (Oxford, 1969), vol.1, p. 229 (9 February 1923).

28 *Ibid.*

29 See David J. Blake, *Window Vision* (Braintree, 1989), and Hentie Louw, 'Crittall, Francis Henry', in *Oxford Dictionary of National Biography* (Oxford, 2004).

30 Henry-Russell Hitchcock, 'Foreign Periodicals', *Architectural Record*, LXIII (1929), p. 598.

31 Quoted in Christian Barman, *The Man Who Built London Transport* (Newton Abbott, 1979).

32 See Alan Powers, 'Britain and the Bauhaus', *Apollo* (May 2006), pp. 48–54.

33 Basil Ward, 'Connell, Ward and Lucas', in *Planning and Architecture*, ed. Dennis Sharp (London, 1967), p. 80.

34 'Connell Ward and Lucas – a note by Peter Smithson', *Architectural Association Journal* (December 1956), p. 138.

35 Lubetkin, 'Samizdat' (unpublished memoir), quoted in John Allan, *Berthold Lubetkin: Architecture and the Tradition of Progress* (London, 1992), p. 99.

36 Dmitri Mirsky, *The Intelligentsia of Great Britain* (London 1935), p. 39.

37 Herbert Read, 'The City of Tomorrow', *The Listener* (18 February 1931), p. 273.

38 Maxwell Fry, *Autobiographical Sketches* (London, 1975), p. 136.

39 *The Times* (11 March 1935), p. 8.

40 See R.A.H. Livett, 'Housing in an Industrial City' (extract from a paper read at the Architectural Association), *Architect and Building News*, CLIV (6 May 1938), pp. 160–61.

41 Adrian Forty, *Words and Buildings* (London, 2000), pp. 180–87. See also Tim Benton, 'The Myth of Function', in *Modernism in Design*, ed. Paul Greenhalgh (London, 1990), pp. 41–53. See also Stanford Anderson, 'The Fiction of Function', *Assemblage*, 2 (February 1987), and Alan Colquhoun, 'Introduction: Modern Architecture and Historicity', in *Essays in Architectural Criticism* (Cambridge, MA, and London, 1982), p. 12.

42 Aldous Huxley, 'Notes on Decoration', *The Studio*, C (1930), p. 242.

43 'Homes of Tomorrow', *The Listener* (11 October 1933), p. 528. The second passage is a quotation from the Arts and Crafts architect and Social Credit enthusiast, A. J. Penty.

44 Nikolaus Pevsner, *Pioneers of Modern Design from William Morris to Walter Gropius* (London, 1936), p. 207.

45 Charles McKean, *The Scottish Thirties: An Architectural Introduction* (Edinburgh, 1987), p. 100.

46 See Bob Jarvis, 'The Enigma of Dunston "B"', *Thirties Society Journal*, II (1982), pp. 31–5. The building was demolished *c.* 1985.

47 'Mars versus Jupiter', *Landscape and Garden*, V (1938), p. 53.

48 Hugh Casson, *Homes by the Million: An Account of the Housing Achievement in the USA, 1940–1945* (Harmondsworth, 1946).

49 Davies, *The Prefabricated Home*, p. 61.

1   Louis MacNeice, *Autumn Journal* (London, 1939), p. 95.
2   Lewis Mumford, *Technics and Civilisation* (London, 1934), pp. 433–4.
3   Lewis Mumford, *The Culture of Cities* (London, 1938), p. 495.
4   See Irene Barclay, *People Need Roots: The Story of the St Pancras Housing Association* (London, 1976).
5   'Russia, busy with essential services, has postponed her architectural development and meanwhile must rely on the only skilled architects she possesses – the academicians of the old regime' was Herbert Read's interpretation of the situation: 'The International Style', *The Listener* (22 May 1935), p. 867.
6   John Summerson, 'Bread and Butter and Architecture', *Horizon*, VI (October 1942), p. 234.
7   Quoted from Emma Goldman, in 'A Laboratory of Anarchy', *Anarchy*, 60 (February 1966), p. 56.
8   Quoted in Colin Ward, 'Peckham Recollected', *Anarchy*, 60 (February 1966), p. 54.
9   The YHA was founded in 1930 with funds from the Carnegie United Kingdom Trust. The earliest buildings were conversions. The Holmbury Hostel stands at the edge of a large tract of publicly accessible woodland, given in trust in 1928. Lobb's contribution included a neo-vernacular hostel at Ewhurst, Surrey, in 1936.
10 Editorial, *Trends in Design*, I/2 (Summer 1936), p. 69.
11 *Miner's Welfare Fund Annual Reports, 1921–26*, vol. I, first report, p. 6, cited in Cheryl Buckley, 'Miner's Welfare', *Architects' Journal* (13 June 1984), pp. 48–59.
12 Nikolaus Pevsner, 'The Modern Movement', unpublished MS in the Getty Archive, Santa Monica, CA; published in *Twentieth Century Architecture, 8: British Modern* (London, 2006).
13 Summerson, 'Bread and Butter and Architecture', p. 242.
14 Tim Bennett, 'The Contribution of the Thirties' (review of Alfred Roth, *The New Architecture*), *Architectural Review*, LXXXVIII (July 1940), p. 30.
15 See 'Scoreboard', *Architects' Journal* (25 May 1939), pp. 851–62.
16 See John Betjeman, 'A Note on Ninian Comper', *Architectural Review*, LXXXV (February 1939); also contributions by Anthony Symondson and Alan Powers to *First and Last Loves: John Betjeman and Architecture* (London, 2006).
17 John Summerson to Ben Nicholson, 31 December 1940, Tate Archive 8717.1.2.4621.
18 Alan A. Jackson, *Semi-Detached London* (London, 1973), 'Epilogue', pp. 319–24.
19 Quoted in Robert Cowan, *Dictionary of Urbanism* (Tisbury, 2005), p. 348.
20 Alison Ravetz, 'From Working Class Tenement to Modern Flat', in *Multi-Storey Living: The British Working Class Experience*, ed. Anthony Sutcliffe (London, 1974), pp. 125.
21 See the final chapter of S. E. Rasmussen, *London: The Unique City* (London, 1937).
22 *Architect and Building News*, CXXXVIII (22 June 1934), p. 330.
23 E.g. Loughborough Park, Brixton, by Edward Armstrong, 1938 (Guinness) or Evelyn Court, Hackney, 1934, by Burnet, Tait and Lorne (4 per cent Industrial Dwellings Company).
24 Elizabeth Denby, 'Kensal House and Urban Village', in *Flats, Municipal and Private Enterprise* (London, 1938), pp. 61–4.
25 The Housing Centre, *New Homes for Old*, cited in Darling note 67.
26 See Elizabeth A. Darling, '"To Induce Humanitarian Sentiments in Prurient Londoners": The Propaganda Activities of London's Voluntary Housing Associations in the Inter-War Period', *London Journal*, XXVII/1 (2002), pp. 42–62.
27 'Rehousing', abstract of paper read before the RIBA on 16 November 1936 by Elizabeth Denby on 'Rehousing from the Slum-Dweller's Point of View', *Architect and Building News*, CXLVIII (20 November 1936), pp. 23–4.
28 Elizabeth Denby, *Europe Rehoused*, (London, 1938), p. 275.
29 F. Yerbury, 'A Housing Survey', *Architectural Review*, LXXXIII (June 1938), pp. 303–4.
30 See Romy Golan, *Modernity and Nostalgia: Art and Politics in France Between the Wars*

(London and New Haven, 1995). There is as yet no international survey of this phenomenon, although a wider range of countries is explored on these lines in Jean-Louis Cohen, ed., *Années 30: l'architecture et les arts de l'espace entre industrie et nostalgie* (Paris, 1997).

31 Marcel Breuer, 'Where Do We Stand?', *Architectural Review*, LXXVII (April 1935), pp. 133–6.

32 Maxwell Fry, 'The Architect's Dilemma – 1', *The Listener* (17 February 1955), p. 282.

33 J. M. Richards, *An Introduction to Modern Architecture* (Harmondsworth, 1940), pp. 79–80.

34 Brenda Colvin, *Land and Landscape* (London, 1948), p. 1.

35 Sonya O. Rose, *Which People's War?* (Oxford, 2003), p. 62.

36 Ralph Tubbs, *Living in Cities* (Harmondsworth, 1942), p. 49.

37 Maxwell Fry, 'The New Britain Must Be Planned', *Picture Post* (4 January 1941), p. 19.

38 Holford to 'Sir Ralph', 9 December 1942, Holford duplicate book, 1942, University of Liverpool d.147/P/17/2; quoted in Gordon Cherry and Leith Penny, *Holford* (London, 1986), p. 95.

39 See *Country and Town: A Summary of the Scott and Uthwatt Reports* (Harmondsworth, 1943), p. 82.

40 Lionel Brett, 'The New Haussmann', *Architectural Review*, XCIII (January 1943), p. 25.

41 The film was *The Way We Live*, Two Cities Films for the Rank Organisation, 1945. See Alan Powers, 'Plymouth: Reconstruction after World War II', in *Out of Ground Zero: Case Studies in Urban Reinvention*, ed. Joan Ockman (Munich and London, 2002), pp. 98–115.

42 The article, 'The New Empiricism', *Architectural Review*, CI (June 1947), pp. 199–204, is unsigned, but attributed by Eric Mumford in *The CIAM Discourse on Urbanism* (2002) to J. M. Richards.

43 Herbert Tayler in conversation with Elain Harwood, May 1996, printed in Elain Harwood and Alan Powers, *Tayler and Green, Architects, 1938–1973: The Spirit of Place in Modern Housing* (London, 1998), p. 66.

44 J. M. Richards, *The Castle on the Ground* (London, 1946), p. 82. The book was illustrated by John Piper. Richards wrote later: 'The book was scorned by my contemporaries as either an irrelevant eccentricity or a betrayal of the forward-looking ideals of the Modern Movement, to which the suburbs were supposed to be an absolute antithesis': *Memoirs of an Unjust Fella* (London, 1980), p. 188.

45 Nikolaus Pevsner, 'Introduction', *The Reith Lectures 1955: The Englishness of English Art* (London, 1955), p. 8. This is the pamphlet intended to provide illustrations for listeners, rather than the book of the lectures published by the Architectural Press in 1956.

46 See Alan Powers, 'The Expression of Levity', in *Festival of Britain*, ed. Alan Powers and Elain Harwood (London, 2001), pp. 48–56, and the other articles and references therein.

47 Commentary to *Brief City*, directed by Jacques Brunius, 1952.

48 Colin Boyne, 'The New Towns as Prototypes', *The Listener* (29 September 1955), p. 502.

49 John Summerson, 'Foreword', *45–55: Ten Years of British Architecture*, exh. cat. (London, 1956), p. 13.

chapter three: Poetics: The Moral Dilemma of Modern Aesthetics

1 John Summerson, 'Foreword', *45–55: Ten Years of British Architecture*, exh. cat. (London, 1956).

2 'The Vertical City', *Observer* (17 February 1952).

3 John Allan, *Berthold Lubetkin: Architecture and the Tradition of Progress* (London, 1992), pp. 384–92.

4 Reyner Banham, 'Façade', *Architectural Review*, CXV (November 1954), p. 306.

5 Paul Thompson, *Architecture or Social Service?* (London, 1963); quoted in William Curtis, *Denys Lasdun* (London, 1994), p. 51.

6 H. T. Cadbury-Brown, 'Goldfinger', *Architects' Journal* (31 January 1973), p. 241.

7 Ian Nairn, *Modern Buildings in London* (London, 1964), p. 47.

8   Ernesto Rogers, 'The Tradition of Modern Architecture in Italy', in *Italy Builds*, ed.
    G. E. Kidder-Smith (London, 1955), pp. 11, 13.

9   Reyner Banham, 'Neo-Liberty: The Italian Retreat from Modern Architecture',
    Architectural Review, cxxv (April 1959), pp. 231–5.

10 See Sarah Williams Goldhagen, 'Coda: conceptualising the modern', in Goldhagen and
    Legault, eds, *Anxious Modernisms: Experimentation in Postwar Architectural Culture*
    (Cambridge, MA, 2000), pp. 301–20.

11 Edward D. Mills, *The New Architecture in Britain* (London, 1953), p. 207.

12 Nairn, *Modern Buildings in London*, p. 111. Gatwick was enlarged by the same architects
    in successive phases into the 1990s, but although the original structure of 1957 survives,
    it no longer reads in any way that corresponds to the original perception.

13 Kenneth Frampton, 'AD in the 60s: A Memoir', *Architectural Design* (June 2000), p. 102.

14 Reyner Banham, 'The Jet Jetty', *New Statesman* (21 June 1958), p. 804.

15 A. Smithson and P. Smithson, *The Charged Void: Architecture* (New York, 2001), p. 40.

16 *Ibid.*, p. 41.

17 [Reyner Banham], 'Design Principles', *Architectural Review*, cxvi (September 1954), p. 152.

18 'Future', *Architectural Review*, cxv (April 1954), p. 274.

19 *Ibid.*

20 Although frequently quoted, apparently this saying has no original printed source.

21 Risinghill (in Penton Street) was renamed Elizabeth Garrett Anderson School, having
    become notorious for the freedom given to pupils in the early 1960s.

22 Reyner Banham, 'The Cool Young Men', *New Statesman* (29 March 1958), p. 404; *The New
    Brutalism* (London, 1966), p. 89.

23 Francesco Tentori, 'Phoenix Brutalism', *Zodiac*, 18 (1968), p. 257. 'Giving a *restrictive* inter-
    pretation of the movement, I shall be inclined from time to time to identify it with
    Banham himself or with the two Smithsons.' In the conclusion of Banham's book on
    New Brutalism, he wrote: 'for all its brave talk of "an ethic, not an aesthetic", Brutalism
    never quite broke out of the aesthetic frame of reference' (p. 134).

24 Arthur Korn, 'The Work of James Stirling and James Gowan', *Architect and Building News*,
    ccxv (7 January 1959), p. 8.

25 Mark Girouard, 'Concluding Address at Royal Gold Medal presentation to James Stirling',
    Architectural Design (July–August 1980), p. 13.

26 James Gowan, 'Curriculum', *Architectural Review*, cxxvi (December 1959), p. 316.

27 Reyner Banham, 'The Style for the Job', *Listener* (14 February 1954), p. 266.

28 Kenneth Frampton, *Modern Architecture: A Critical History* (London, 1980), p. 265.

29 John Voelcker, 'Team x', *Arena* (June 1965), p. 12.

30 Alison Smithson and Peter Smithson, *Urban Structuring* (London, 1967), pp. 34–5.

31 Smithson and Smithson, *Urban Structuring*, p. 34.

32 Reyner Banham, 'Corbolatry at County Hall', *New Society* (4 November 1965), p. 26.

33 See Gavin Stamp, 'McMorran and Whitby: A Progressive Classicism', in *Modern Painters*, 4
    (Winter 1991), pp. 56–60, where the Lammas Green Estate, Sydenham Hill (1957), and the
    Holloway Estate are illustrated. See also Elain Harwood, *England: A Guide to Post-War
    Listed Buildings* (London, 2000), example 9/26.

34 See Edward Hollamby and David Gregory-Jones, 'The Structure and Personality of the
    LCC Architects Department', *Architecture and Building*, xxxii (May 1957), pp. 170–80.

35 E.g. Backström & Reinius, Danviksklippan, Hästholmsvägen, Stockholm, 1943.

36 Nikolaus Pevsner, 'Roehampton', *Architectural Review*, cxxvi (July 1959), p. 22. When
    Peter Smithson travelled to Sweden in 1946 with Ron Simpson, he was strongly influenced
    by the housing designs of Backström and Reinius, which consisted of towers with
    cut-off corners, forming part of the range of sources that informed Alton East, as
    well as more connected blocks with Y-form plans. See Ron Simpson, 'From the
    Beginning', in *Architecture Is Not Made with the Brain* (London, 2005), pp. 78–9.

37 Jack Lynn, 'Park Hill Development, Sheffield', *RIBA Journal* (December 1962), p. 447.

38 Ivor Smith, 'Architects' Approach to Architecture', *RIBA Journal* (July 1967), p. 274.

39   Reyner Banham, 'The Vertical Community', *New Statesman* (30 June 1961), p. 1056.
40   Robert Maxwell, *New British Architecture* (London, 1972), p. 20.
41   Robert Maxwell, 'Rowe, Colin', *Oxford Dictionary of National Biography* (Oxford, 2004).
42   A.J.P. Taylor, 'Look Back at the Fifties', *New Statesman* (2 January 1960), pp. 5–6.
43   James Stirling, 'Ronchamp – Le Corbusier's Chapel and the Crisis of Rationalism' *Architectural Review*, vol. 119 (March 1956), pp. 155–61.
44   Voelcker, 'Team x", *Arena/AAJ* (June 1965), p. 19.
45   Fred Vanderschmidt, *What the English Think of Us*, quoted in Harry Hopkins, *The New Look* (London, 1963), p. 109.
46   See F. R. Leavis and Denys Thompson, *Culture and Environment* (London, 1933); Richard Hoggart, *The Uses of Literacy* (London, 1957), and Raymond Williams, *Culture and Society, 1780–1950* (Harmondsworth, 1958).
47   John McHale, 'The Expendable Ikon 1', *Architectural Design* (February 1959), pp. 82–3, and (March 1959), pp. 116–17.
48   *Architectural Review*, CXXI (May 1957), p. 293.
49   *Ibid.*, p. 297.
50   Denys Lasdun, 'An Architect's Approach to Architecture', *RIBA Journal* (April 1965), p. 184.
51   *Ibid.*, p. 194; 'A Sense of Place and Time', *Listener* (17 February 1966), p. 229.
52   Louis Kahn, 'Towards a Plan for Modern Philadelphia', *Perspecta*, 2 (1953), p. 11.
53   Reyner Banham, 'Apropos the Smithsons', *New Statesman* (8 September 1961), p. 317.
54   *Ibid.*, p. 318.
55   Ian Nairn, *Nairn's London* (Harmondsworth, 1968), p. 80.
56   Peter Blake, 'The Establishment Strides Again!', *Architectural Forum*, CXXII (May 1965), p. 18; Brian Henderson in conversation with the author, 1992; Alvin Boyarsky, 'The Architecture of Etcetera', *Architectural Design* (June 1965), p. 268.
57   Reyner Banham, *The New Brutalism* (London, 1966), p. 134.
58   Peter Smithson, 'Planning Today', *Architectural Design* (June 1957), p. 186.
59   Robin Middleton, 'The New Brutalism as a Clean and Well-Lighted Place', *Architectural Design* (January 1967), pp. 7–8.

chapter four: **Production: White Heat and Burnout**

1   H.C.G. Matthew, 'Macmillan, Harold', *Oxford Dictionary of National Biography* (Oxford, 2004).
2   In response to a talk at the RIBA by Alistair Cooke, *RIBA Journal* (July 1961), p. 343.
3   E. W. Cooney, 'High Flats in Local Authority Housing in England and Wales since 1945', in *Multi-Storey Living: The British Working Class Experience*, ed. Anthony Sutcliffe (London, 1974), p. 151.
4   See Patrick Dunleavy, *The Politics of Mass Housing in Britain, 1945–1975* (Oxford, 1981), p. 170.
5   RIBA Journal (March–April 1955), p. 201; Herbert Tayler, 'Flats and Houses, 1958: A Critical Review', *Architect and Building News*, CCXV (27 May 1959), pp. 693–8.
6   Fred Berry, *Housing: The Great British Failure* (London, 1974), p. 53.
7   Ibid., p. 57. 'The Twilight Zone' was the title of an American TV science-fiction series of 1959–64.
8   Miles Glendinning, ed., *Rebuilding Scotland* (East Linton, 1997), p. 107.
9   Charles Robertson, in *Rebuilding Scotland*, p. 101.
10 Bridget Cherry and Nikolaus Pevsner, *The Buildings of England: London 2: South* (London, 1983), p. 595.
11 A. W. Davey, *Architectural Design* (July 1959), p. 282.
12 Colin Amery and Lance Wright, 'Foreword: Lifting the Witch's Curse', in *The Architecture of Darbourne & Darke* (London, 1977).
13 Quoted in Elain Harwood, *England: A Guide to Post-War Listed Buildings* (London, 2003),

p. 312.

14   See Reyner Banham, *Megastructure: Urban Futures of the Recent Past* (London, 1976).

15   Nicholas Taylor, 'The Failure of "Housing", *Architectural Review*, CXLII (November 1967), pp. 341, 359.

16   J. M. Richards, 'Rebuilding the City: The City of London on the Brink of Disaster', *Architectural Review*, CXV (June 1954), pp. 379–86.

17   Ian Nairn, *Modern Buildings in London* (London, 1964), p. 20.

18   Oliver Marriott, *The Property Boom* (London, 1967), p. 44.

19   See John Smith, 'Anti-Ugly Action', *Architecture and Building* (April 1959), pp. 126–8; Ken Baynes, 'Where Do We Go From Here, Boys?', *Architects' Journal* (21 January 1961), pp. 105–6; Gavin Stamp, 'Anti-Ugly', *Apollo* (January 2005), pp. 88–9.

20   Rodney Gordon, 'Modern Architecture for the Masses: The Owen Luder Partnership, 1960–67', *Twentieth Century Architecture 6: The Sixties – Life, Style, Architecture*, ed. Elain Harwood and Alan Powers (London, 2002), p. 75.

21   Marriott, *The Property Boom*, p. 140.

22   *Ibid.*, chapter 11.

23   The RFAC was founded in 1924 as an advisory body. Following the death of its first secretary, H. Charlton Bradshaw, in 1946, the position was taken by Godfrey Samuel, a leading member of the pre-war MARS Group. Samuel brought Modernist sympathies to the role, but the committee was balanced between conservative members, including Sir Albert Richardson, Raymond Erith and John Betjeman, and, after 1958, an increase in the radical faction, led by J. M. Richards. The Commission made it known by its actions that it would tend not to support traditional schemes.

24   Lord Annan, *Report of the Disturbances in the University of Essex* (Wivenhoe, 1974), p. 32.

25   Stefan Muthesius, *The Post-War University* (London and New Haven, 2000), p. 181.

26   Lance Wright, 'Enquiries Welcome', *Architectural Review*, CXLIX (March 1971), p. 161.

27   Leslie Martin, *Buildings and Ideas, 1933–83* (Cambridge, 1983), p. 121.

28   Editorial, 'Too Big for its Site', *Architectural Review*, CXLV (February 1974), p. 69.

29   Peter Hall, *Great Planning Disasters* (London, 1980), p. 152.

30   Alan Bennett, 'Views', *Listener* (30 November 1967), p. 692. Commenting on the proposal drawings, he wrote: 'How many times in the last ten years has one seen the same drawing: that spacious sun-baked piazza, the motor-cars tucked vaguely away somewhere, those fine flourishing trees, those outdoor restaurants, the whole thronged by Precinct People, a race of tall, long-headed men, Municipal Masai, who lounge about in every architect's drawing in a languor presumably induced by the commodiousness of their surroundings.'

31   Terence Bendixson, 'Knights in Shining Architecture', *Spectator* (31 March 1967), p. 374.

32   'I. de Wolfe' (H. de Cronin Hastings) and Gorden Cullen, 'Townscape' and 'Townscape Casebook' in *Architectural Review* (December 1949), pp. 354–74.

33   Colin Buchanan, *Mixed Blessing: The Motor Car in Britain* (London, 1958), p. 99.

34   Sir Colin Anderson (chair), *Motorway Signs: Final Report of Advisory Committee on Traffic Signs for Motorways* (London, 1962); Phil Baines, 'A design (To Sign Roads By)', *Eye*, 34 (Winter 1999), pp. 26–36. The Morris Mini Minor and Austin Seven (the same model under different names) were introduced in 1959. One major innovation was to position the engine laterally to save length. Edward de Bono's *Lateral Thinking* was published by Ward Lock Education in 1970.

35   See Peter J. Larkham and Keith D. Lilley, *Planning the 'City of Tomorrow': British Reconstruction Planning, 1939–1952: An Annotated Bibliography* (Pickering, 2001).

36   Buchanan, *Mixed Blessing*, caption to plate XLIII.

37   Ian Nairn, 'Birmingham, Liverpool, Manchester', *Architectural Review*, CLXXXVII (August 1960), p. 111.

38   James P. McCafferty, 'The Glasgow Inner Ring Road: Past, Present and Future', in *Rebuilding Scotland*, ed. Glendinning, p. 77.

39   *Glasgow Herald* (22 February 1960), quoted in McCafferty, 'The Glasgow . . . Road'.

40 Cyril Winskell, 'Newcastle upon Tyne, 1945–2003', in *Twentieth Century Architecture 7: The Heroic Period of Conservation*, ed. Elain Harwood and Alan Powers (London, 2004).

41 *Ibid.*, p. 102.

42 *Ibid.*, p. 103. This is what actually happened by 2000, as Winskell comments.

43 *Traffic in Towns: A Study of the Long Term Problems of Traffic in Urban Areas. Report of the Steering Group and Working Group Appointed by the Minister of Transport* (London, 1963).

44 For a grim appraisal of Cumbernauld, see p. 166.

45 Anonymous, 'Covent Garden Carve Up', *Architectural Design* (July 1971), p. 402.

46 In the *Architectural Design* article cited, p. 404, the community was described as 'a sort of Cow Green of social relationships', a reference to 'an incomparable and unique survival of flora dating back to the Ice Age, which was callously flooded, after a ministerial enquiry, to provide a reservoir for an ICI plant'.

47 For a group of papers on these themes, introduced by Royston Landau, see *Architectural Design* (October 1972).

48 Martin Pawley, 'Fifty Years of Phantom Pregnancy', *Architectural Design* (December 1971).

49 Martin Pawley, 'It's Alright Ma, Everybody Loves Ya', *Architectural Design* (November 1970), p. 585.

50 Martin Pawley, 'Architecture on TV; or, It Won't Always Be This Easy', *Architectural Design* (September 1971), pp. 572–3.

chapter five: Happiness: The Reintegration of Architecture

1 Udo Kultermann, *Architecture in the Seventies* (London, 1980), p. 1.

2 Books on happiness include Ziyad Marar, *The Happiness Paradox* (London, 2003), and Richard Layard, *Happiness: Findings from a New Science* (London, 2004). In the autumn of 2005, a television series, 'Making Slough Happy', was broadcast, based on an attempt to apply Layard's ideas. Alain de Botton's *The Architecture of Happiness* (London, 2006) uses the idea of happiness as a way of defining beauty in modern architecture.

3 The calculation has been made by the New Economics Foundation in London.

4 *Listener* (6 February 1964), p. 224.

5 Peter Smithson, 'Just a Few Chairs and a House: An Essay on the Eames-Aesthetic', *Architectural Design* (September 1966), pp. 444–5.

6 'A Matter of Taste', *Listener* (13 October 1966), p. 528. Bruce Archer, 'Who Profits By Design?', *ibid.*, pp. 533–4, including the conclusion, 'efficient designing includes proper respect for popular tastes'.

7 Stephen Mullin, 'Day Tripper: Two Legs Good, Four Wheels Bad', *Architectural Design* (September 1968), p. 409.

8 AA *Journal* (October 1964), p. 63.

9 Theo Crosby, *Architecture: City Sense* (London, 1967).

10 Royston Landau, 'A Philosophy of Enabling', *Cedric Price: The Square Book* (London, 1984).

11 'Obituary: Joan Littlewood', *The Guardian* (23 September 2002).

12 B. N. Lewis, 'Fun Palace: Counterblast to Boredom', *New Society* (15 April 1965), p. 8.

13 The Open University did, however, erect its own buildings at Milton Keynes designed by Jane Drew of Fry, Drew and Partners (1969).

14 Paul Barker, 'Thinking the Unthinkable', in *Non-Plan: Essays on Freedom, Participation and Change in Modern Architecture and Urbanism*, ed. Jonathan Hughes and Simon Sadler (Oxford, 2000), p. 4.

15 See Simon Sadler, 'The Brutal Birth of Archigram', in *Twentieth Century Architecture 6: The Sixties – Life, Style, Architecture*, ed. Elain Harwood and Alan Powers (London, 2002), pp. 120–28.

16 *Architects' Journal* (19 June 1968), p. 1300.

17 Simon Sadler, *Archigram: Architecture without Architecture* (Cambridge, MA, 2005).

18 Martin Pawley, 'Miraculous Expanding Tits Versus Lacquered Nipples', *Architectural Design*

(February 1972), p. 80.

19 Susan Sontag, *Against Interpretation* (London, 2001), p. 291.

20 Peter Cook, 'Arcadia', *Architectural Design* (April 1971), p. 235. The derogatory comments on Hoover (designed by Wallis, Gilbert & Partners, 1932–5) from Nikolaus Pevsner's *Middlesex* (Harmondsworth, 1951) were probably the only references in print to a building well known from the roadside view on the A40 Western Avenue.

21 *Ibid.*

22 Peter Cook, 'Towards a Quietly Technologised Folk-Suburbia', *Architectural Design* (April 1972), pp. 241–2.

23 *Ibid.*

24 Robin Middleton, 'Foreword', in *The Idea of the City*, ed. Robin Middleton (London and Cambridge, 1996), p. 7.

25 Bernard Tschumi, 'City and Void', in *The Idea of the City*, ed. Middleton, p. 143.

26 George Baird, 'Meaning in Architecture: An Introduction', *Arena/AAJ*, LXXXIII (June 1967), p. 7.

27 Charles Jencks, *Modern Movements in Architecture* (Harmondsworth, 1973), pp. 11–12.

28 Charles Jencks, *The Language of Post-Modern Architecture* (London, 1977), p. 101.

29 The Mark I New Towns were those begun or designated between 1946 and 1950: Stevenage (1946), Crawley, East Kilbride, Harlow, Hemel Hempstead, Newton Aycliffe, (1947), Glenrothes, Hatfield, Peterlee, Welwyn (1948), Basildon, Bracknell, Cwmbran (1949), Corby (1950). Mark II were designated in response to an increasing birth rate after 1950: Cumbernauld (1955), Skelmersdale (1961), Livingston (1962), Redditch, Runcorn (1964), Washington (1964), Irvine (1966), Newton (1967). Mark III New Towns were created specifically to deal with London 'overspill' and larger populations in the region of 170,000–250,000. Peterborough (1967) and Northampton (1968) were enlargements of existing Midland towns. Milton Keynes (1967) incorporated some existing settlements, but created a new centre and name.

30 John Weeks, 'Scientific Fitness', *Architectural Review*, CL (November 1971), p. 264.

31 Robert Maxwell, 'The Beautiful City', *AA Quarterly*, VI/3–4 (1974), p. 12.

32 Peter Aldington was at the Manchester University School of Architecture, where the Head of School, R. A. Cordingley, was an enthusiast for vernacular, and one of the staff, Ronald Brunskill, one of the leading experts in the country on such matters. Norman Foster's student notebooks from the same course show an early understanding of framed and jointed structures.

33 See Mats Egelius, *Ralph Erskine* (Stockholm, 1990), p. 136; Peter Colleymore, *The Architecture of Ralph Erskine* (London, 1985), p. 1.

34 'Martin Richardson', *Architectural Design* (September–October 1977), pp. 716–17.

35 Robert Maxwell, 'The Beautiful City', p. 38 (review first published in *Progressive Architecture*, August 1979).

36 Arthur Edwards, *The Design of Suburbia* (London, 1981), p. 160.

37 Sutherland Lyall, *The State of British Architecture* (London, 1980), pp. 79–80.

38 *Ibid.*, p. 84. See Paul Ricoeur, 'Universalisation and National Cultures', in *History and Truth* (Evanston, IL, 1961), pp. 276–83; A. Tzonis, L. Lefaivre and A. Alofsin, 'Die Frage des Regionalismus', in *Für eine andere Architektur*, ed. N. Andritzky, L. Burchardt and O. Hoffman (Frankfurt, 1981). Texts by Frampton (1983) and Tzonis and Lefaivre (1991) are found in *Theorizing a New Agenda for Architecture, 1965–1995*, ed. Kate Nesbitt (Princeton, NJ, 1996), and in other collections.

39 Kenneth Frampton, 'Towards a Critical Regionalism: Six Points for an Architecture of Resistance', in Hal Foster, ed., *The Anti-Aesthetic: Essays on Postmodern Culture* (Port Townsend, WA, 1983).

40 According to Jeremy Dixon, the phrase came from Michael Gold's manner of clearing his throat before speaking.

41 Walter Segal, 'The Neo-Purist School of Architecture', *Architectural Design* (June 1972), pp. 344–5.

42   Walter Segal, 'Less Is More', *Architects' Journal* (20 February 1974), p. 371.
43   The Solar House at 14 Beacon Way, Rickmansworth, is described in *Architecture and Build-
     ing News* (11 October 1956), pp. 490–97. On Wallasey, see Dean Hawkes, 'Energy Revisit:
     Wallasey School, Pioneer of Solar Design', *Architects' Journal* (6 May 1987), pp. 55–9.
44   An account of the movement in the 1970s is given in Colin Porteous, *The New Eco-
     Architecture: Alternatives from the Modern Movement* (London, 2002). Another narrative
     with more historical depth is John Farmer, *Green Shift: Changing Attitudes in Architecture
     to the Natural World* (Oxford, 1996; revd edn, 1999).
45   The concept was apparently formulated by the architectural teacher and historian Robert
     Macleod in 1971. See Alex Gordon, 'Architects and Resource Conservation', *RIBA Journal*
     (January 1974), p. 9.
46   See John Littler and Randall Thomas, 'Solar Energy Use in the Autarkic House', *Martin
     Centre for Architectural and Urban Studies: Transactions*, II (1977), pp. 93–110.
47   Bryan Appleyard, *Richard Rogers: A Biography* (London, 1986), p. 126.

chapter six: **Conscience: The Architecture of Fruitful Anxiety**

1   Eric Lyons, 'Debate', *RIBA Journal* (March 1980), p. 9.
2   Roger Zogolovitch, 'Developing Talent', *Architects' Journal* (6 March 1985), p. 40.
3   Michael Heseltine, speaking at Financial Times Industrial Architecture Award luncheon
     (1980); quoted in Colin Amery, *The National Gallery Sainsbury Wing: A Celebration of Art
     and Architecture* (London, 1991), p. 43.
4   'Sense and Sensibility: The Architecture of Romantic Pragmatism' was the title of an
     article in the *Architectural Review*, CLXXIV (September 1983), by Gillian Darley and Peter
     Davey, covering Cullinan, Robert Maguire, Peter Aldington and other architects.
5   Alison Ravetz, letter, *Architects' Journal* (2 April 1980), p. 653.
6   See Chris Holmes, *A New Vision for Housing* (London, 2006), p. 89.
7   'Aids, Education and the Year 2000' (interview with Margaret Thatcher by Douglas Keay),
     Woman's Own (31 October 1987), pp. 8–10.
8   See Colin St John Wilson, 'England Builds', *Architectural Reflections* (Oxford, 1992),
     pp. 198–203.
9   Wilson, quoted in Michael Stonehouse and Gerhard Stromberg, *The British Library at St
     Pancras* (London, 2004), p. 111.
10   Quoted in Amery, *The National Gallery Sainsbury Wing*, p. 43.
11   'The British Way of Death', Leader, *Architects' Journal* (10 April 1985), p. 15.
12   For example, Peter Smithson, 'The Viceroy's House in New Delhi', *RIBA Journal*
     (April 1969), pp. 152–4.
13   Jonathan Dimbleby, *The Prince of Wales* (London, 1994), p. 314.
14   The Hampton Court speech and the other principal speeches made by the Prince up to
     1988 are printed in full in Charles Jencks, *The Prince, the Architects and the New Wave
     Monarchy* (London, 1988).
15   Lionel Esher drew attention to these in the conclusion of *A Broken Wave: The Rebuilding
     of England, 1940–1980* (London, 1981), p. 296.
16   Nick Wates, 'Co-Op Consolidation', *Architectural Review*, CLXXVII (April 1985), pp. 57–60.
17   Dennis Hardy, *Poundbury: The Town That Charles Built* (London, 2006), p. 37.
18   Terry Farrell, 'Buildings as Resources', *RIBA Journal* (May 1976), p. 172.
19   Jürgen Habermas, 'Modernity – An Incomplete Project', in *Postmodern Culture*, ed. Hal
     Foster (London, 1983), pp. 3–15.
20   Berthold Lubetkin, 'Letters', *Architects' Journal* (29 October 1986), p. 22.
21   Richard MacCormac, 'Introduction', in *The Art of the Process* (London, 1993), p. 4.
22   Francis Duffy, *The Changing Workplace* (London, 1992), p. 125 (reprinted from *Architects'
     Journal*, 18 November 1981, pp. 997–9).
23   Two of the best of Richardson's early City buildings were victims of 1980s redevelopment,

replaced by crude Postmodern monsters: Moorgate Hall, Moorgate, and Leith House, Gresham Street.

24 Murray Fraser, review of 'Zaha Hadid: The Complete Works', *Architects' Journal* (13 January 2005), p. 40.

25 Donald Schon and Robert Gutman, *Architectural Practice: A Critical View* (Princeton, NJ, 1988).

26 Michael Spens, 'AR Critique, 1980–1995', *The Recovery of the Modern* (Oxford, 1996), p. 17.

27 *Ibid.*, p. 23.

28 'The New Spirit', *Architectural Review*, CLXXX (August 1986); reprinted *ibid.*, p. 58.

29 Quoted in Michael Jenner, *New British Architecture in Germany* (Munich, 2000), p. 25.

30 Peter Davey, 'Regional Meaning', *Architectural Review*, CLXXXIII (May 1988), p. 164.

31 Tony Fretton: *Conversation with David Turnbull* (Barcelona, 1995), pp. 8–9.

32 Kenneth Frampton, 'The Lessons of Lisson', *AA Files*, 23 (1992), p. 23.

33 Christopher Woodward, 'A London Practice', in *As Built: Caruso St John Architects*, ed. Aurora Fernández Per (Vitoria-Gasteiz, 2005), p. 7.

34 See www.screenonline.org.uk/film/id/497617/index.html (accessed 5 October 2006).

35 Transcription from videotape; punctuation invented.

36 Richard Rogers and Philip Gumuchdjian, *Cities for a Small Planet* (London, 1997), p. 170.

37 *Towards an Urban Renaissance* (London, 1999).

38 Hugh Aldersley Williams, 'Building on Tradition', *New Statesman* (3 May 1999); quoted in Ken Worpole, *The Value of Architecture: Design, Economy and the Architectural Imagination* (London, 2000), p. 18.

39 *Ibid.*, p. 36.

40 *Bennetts Associates: Four Commentaries* (London, 2005), p. 40.

41 For example, 'Not All Houses Are Square' (presenter Charlie Luxton, Channel 4, October 2001) and 'The Perfect House' (presenter Alain de Botton, Channel 4, March 2006).

42 Peter Buchanan, 'Now and Then: British Architecture since 1950', *AV Monographs*, 107 (2004), p. 13.

chapter seven: Difference: Local Action and Global Thought

1 Paul Ward, *Britishness since 1870* (London, 2004), p. 1.

2 Quoted in John Davies, *A History of Wales* (London, 1994), p. 418.

3 No surviving copy of the Dewi-Prys Thomas manifesto has been traced. David Jones, 'Wales and Visual Form' (*c.* 1944), in *The Dying Gaul and Other Writings* (London, 1978).

4 Greg Stevenson, 'Foreword' to Iorwerth C. Peate, *The Welsh House: A Study in Folk Culture* [1940] (Cribyn, 2004).

5 George Scott-Moncrieff, text for *The Little Houses*, exh. cat., National Trust touring exhibition (1952).

6 Quoted in Charles McKean, *The Scottish Thirties* (Edinburgh, 1987), p. 14.

7 Robert Hurd, 'Scotland's Mirror', *Listener* (6 June 1934), p. 948.

8 Colin McWilliam, *Scottish Townscape* (London, 1975), p. 180.

9 J. M. Richards, 'Glasgow 1938: A Critical Survey', *Architectural Review*, LXXXIV (July 1938), p. 4.

10 Quoted in the entry on Mackintosh by Robert Furneaux Jordan in J. M. Richards, ed., *Who's Who in Architecture* (London, 1977).

11 See Paul Larmour, 'Cinema Paradiso', *Perspective*, V/4 and 'The Big Feature', (March–April 1997), pp. 26–37.

12 A selection is illustrated in McKean, *The Scottish Thirties*, pp. 124–5.

13 See Andrew Cowser, 'Bendhu', *Perspective* (May–June 1995), pp. 21–3.

14 Robert McKinstry, 'Contemporary Architecture', in *Causeway: The Arts in Ulster*, ed. M. Longley (Belfast, 1971), p. 28.

15 See Paul Larmour, 'Style Master', *Perspective* (July–August 1997), pp. 18–31.

16 See Paul Larmour, 'In the Name of the Father', *Perspective* (November–December 1996), pp. 30–43.

17 Peter Murray and Stephen Trombley, eds, *Modern British Architecture since 1945* (London, 1984), p. 156.

18 See Paul Clarke, 'Belfast's Upward Spiral', *Perspective* (May–June 2004), pp. 72–5.

19 Patrick Nuttgens, 'Scottish Architecture Today', *Architectural Design* (January 1962), p. 11.

20 Peter Willis, *New Architecture in Scotland* (London, 1977), p. 14.

21 See *House and Garden Book of Modern Houses and Conversions* (London, 1966), pp. 134–5; Entwood, Birkenhead (1959), illustrated in Elain Harwood, *England: A Guide to Post-War Listed Buildings* (London, 2003), pp. 72–3.

22 Jacobsen's Søholm houses at Klampenborg, Copenhagen (1946–55), are the model. The high windows producing the split-roof section were included to catch the setting sun in what were otherwise east-facing houses.

23 Ian Nairn, 'The Burghs of Fife', *The Listener* (12 November 1964), p. 756.

24 See Miles Glendinning and Stefan Muthesisus, *Tower Block* (New Haven and London, 1994), p. 263.

25 Nuttgens, 'Scottish Architecture Today', p. 8.

26 Ian Nairn, 'The Burghs of Fife', *Listener* (12 November 1964), p. 756.

27 See Diane Watters, '"Sturdy Homes, Living Homes": The National Trust for Scotland's Little Houses Improvement Scheme', in *Twentieth-Century Architecture 7: The Heroic Period of Conservation*, ed. Alan Powers and Elain Harwood (London, 2004), pp. 111–26, and Diane Watters and Miles Glendinning, *Little Houses* (Edinburgh, 2006).

28 Peter Lord, 'The Genius Loci Insulted', in *Gwenllian: Essays on Visual Culture* (Llandysal, Dyfed, 1994), pp. 142, 144.

29 'Masterwork or Missed Opportunity?', *Touchstone*, 2 (May 1997), p. 17.

30 Richard Weston, 'Revisiting Our Roots', *Touchstone*, 10 (Spring 2002), p. 19.

31 Malcolm Fraser, 'Architecture and the Wee Blue Ball', in *Architecture in Scotland, 2002–2004*, ed. Stuart MacDonald (Glasgow, 2004), p. 27.

32 Michael Keating, *The City That Refused To Die. Glasgow: The Politics of Urban Regeneration* (Aberdeen, 1988).

33 Stephen Evans, 'In Steel and Stone', *Planet*, 140 (April–May 2000), p. 9.

34 Quoted in Deyan Sudjic, 'The Scottish Parliament', in *Architecture in Scotland*, p. 9.

35 Neil Gillespie, 'Seat of Power', *Architects' Journal* (30 September 2004), p. 30.

36 *Architects' Journal* (24 October 1996), p. 9.

37 David Lea, 'Fake or Real?', *Planet*, 138 (December 1999–January 2000), p. 81.

38 Adam Voelcker, 'Could This Be Wales?', *Touchstone*, 4 (April 1998), pp. 25–6.

39 Peter Fawcett, 'Master of Arts', *Architects' Journal* (22 June 2000) , p. 34.

40 The unique features of timber framing in the British Isles are the unequal spacing of the principal trusses and bays, the distinction between the upper and lower face of the truss, and the tie beam lap dovetail assembly of the truss. See Richard Harris, *Discovering Timber Framed Buildings* (Princes Risborough, 1997).

41 John Summerson, *Architecture in England* (London, 1946), p. 20.

42 Perry Anderson, 'Components of the National Culture' (1968), in *English Questions* (London, 1992).

43 Stefan Collini, *Absent Minds: Intellectuals in Britain* (Oxford, 2006).

44 David Chipperfield quoted by Jonathan Glancey, *The Guardian* 'Culture' (21 November 2005), p. 19.

45 *Icon*, 28 (October 2005), p. 163.

46 *Ibid.*, p. 139.

47 Deyan Sudjic, 'The Stirling Prize 2005', in *The Stirling Prize: Ten Years of Architecture and Innovation*, ed. Tony Chapman (London, 2006), p. 216.

48 *Icon*, p. 169.

49 Zygmunt Bauman, *Liquid Modernity* (Cambridge, 2000).

Select Bibliography

Allan, John, *Berthold Lubetkin: Architecture and the Tradition of Progress* (London, 1992)
—, *Berthold Lubetkin* (London, 2002)
Amery, Colin, *The National Gallery Sainsbury Wing: A Celebration of Art and Architecture* (London, 1991)
Anderson, Perry, *English Questions* (London, 1992)
Archer, J. H., *Partnership in Style: Edgar Wood and J. Henry Sellars* (Manchester, 1975)
Arnell, Peter, and Ted Bickford, eds, *James Stirling: Buildings and Projects* (London, 1984)
Arts Council of Great Britain, *45–55: Ten Years of British Architecture* (London, 1955)
—, *Thirties* (London, 1979)
As Built: Caruso St John Architects (Vitoria-Gasteiz, 2005)
Auden, W. H., *The English Auden: Poems, Essays and Dramatic Writings, 1927–1939* (London, 1977)
Barclay, Irene, *People Need Roots: The Story of the St Pancras Housing Association* (London, 1976)
Bauman, Zygmunt, *Liquid Modernity* (Cambridge, 2000)
Bertram, Anthony, *The House: A Machine for Living In* (London, 1935)
—, *Design* (Harmondsworth, 1938)
Banham, Reyner, *The New Brutalism: Ethic or Aesthetic?* (London, 1966)
—, *Megastructure: Urban Futures of the Recent Past* (London, 1976)
—, *Design by Choice* (London, 1981)
—, *A Critic Writes* (London, 1996)
Barker, Paul, ed., *Arts in Society* (London, 1977)
Barman, Christian, *The Man Who Built the London Transport* (Newton Abbot, 1979)
Berry, Fred, *Housing: The Great British Failure* (London, 1974)
Blake, David, *Window Vision* (Braintree, 1989)
Blomfield, Reginald, *Modernismus: A Study* (London, 1934)
Booker, Christopher, *The Neophiliacs: A Study of the Revolution in English Life in the Fifties and Sixties* (London, 1969)
Brett, David, *The Plain Style* (Cambridge, 2004)
British Architecture Today: Six Protagonists (Milan, 1992)
Buchanan, Colin, *Mixed Blessing: The Motor Car in Britain* (London, 1958)
Bullivant, Lucy, *Anglo-Files: UK Architecture's Rising Generation* (London, 2005)
Bullock, Nicholas, *Building the Post-War World: Modern Architecture and Reconstruction in Britain* (London, 2002)
Calabi, Donatella, ed., *Architettura domestica in Gran Bretagna, 1890–1939* (Milan, 1982)
Campbell, Louise, *Coventry Cathedral: Art and Architecture in Post-War Britain* (Oxford, 1996)
Cantacuzino, Sherban, *Wells Coates* (London, 1978)
Casson, Hugh, *New Sights of London* (London, 1938)
Chapman, Tony, ed., *The Stirling Prize: Ten Years of Architecture and Innovation* (London, 2006)
Cherry, Gordon, and Penny Leith, *Holford: A Study in Architecture, Planning and Civic Design* (London, 1986)
Cherry, Monica, *Building Wales* (Cardiff, 2005)

Chipperfield, David, *David Chipperfield: Architectural Works, 1990–2002* (New York, 2003)

Colleymore, Peter, *The Architecture of Ralph Erskine* (London, 1985)

Collini, Stefan, *Absent Minds: Intellectuals in Britain* (London, 2006)

Colquhoun, Alan, *Essays in Architectural Criticism* (Cambridge, MA, and London, 1982)

Colvin, Brenda, *Land and Landscape* (London, 1948)

Cottam, David, *Sir Owen Williams, 1890–1966* (London, 1986)

Country and Town: A Summary of the Scott and Uthwatt Reports (Harmondsworth, 1943)

Crosby, Theo, *Architecture: City Sense* (London, 1965)

—, *Playing the Environment Game* (Harmondsworth, 1973)

Curtis, William, *Denys Lasdun* (London, 1994)

—, *Modern Architecture since 1900* (London, 1982, with subsequent revisions)

Dannatt, Trevor, *Modern Architecture in Britain* (London, 1959)

Darling, Elizabeth, *Re-forming Britain: Narratives of Modernity before Reconstruction* (London, 2006)

Davies, Colin, *High Tech Architecture* (London, 1988)

—, *Michael Hopkins*, 2 vols (London, 1993–2001)

—, *The Prefabricated Home* (London, 2005)

Dean, David, *The Thirties: Recalling the English Architectural Scene* (London, 1983)

Denby, Elizabeth, *Europe Re-Housed* (London, 1938)

Drew, Philip, *The Third Generation: The Changing Meaning of Architecture* (London, 1972)

Duffy, Francis, *The Changing Workplace* (London, 1992)

Duncan, R. A., *The Architecture of a New Era: Revolution in the World of Appearance* (London, 1933)

Dunleavy, Patrick, *The Politics of Mass Housing in Britain, 1945–1975* (Oxford, 1981)

Dunnett, James, and Gavin Stamp, eds, *Ernö Goldfinger* (London, 1983)

Dunster, Bill, *From A to Zed: Realising Zero (Fossil) Energy Developments* (Wallington, 2003)

Edwards, Brian, *Basil Spence, 1907–1976* (Edinburgh, 1995)

Egelius, Mats, *Ralph Erskine* (Stockholm, 1990)

Elwall, Robert, *Building a Better Tomorrow: Architecture of the 1950s* (Chichester, 2000)

—, *Ernö Goldfinger* (London, 1996)

Esher, Lionel, *A Broken Wave: The Rebuilding of England, 1940–1980* (London, 1981)

Farmer, John, *Green Shift: Changing Attitudes in Architecture to the Natural World* (Oxford, 1996)

Fairbrother, Nan, *New Lives, New Landscapes* (London, 1970)

Flats, Municipal and Private Enterprise (London, 1938)

Ford, Boris, ed., *The Cambridge Guide to the Arts in Britain*, vols 8 and 9 (Cambridge, 1989)

Forty, Adrian, *Objects of Desire* (London, 1986)

—, *Words and Buildings* (London, 2000)

Frampton, Kenneth, *Modern Architecture: A Critical History* (London, 1980)

—, *Labour, Work and Architecture* (London, 2002)

Fry, Maxwell, *Fine Building* (London, 1944)

—, *Autobiographical Sketches* (London, 1975)

Fry, Roger, *Architectural Heresies of a Painter* (London, 1921)

Girouard, Mark, *Big Jim: The Life and Work of James Stirling* (London, 1998)

Glancey, Jonathan, *New British Architecture* (London, 1989)

Glendinning, Miles, ed., *Rebuilding Scotland: Post-War Vision, 1945–1975* (East Linton, 1997)

—, and Stefan Muthesius, *Tower Block* (London, 1994)

Gloag, John, ed., *Design in Modern Life* (London, 1934)

Gold, John, *The Experience of Modernism: Modern Architects and the Future City, 1928–1953* (London, 1997)

Goldhagen, Sarah Williams, and Réjean Legault, *Anxious Modernisms: Experimentation in Postwar Architectural Culture* (Montreal and Cambridge, MA, 2000)

Goodhart-Rendel, H. S., *English Architecture since the Regency: An Interpretation* (London, 1953)

Gould, Jeremy, *Modern Houses in Britain, 1919–1939* (London, 1977)

Hall, Peter, *Urban and Regional Planning* (Harmondsworth, 1975)

—, *Great Planning Disasters* (London, 1980)

Hardy, Dennis, *Poundbury: The Town That Charles Built* (London, 2006)

Harwood, Elain, *England: A Guide to Post-War Listed Buildings* (London, 2003)

—, and Alan Powers, *Tayler and Green, Architects, 1938–1973: The Spirit of Place in Modern Housing* (London, 1998)

Higgott, Andrew, *Mediating Modernism: Architectural Cultures in Britain* (London, 2006)

Hitchcock, Henry-Russell, *Modern Architecture in England* (New York, 1937)

Holmes, Chris, *A New Vision for Housing* (London, 2006)

Hughes, Jonathan, and Simon Sadler eds, *Non-Plan: Essays on Freedom, Participation and Change in Modern Architecture and Planning* (London, 2000)

Jackson, Anthony, *The Politics of Architecture: A History of Modern Architecture in Britain* (London, 1970)

Jacobs, Jane, *The Death and Life of Great American Cities* (London, 1962)

Jencks, Charles, *Modern Movements in Architecture* (Harmondsworth, 1973)

—, *The Language of Post-Modern Architecture* (London, 1977)

—, *The Prince, the Architects and the New Wave Monarchy* (London, 1988)

—, and George Baird, eds, *Meaning in Architecture* (London, 1969)

Jenkins, David, ed., *On Foster . . . Foster On* (Munich and London, 2000)

—, ed., *Norman Foster: Works*, 4 vols (London 2002–)

Jenner, Michael, *New British Architecture in Germany* (Munich, 2000)

Keiller, Patrick, *Robinson in Space* (London, 1999)

Kitchen, Paddy, *A Most Unsettling Person: An Introduction to the Life and Ideas of Patrick Geddes* (London, 1975)

Latham, Ian, and Mark Swenarton, eds, *Jeremy Dixon and Edward Jones: Buildings and Projects, 1959–2002* (London, 2002)

Landau, Royston, *New Directions in British Architecture* (London, 1968)

Lasdun, Denys, ed., *Architecture in an Age of Scepticism* (London, 1984)

Latimer, Karen, ed., *Modern Ulster Architecture* (Belfast, 2006)

Loveday, Donna, and James Peto, eds, *Modern Britain* (London, 1999)

Lyall, Sutherland, *The State of British Architecture* (London, 1980)

MacDonald, Stuart, ed., *Scottish Architecture, 2000–2002* (Glasgow, 2002)

—, ed., *Architecture in Scotland, 2002–2004* (Glasgow, 2004)

McGrath, Raymond, *Twentieth Century Houses* (London, 1934)

McKean, Charles, *The Scottish Thirties: An Architectural Introduction* (Edinburgh, 1987)

McKean, John, *Learning from Segal* (Basel, 1989)

—, *Leicester University Engineering Building* (London, 1994)

—, *Royal Festival Hall* (London, 1992)

MacNeice, Louis, *Autumn Journal* (London, 1939)

Marriott, Oliver, *The Property Boom* (London, 1967)

Martin, J. L., *Buildings and Ideas, 1933–83* (Cambridge, 1983)

—, Ben Nicholson and Naum Gabo, *Circle: International Survey of Constructive Art* (London, 1937)

Maxwell, Robert, *New British Architecture* (London, 1967)

—, *Sweet Disorder and the Carefully Careless* (London, 1993)

Michelaides, Byron, ed., *Architecture for People* (London, 1980)

Mills, Edward D., *The New Architecture in Britain* (London, 1953)

Mirsky, Dmitri, *The Intelligentsia of Great Britain* (London, 1935)

Moore, Rowan, ed., *Structure Space and Skin: The Work of Nicholas Grimshaw and Partners* (London, 1993)

Mumford, Eric, *The CIAM Discourse on Urbanism, 1928–1960* (Cambridge, MA, 2000)

Mumford, Lewis, *Technics and Civilisation* (London, 1934)

—, *The Culture of Cities* (London, 1938)

—, *The Letters of Lewis Mumford and Frederick J. Osborn* (Bath, 1971)

Murray, Peter, and Stephen Trombley, *Modern British Architecture since 1945* (London, 1984)

Muthesius, Hermann, *The English House*, ed. Dennis Sharp (London, 1979)

Muthesius, Stefan, *The Post-War University* (London and New Haven, CT, 2000)

Nairn, Ian, *Modern Buildings in London* (London, 1964)

—, *Nairn's London* (Harmondsworth, 1968)

Osborn, Frederick, and Arnold Whittick, *New Towns: The Answer to Megalopolis* (London, 1969)

Pawley, Martin, ed., *Norman Foster: A Global Architecture* (London, 1999)

Pearman, Hugh, *Equilibrium: The Work of Nicholas Grimshaw and Partners* (London, 2000)

Pevsner, Nikolaus, *Pioneers of the Modern Movement from William Morris to Walter Gropius* (London, 1936)

—, *The Englishness of English Art* (London, 1956)

—, *Studies in Art, Architecture and Design. Volume Two: Victorian and After* (London, 1968)

—, et al., Pevsner Buildings of England series

—, et al., Pevsner Buildings of Ireland series

—, et al., Pevsner Buildings of Scotland series

—, et al., Pevsner Buildings of Wales series

Porteous, Colin, *The New Eco-Architecture* (London, 2002)

Powell, Kenneth, *Edward Cullinan Architects* (London, 1995)

—, *New Architecture in Britain* (London, 2003)

—, *New London Architecture* (London, 2001)

—, *Richard Rogers*, 3 vols (London, 1998–2006)

Powers, Alan, *Look Stranger at this Island Now: English Architectural Drawings of the 1930s* (London, 1983)

—, *Oliver Hill: Architect and Lover of Life* (London, 1989)

—, *Serge Chermayeff* (London, 2001)

—, *The Twentieth Century House in Britain* (London, 2004)

—, *Modern: The Modern Movement in Britain* (London, 2005)

Price, Cedric, *Cedric Price* (London, 1984)

Rasmussen, Steen Eiler, *London: The Unique City* (London, 1937)

Ravetz, Alison, *Model Estate: Planned Housing at Quarry Hill, Leeds* (London, 1974)

Read, Herbert, ed., *Unit One: The Modern Movement in English Architecture, Painting and Sculpture* (London, 1934)

Richards, J. M., *Introduction to Modern Architecture* (Harmondsworth, 1940)

—, *The Castles on the Ground* (London, 1946)

—, *Memoirs of an Unjust Fella* (London, 1980)

Richmond, Peter, *Marketing Modernisms: The Architecture and Influence of Charles Reilly* (Liverpool, 2001)

Risselada, Max, and Dirk van den Heuvel, eds, *Team 10: 1953–81 in Search of a Utopia of the Present* (Rotterdam, 2005)

Robbins, David, ed., *The Independent Group: Postwar Britain and the Aesthetics of Plenty* (Cambridge, MA, 1990)

Robertson, Howard, *Modern Architectural Design* (London, 1932)

Rogers, Richard, and Mark Fisher, *A New London* (London, 1992)

Rowe, Colin, *The Mathematics of the Ideal Villa and Other Essays* (Cambridge, MA, and London, 1982)

—, and Fred Koetter, *Collage City* (London, 1975)

Royal Institute of British Architects, *The Art of the Process* (London, 1993)

Sadler, Simon, *Archigram: Architecture without Architecture* (Cambridge, MA, 2005)

Saler, Michael T., *The Avant-Garde in Interwar England: Mediaeval Modernism and the London Underground* (New York, 1999)

Saint, Andrew, *Towards a Social Architecture* (New Haven, CT, and London, 1987)

Samuel, Raphael, *Theatres of Memory* (London, 1994)

—, *Island Stories* (London, 1998)

Scott, Geoffrey, *The Architecture of Humanism* (London, 1914, revised 1923)

Sharp, Dennis, ed., *Connell, Ward and Lucas: Modern Movement Architects in Britain, 1929–1939* (London, 1994)

Sharp, Thomas, *Town Planning* (Harmondsworth, 1940)

Sharples, Joseph, ed., *Charles Reilly and the Liverpool School of Architecture, 1904–1933* (Liverpool, 1998)

Silver, Nathan, and Jos Boys, eds, *Why Is British Architecture So Lousy?* (London, 1980)

Smithson, Alison, and Peter Smithson, *Urban Structuring* (London, 1967)

—, —, *Without Rhetoric: An Architectural Aesthetic, 1955–1972* (London, 1973)

—, —, *The Charged Void: Architecture* (New York, 2001)

Spens, Michael, ed., *The Recovery of the Modern: Architectural Review, 1980–1995: Key Text and Critique* (London, 1996)

Stamp, Gavin, ed., *Britain in the Thirties* (London, 1979)

Stephen, Douglas, Kenneth Frampton and Michael Carapetian, *British Buildings, 1960–1964* (London, 1965)

Stirling, James, *James Stirling: Buildings and Projects, 1950–1974* (London, 1975)

Stonehouse, Michael, and Gerhard Stromberg, *The British Library at St Pancras* (London, 2004)

Sudjic, Deyan, *Norman Foster, Richard Rogers, James Stirling: New Directions in British Architecture* (London, 1986)

Summerson, John, *Heavenly Mansions* (London, 1949)

Sutcliffe, Anthony, *Multi-Storey Living: The British Working Class Experience* (London, 1974)

Swenarton, Mark, *Homes for Heroes* (London, 1981)

Taylor, Nicholas, *The Village in the City* (London, 1973)

Taylor, Nigel, *Urban Planning Theory since 1945* (London, 1998)

Towards an Urban Renaissance (London, 1999)

Towndrow, F. E., *Architecture in the Balance: An Approach to the Art of Scientific Humanism* (London, 1933)

Traffic in Towns: A Study of the Long Term Problems of Traffic in Urban Areas. Report of the Steering Group and Working Group Appointed by the Minister of Transport (London, 1963)

Tubbs, Ralph, *Living in Cities* (Harmondsworth, 1942)

—, *The Englishman Builds* (Harmondsworth, 1944)

Tyrwhitt, J., et al., *The Heart of the City: Towards the Humanisation of Urban Life* (London, 1952)

Venturi, Robert, *Complexity and Contradiction in Architecture* (New York 1966)

Ward, Paul, *Britishness since 1870* (London, 2004)

Watkin, David, *Morality and Architecture* (Oxford 1977)

Watters, Diane, and Miles Glendinning, *Little Houses: The National Trust for Scotland's Scheme for Small Houses* (Edinburgh, 2006)

Webb, Michael, *Architecture in Britain Today* (London, 1969)

Williams-Ellis, Clough, and Amabel Williams-Ellis, *The Pleasures of Architecture* (London, 1924)

Willis, Peter, *New Architecture in Scotland* (London, 1977)

Wilson, Colin A. St John, *Architectural Reflections* (Oxford, 1992)

—, *The Other Tradition of Modern Architecture* (London, 1995)

Worpole, Ken, *The Value of Architecture: Design, Economy and the Architectural Imagination* (London, 2000)

Wright, Myles, *Design of Nursery and Elementary Schools* (London, 1938)

Yorke, F.R.S., *The Modern House* (London, 1934)

—, *The Modern House in England* (London, 1937)

—, and Frederick Gibberd, *The Modern Flat* (London, 1938)

Journals

Architectural Association Journal
Architectural Design
Architectural Review
Architect and Building News
Architecture Today
Architects' Journal
Architects' Year Book
Builder (retitled *Building* in 1966)
Building (retitled *Architecture and Building* in 1953)
Design for Today
Perspective (Northern Ireland)
Perspectives on Architecture
Prospect (Scotland)
RIBA Journal
Studio
Thirties Society Journal
Touchstone (Wales)
Twentieth Century Architecture

Acknowledgements

My first debt is to Professor Adrian Forty, who recommended me as author of this book, and my second to my editor, Vivian Constantinopoulos, who has been as encouraging and patient as any author could possibly hope. In the later stages, other editors at Reaktion Books have also been most helpful. My wife and children have provided a valuable domestic support.

The book brings together the results of conversations and encounters lasting a lifetime and still in progress, and they cannot be listed individually. I would, however, like to give a special mention to Elain Harwood, a colleague in many ventures and a constant source of detailed and accurate information. In addition, my visual coverage of 'outer Britain' in the final chapter would have been poorer without the generous contributions of Monica Cherry, Paul Larmour, and Gavin Stamp. Many other people and architectural practices have been generous in providing photographs or helping me to obtain them, and their names are listed on the following page. Among those concealed behind the names of their institutions, I would like to thank Robert Elwall of the RIBA and Nigel Wilkins of the National Monuments Record.

The British Academy awarded a Small Research Grant towards the cost of illustrations, and the Paul Mellon Centre for Studies in British Art supported the illustration and production costs. I am grateful to Gavin Stamp, Louise Campbell, John Allan and John Gold, who supported these applications.

Photo Acknowledgements

The author and publishers wish to express their thanks to the below sources of illustrative material and/or permission to reproduce it.

John Allan/Avanti Architects: p. 68; Andrew Wright Associates: p. 235; Archigram Archives: pp. 170, 173; Peter Baistow: 160; Florian Beigel: p. 231; Stephenson Bell: p. 233 (both); Benson & Forsyth: p. 266; photo Hélène Binet (courtesy of Caruso St John): p. 230; John S. Bonnington: p. 124; Dirk Bouwens: p. 30 (left); Braintree District Council: p. 31; Graham Brooks: p 261; Cheryl Buckley: p. 61 (bottom); H. T. Cadbury-Brown: p. 84; Louise Campbell: p. 256; Canadian Centre for Architecture/Collection Centre Canadien d'Architecture (Cedric Price Fonds): p. 167; Capita Percy Thomas: p. 272; Centre for Alternative Technology, Machynlleth: p. 187 (left); Martin Charles: pp. 116, 139, 203, 219; Monica Cherry: pp. 258, 264; Nev Churcher: p. 200; Country Life Picture Library: p. 21; Tim Crocker: p. 138 (top); Gillian Daniell: p. 134; Jeremy Dixon: p. 201; James Dunnett: pp. 81, 91 (right); photo Richard Einzig/arcaid. co. uk: p. 103; photo © English Heritage/NMR: p. 52; Foster & Partners: pp. 192, 194; Grimshaw Architects: p. 189; Zaha Hadid: p. 267; Michael Carapetian: p. 121; Elain Harwood: pp. 179 (right), 180, 182 (top); courtesy of Louis Hellman: pp. 8–9, 129, 158, 161, 165, 196, 208 (bottom), 213, 238 (top), 239; Judith Henderson: p. 105; History of Advertising Trust: p. 12; Ken Kirkwood: pp. 191, 265; Charles Knevitt: p. 208 (top);Paul Larmour: p. 20 (top), 253, 254, 255, 259, 273; Leeds City Council: p. 44; Len Grant Photography: p. 243; Liverpool City Council: p. 17; London Borough of Camden Local Studies & Archives Centre: p. 55; MacCormac, Jamieson & Pritchard: p. 220; Maggie's Centres: p. 269; Martin Centre, Cambridge: p. 187 (right); Roger Mayne: pp. 88, 113; National Monuments Record: pp. 26, 146; *New Society*: p. 169; O'Donnell & Tuomey: p. 246; Pollinger Ltd: p. 45; from Margaret Potter and Alexander Potter, *The Building of London* (West Drayton, 1944): p. 79 (top); Proctor and Matthews Architects: p. 244; RCAHMS: pp. 260, 263; Richard Rogers Partnership/Redshift Photography: p. 271; David Richmond & Partners: p. 238 (bottom); Royal Academy of Arts, London: p. 212; photos courtesy of the Royal Institute of British Architects Library: pp. 27, 77 (top) (both RIBA Library Drawings Collection), 6, 29, 34, 39, 47, 49, 50, 58 (top), 60, 64, 65, 72, 79 (bottom), 108, 135, 143 (all RIBA Photographs Collection); photo Royal Borough of Kensington and Chelsea Libraries, London: p. 144; Phil Sayer: p. 186 (foot); Scottish Parliament Public Information Service: p. 268; Simon Smithson: p. 107; Gavin Stamp: pp. 206, 252; Tim Street-Porter: p. 193; Swansea Town Council: p. 15; Whitechapel Art Gallery and Whitechapel Archive, London: p. 106; Matthew Wickens: p. 257; Charlotte Wood: p. 270; and courtesy of the author: pp. 16, 20 (bottom), 22, 23, 30 (right), 32, 33, 35, 37, 38, 40, 42, 46, 51, 57, 58 (bottom), 59, 61 (top), 67, 69, 71, 76, 77 (bottom), 78, 80, 82, 85, 86, 87, 90, 91 (left), 93, 94, 95, 96, 97, 98, 100, 102, 109, 110, 111, 117, 118, 119, 130, 133, 137, 138 (bottom), 140, 141, 142, 145, 148, 150, 151, 153, 157, 159, 162, 164, 171, 175, 177, 179 (left), 181, 182 (bottom), 183, 184, 186 (top), 188, 205, 207, 209, 211, 214, 215, 216, 217, 221, 222, 224, 228, 229, 237, 241 and 242.

Index